Jacqueline Ann Ziegler

Winter Star

6/93

RETURNING

by Dan Wakefield:

RETURNING
A Spiritual Journey

by DAN WAKEFIELD

Doubleday
New York
1988

Parts of the first chapter of this book appeared in somewhat altered form in the New York *Times Magazine,* December 22, 1985; *GQ,* December 1985; and the Boston *Globe,* November 28, 1984. Excerpt from "Little Gidding" in *Four Quartets* by T. S. Eliot, copyright 1936 by Harcourt Brace Jovanovich, Inc.; copyright © 1963, 1964 by T. S. Eliot. Reprinted by permission of Harcourt Brace Jovanovich, Inc., New York, and Faber and Faber, Ltd., London.

Library of Congress Cataloging-in-Publication Data

Wakefield, Dan.
Returning: a spiritual journey/by Dan Wakefield.
p.   cm.
1. Wakefield, Dan—Religion.
2. Unitarian Universalists—United States
—Biography.
I. Title.
BX9869.W18A3   1987
288'.32'0924—dc19   87-21926
[B]   CIP
ISBN 0-385-23722-7

To the Reverend Norman Eddy,
the Reverend Carl Scovel,
and the men and women of all faiths
who "come not to be ministered unto,
but to minister,"
this book is dedicated.

Contents

Acknowledgments

The author wishes to express special thanks to Sally Arteseros, editor and friend, whose belief in his work over the years has been a sustaining factor, and whose belief in this book has made it possible.

The origin of this book was an article written in the religious autobiography course at King's Chapel, taught by the minister, the Reverend Carl Scovel. That article, "Returning to Church," was originally published in the New York *Times Magazine,* and the author wishes to thank its editors, especially Ed Klein, Harvey Shapiro, and Gerald Walker.

The following people read the manuscript in progress and offered invaluable comments and support: Merloyd Lawrence, Ned Leavitt, Robert Manning, the Reverend Carl Scovel, and Father Thomas Shaw, S.S.J.E. They are not responsible for the author's experiences or opinions, but have earned his deepest gratitude.

The author wishes to thank the following people, knowing it is only a partial list of those whose professional trust and support during the writing of this book as in all his work is deeply appreciated: Leo Bookman, David Hollander, Owen Laster, Ned Leavitt, Sam Weintraub.

Author's Preface

This book originated in the living room of the King's Chapel parish house in Boston, where a group of ten people sat around a table sharing their life experiences in a course on "religious autobiography" taught by the minister. It was there that for the first time I began to understand how my life could be viewed as a spiritual journey as well as a series of secular adventures of accomplishment and disappointment, personal and professional triumph and defeat. I started to see the deeper connections and more expansive framework offered by the sense of our small daily drama in relation to the higher meaning that many people call God.

Because of the intimacy and trust of that small group of people, I began to write of my earliest experiences of a spiritual nature in the most unguarded and open manner. When I later returned to pick up the thread of that narrative and expand it first into an article that appeared in the New York *Times Magazine* and then into this book, I continued to write in the same intimate tone when dealing with the most personal experiences of my life, whether sexual, psychological, or spiritual. It was not my purpose in doing so to shock anyone, or to gain some sort of absolution through literary confession, but rather to share with readers as I had with the people in that room in the parish house the deepest currents of my experience in the most honest and open way I knew how. To do less seemed a violation of the spirit of the enterprise, the effort to look as deeply as possible into the self in order to try to connect as best we could, no matter how brokenly, with the very source of our being. In doing so, I felt that those of us at the parish house made a contribution not only to our own self-understanding but to that of one another. It is with this goal and on this level I hope to communicate with the readers of this book.

I think the attempt to see one's life in spiritual terms is increasingly of interest and value to people. I watched some of my fellow seekers in the class grow and change, and in deep and quiet ways experience the power of healing simply through becoming closer to the spiritual element in their lives. I was one of them. I recommend the experience and, with gratitude and humility, I offer you mine.

"We and God have business with each other; and in opening ourselves to His influence our deepest destiny is fulfilled. The universe, as those parts of it which our personal being constitutes, takes a turn genuinely for the worse or for the better in proportion as each one of us fulfills or evades God's demands. As far as this goes I probably have you with me, for I only translate into schematic language what I may call the instinctive belief of mankind: God is real since He produces real effects."

—William James, *The Varieties of Religious Experience*

"I believe that humans are unable to live without some contact with what I call the third parent: God, or some culture growing up around a tradition of thinking about God or gods."

—George W. S. Trow, "The Third Parent,"
Harper's magazine, July 1987

I

TURNING

One balmy spring morning in Hollywood, a month or so before my forty-eighth birthday, I woke up screaming. I got out of bed, went into the next room, sat down on a couch, and screamed again. This was not, in other words, one of those waking nightmares left over from sleep that is dispelled by the comforting light of day. It was, rather, a response to the reality that another morning had broken in a life I could only deal with sedated by wine, loud noise, moving images, and wired to electronic games that further distracted my fragmented attention from a growing sense of blank, nameless pain in the pit of my very being, my most essential self. It was the beginning of a year in which I would have scored in the upper percentile of these popular magazine tests that list the greatest stresses of life: I left the house I owned, the city I was living in, the work I was doing, the woman I had lived with for seven years and had hoped to remain with the rest of my life, ran out of money, discovered I had endangered my health, and attended the funeral of my father in May and my mother in November.

The day I woke up screaming I grabbed from among my books an old Bible I hadn't opened for nearly a quarter of a century. With a desperate instinct I turned to the Twenty-third Psalm and read it over, several times, the words and the King James cadence bringing a sense of relief and comfort, a kind of emotional balm. In the coming chaotic days and months I sometimes recited that psalm over in my mind, and it always had that calming effect, but it did not give me any sense that I suddenly believed in God again. The psalm simply seemed an isolated source of solace and calm, such as any great poem might be.

In that first acute stage of my crisis I went to doctors for help, physical and mental. I told an internist in Beverly Hills that I had an odd feeling my heart was beating too fast and he confirmed my suspicion. My "resting" pulse rate was 120, and the top of the normal range is 100. An EKG showed there was nothing wrong with my heart, and the doctor asked if I was in the entertainment business. I confessed to television; I had been co-producer of a TV movie I wrote and so earned the title of "writer-producer," giving me the high Hollywood status of a "hyphenate." The doctor nodded and smiled, saying many of his patients in The Industry suffered from stress, as I evidently did now. He prescribed medication that would lower my racing pulse.

The "beta blockers" lowered my pulse but not my anxiety, and I explained to a highly recommended psychiatrist in nearby Westwood (home of UCLA) how I had come out to Los Angeles from Boston nearly three years before to write a TV series called "James at 15" that ran for a season, and then I stayed on doing TV movies and a feature film rewrite I was fired from. I told her how I had grown to feel alien and alienated in Los Angeles; the freeways and frantic pace and the roller coaster of show business were driving me nuts and I couldn't stand the sight of a palm tree. The psychiatrist said I should take a vacation; she suggested Santa Barbara. At that moment the voice of Bob Dylan wailed in my mind the line from "Just Like Tom Thumb Blues"—that my best friend the doctor won't even tell me what I got.

Watching the national weather forecast on "Good Morning, America," I pictured myself on the bottom left-hand corner of the map in the dot of Los Angeles and felt I had slid to the wrong hole on a giant pinball machine, wanting to tilt the whole thing so I could get back to the upper right-hand corner to Boston, where I felt pulled by internal gravity. My Southern California disorientation deepened because I no longer knew when anything happened in the course of a year since all the seasons looked the same to me; when I saw a videotape of Henry James's *The Europeans* the New England autumn leaves and sunlight falling on plain board floors brought tears to my eyes.

I tried to forget about Hollywood by starting a new novel but the room I worked in was next to the swimming pool and the service people who came to test the chlorine were unemployed actors discussing casting calls, making it hard to concentrate; besides, the damp seeped into the pages and stiffened them, giving the manuscript the texture of corpse. I wondered if I might end up as one of those bodies in the movies of Hollywood who float face down in their own swimming pool.

A plumber who came to fix the toilet saw the typewriter and tried to pitch me an idea for a TV pilot about a jewel thief who gains access to rich people's houses by working as a plumber. When he asked if I wanted to get involved I wasn't sure if he meant in a criminal operation or a TV series and each seemed equally unappealing. I longed to leave the land of deals and palm trees and live in a building made of solid brick with a tree outside I could tell the time of year by. Finally, on one of those frantic mornings I stopped in the midst of all I was doing (and failing to do) and called American Airlines, booking a seat on the next flight to Boston.

The city itself was succor, a feast of familiar tradition from the statues of heroes (Alexander Hamilton, William Lloyd Garrison, Samuel Eliot Morison among them) in the wide swath of Commonwealth Avenue to the long wharves on the waterfront reaching out toward Europe. Walking the brick streets of my old neighborhood on Beacon Hill, I felt in balance again with the universe, and a further pull to what seemed the center of it, the source of something I was searching for, something I couldn't name that went far beyond the satisfaction of scenery or local color. I headed like a homing pigeon to the pond in the Public Garden and, without having planned it, sat down on a bench, and at the same time that tears of gratitude came to my eyes the words of the psalm also came to my mind:

". . . he leadeth me beside the still waters. He restoreth my soul."

I recited the psalm from the start and at the end said "Amen" as if it were a prayer, and it was, of thanks. It would not have occurred to me to go to any church or chapel, but the pond in the Public Garden seemed precisely the place to have offered this.

I thought no further about "religion" on that trip but concerned myself with the more pressing problem of my physical health, which my Boston doctor told me he was frankly worried about. He too found I had a pulse rate of 120, a condition called tachycardia. The EKG showed no heart disease or damage ("yet," he added) but, unlike the internist in L.A., he prescribed not pills but a program of exercise and diet conducted at something called a Stress Lab at Massachusetts General Hospital. I went out of fear, grumbling all the way, wanting a chilled glass of dry white wine instead.

When I came back to Boston a month later, after finishing (or in some cases giving up or fleeing from) my business in Los Angeles, the last thing I wanted to do was return to that damned stress clinic and start their Exercycle program. The principal exercise I had been engaged in the past few years was carrying from the car to the house the case of Almaden chablis half gallons I bought every week as basic sustenance. I was in grief over the breakup of my seven-year relationship that had not survived my move back East from L.A., which was followed a week later by my father's death. The only way I knew how to ease the pain was by drowning it with alcohol, the same "cure" I'd been using for nearly a quarter of a century. I had not done anything for my physical health since I left Boy Scout Camp Chank-tun-un-gi the summer of '48, and only some frayed, shrunken instinct for survival enabled me to make myself go back to see the Exercycle people.

I told Dr. Howard Hartley, the director of the Stress Lab, and the nurse who assisted him, Jane Sherwood, that I was going through a difficult time, I was drinking a lot of wine, and that I did not intend to stop or even cut down. I thought this might provoke them and get me out of the whole thing, but neither of them even blinked. Dr. Hartley was a quiet, thoughtful man about my own age with graying hair and my own sort of Midwestern accent, and Jane was an attractive young blond woman who seemed genuinely concerned about my health. They had disappointed my preconceptions (based on painful experience) about medical people as condescending martinets, and even my aggressive announcement about wine consumption failed to rattle them. Dr. Hartley said all they were asking me to do at that point was work out on the Exercycle a half hour every day, or at least three times a week. I gruffly said if I was going to do it at all I would do the damn thing every day.

I rode for dear life. I rode for my life when I wondered if trying to save it or keep it together was worth the effort. I rode in a fifth-floor walkup apartment I had sublet on Beacon Hill that stifling summer of 1980 in stuffy heat broken by sudden dark thunderstorms that crashed around me like the pieces of my life breaking apart. I rode on a BH Home Bike my old friend Shaun O'Connell helped me buy in some suburban mall sporting goods store and lugged up the stairs for me on a day I was so depressed that after assembling the bike, while I looked on in a sort of paralysis of will, he turned to me before leaving and said in the most optimistic summation of my situation he could muster: "Well, at least you're alive."

I rode watching "All My Children" on a portable black and white television set to see other people's problems in hopes of temporarily forgetting my own; I rode while reading Henri

Troyat's biography of Tolstoy and was cheered to learn that the author of *War and Peace* took up bicycle riding for his health at age sixty-seven (he read *Scientific Notes on the Action of the Velocipede as Physical Exercise* by L. K. Popov) and that he and his wife Sonya kept records of their pulse rates in their respective journals, especially noting the elevation after domestic arguments. ("After she left he felt his pulse . . . and noted 'Ninety.' ") I rode every day, as ritually as I guzzled my wine every night, and sometimes at lunch to help me make it through to "cocktail time." I rode on days when I didn't even want to get out of bed or get dressed, I rode when I couldn't yet begin the rewrite of the script I had to do to make enough money to pay the rent, I rode when I had a hangover and feared any exertion would make me sick. I rode because some vital if battered part of me wanted to survive, and more than that to live, and when everything else seemed illusory or elusive and out of my control, I knew there was one specific thing I could do to help myself, to keep going, and that was to ride the damned bike. I did it, each day, and nothing I had ever done felt quite so essential as gripping those handlebars and holding on.

There was consolation in being back not only in Boston but in my old neighborhood, the Hill; walking down the main drag of Charles Street, I knew how a soldier felt returning home from war. Old neighbors stopped to shake my hand, and merchants greeted me with welcome and asked what they could do to help me get settled again ("rehabilitated," I thought of it). Ed Jones, a bachelor I thought of as "King of the Hill," reintroduced me to the regulars at the bar of the Charles Restaurant, and it seemed a haven and shelter, comfortably friendly and dim.

That sodden summer was shot through with shafts of the most intense and unexpected joy, like the moment I came up out of the subway at Harvard Square to the strains of Bach being vigorously played in the foyer of the Coop for coins by street musicians with violins and cellos and it felt like being bathed with love; and the evening Joe Massik took us sailing out of

Boston Harbor and we watched the sun go down and the lights come on in the towers downtown like golden signals. Afterward we went to Brandy Pete's for huge platters of chicken and pasta and baskets of fresh bread, and I felt fed as well by friendship and fortune of place.

That fall I found an apartment up on Mt. Vernon Street with big bay windows that looked out on another brick building across the street and a tree, just as I'd dreamed of in Hollywood. I got out the novel whose pages were still stiff from the damp of my poolside studio—it felt like something exhumed—and set to work, with the Hill serving not only as home but as inspiration. I could see a slice of the Boston Common from the window I faced when I worked, and as the late autumn sky above it turned the cold royal purple and silver-gray colors I remembered and loved, I told myself I had to finish the book to earn the money—the privilege—of staying on and living here. The Hill was family, too. When my mother died in early November Ed Jones gathered friends from the neighborhood who mourned with me; he made a stew and we drank and dined, and I was comforted. They drove me to the airport and met me when I returned. Home.

Just by moving back to Boston my pulse went down from 120 to 100, and after faithfully riding the Exercycle for three months it was down to the eighties. I was elated by actually making an improvement in my physical condition for the first time in my life, an accomplishment that prompted me to tell Dr. Hartley I'd be willing to try the diet he recommended (a high-complex-carbohydrate regime with no oil, butter, or fat, similar to but not as strict and restrictive as the Pritikin diet). I would try it with the proviso, of course, that I could still drink all the wine I wanted. They told me to do the best I could. In another three months I had lost eighteen pounds and felt almost as miraculously lean as my idol Paul Newman in *The Hustler*.

My faith in Dr. Hartley and Jane Sherwood was now so awesome that they could have asked me to do the impossible, and they did. They asked me to stop drinking for a month. No alcohol of any kind. No wine. Not a glass, not a sip. Zilch. Cold turkey. Why, I wondered, was such an extreme (inhuman) measure necessary? Dr. Hartley explained that, while they were very pleased with my progress—the weight loss, the increased "work load" as measured on their Exercycle stress test, and my pulse down to the eighties—they felt that, in line with this very improvement, my pulse should really now be in the sixties. They said the only factor they could think of that was keeping it above that was the wine consumption, and they wanted to see for sure if that were true. The only way to find out was for me to stop consuming it for a month.

The longest stretch of time I had done without a drink in twenty years was one week, and the four occasions on which I had performed such a miracle of abstinence had been the most extreme tests of my character, will power, and stamina. In fact, they were torture. I had not had the DTs, but I had suffered such anguish, such torment of desire, such depths of deprivation, that the idea of holding out a day or even an hour longer seemed impossible. Now I was being asked to do it for a month.

I said I would start tomorrow. Declaring it was like diving off the high board; I had to do it right away without thinking or I'd never get up the courage. Dr. Hartley pointed out that this was the end of November, and I'd be having to endure this unaccustomed sobriety during the most difficult time of all, the holiday season. Perhaps I'd prefer to put it off to the first of the year. "No," I said, "I am perverse, and the fact that this is more difficult, that it goes against the grain of society, will somehow make it easier for me." I would start the next day, I pledged, and I meant it.

That night I found one of my drinking pals, a regular from the Charles Restaurant bar, and asked her to join me for a final fling. I was going to load up for the holidays, get loaded in order to endure, as if I could so soak myself in wine that it would somehow sustain me through the dry period. I did my best. I guzzled

and gulped, I drank with steady purpose at favorite neighborhood bars, then bought us a half gallon of cheap dry white that I
lugged up to my friend's apartment. I poured the stuff down as
though I were trying to extinguish a fire (the fear of going
without for so long).

I woke not knowing at first who or where I was. Me. Boston.
Beacon Hill. My friend's living-room couch. Ouch. I sank back
down, dizzy. This was a beaut, this was one of the worst pounding hangovers in my painfully hung-over history. I reeled to the
refrigerator for orange juice, gulped, gasped, and flopped back
down on the couch. The traumas of the past year began to
bloom in my head, and I sought some way of turning them off. It
was too early to tune in television in hopes of having my mind
blasted empty by the tube, for my faithful drinking companion
was still asleep in her bed. Instead, I groped for a magazine or
book, some distracting piece of reading matter from the coffee
table by the couch where I lay.

I picked up off the top of a pile a book I had never seen before.
It turned out to be a journal with sketches that Françoise Sagan
had kept while taking the cure in an alcoholic dry-out clinic. It
was not the youthfully bittersweet romance of *Bonjour Tris-
tesse*. It was gritty, tough experience, painful and true. Too true.
Too close to the mark of the path on which I was painfully about
to embark. But so true I couldn't stop reading, either. It was like
a personal letter to a fellow boozer on the brink of trying the
cure. The last entry, made when the author was sobered and
clean and ready to leave, seemed like a message to sustain me in
the dry month ahead, a goal to think about during my thirty
days in the wilderness of sobriety, a goal that must have seemed
as distant and as painful to reach for Mlle. Sagan when she
started her cure as it did to me at that moment, but one whose
attainment would indeed be worth every deprivation, every
exercise of discipline, every resource of nerve and courage it
was possible to summon:

"Now I begin to live and write in earnest."

Just before Christmas I was sitting in The Sevens, a neighborhood bar on Charles Street, drinking a mug of coffee while friends sipped their beers. I didn't mind being in bars and around other people who were drinking while I was on the wagon, in fact I preferred it. I was comfortable in the atmosphere, and if I couldn't drink any booze at least I could inhale its nirvanic scents and maybe I even got a kind of "contact high" as musicians were said to do off others smoking grass. A house painter named Tony who was sitting at the table with me and some other neighbors remarked out of the blue that he'd like to go to mass somewhere on Christmas Eve. I didn't say anything, but a thought came into my mind, as swift and unexpected as it was unfamiliar: *I'd like to do that too.*

Since leaving my boyhood Protestant faith as a rebellious Columbia College intellectual more than a quarter century before, I had only once gone to church. Yet I found myself that Christmas Eve in King's Chapel, which I finally selected from the ads on the Boston *Globe* religion page because it seemed least threatening. It was Unitarian, I knew the minister slightly as a neighbor, and I assumed "Candlelight Service" meant nothing more religiously challenging than carol singing.

As it happened, the Reverend Carl Scovel gave a sermon about "the latecomers" to the Church on a text from an Evelyn Waugh novel called *Helena.* There was a passage in which Helena, the mother of Constantine, addressed the magi, the three wise men who came late to the manger to bring their gifts to the Christ child, and it ended like this:

" 'You are my special patrons,' said Helena, 'and patrons of all late-comers, of all who have had a tedious journey to make to the truth, of all who are confused with knowledge and speculation, of all who through politeness make themselves partners in guilt, of all who stand in danger by reason of their talents. . . .

" 'For His sake who did not reject your curious gifts, pray always for the learned, the oblique, the delicate. Let them not be quite forgotten at the Throne of God when the simple come into their kingdom.' "

I slunk down in my pew, literally beginning to shiver from what I thought was only embarrassment at feeling singled out for personal attention, and discomfort at being in alien surroundings. It turned out that I had a temperature of 102 that kept me in bed for three days with a violent case of the flu and a fearful suspicion that church was a very dangerous place, at least if you weren't used to it.

Maybe my flesh was rebelling against not only the unaccustomed intrusion of spirit but the equally unusual exclusion of alcoholic spirits from my system. For the first time in my adult life I went without wassail through the Yuletide, strictly keeping my pledge of abstinence from alcohol—though the help of a small stash of marijuana from a friend kept it from being a truly cold-turkey Christmas season.

I showed up for my stress test appointment the last day of my most stressful year with my blood completely pure of booze, and Dr. Hartley counted my pulse at an even sixty, exactly as he had predicted it ought to be if I cut out the wine. I was both elated to have reached this healthy rate and disturbed at what it meant. Dr. Hartley's suspicion was correct: the wine was acting as a stimulant to my sympathetic nervous system (the part of the nervous system that controls the heart and blood vessels) and keeping my pulse elevated. Before I could get depressed at the distressing implication—it obviously meant cutting wine drastically down if not altogether out of my daily diet if I wanted to maintain my healthy heartbeat—I took the Exercycle stress test. When I finished pumping and sweating through the last stationary miles, Jane Sherwood announced with elation that I had increased my "work load" by a third, from 120 to 180 watts (units of power generated), since starting the program eight months before.

I was exhilarated by making such dramatic improvement and immediately felt competitive. I wanted to know where I stood now in relation to *other* people, and Jane hurried to her files, coming back smiling and waving a folder. The Stress Lab people kept records of different professional groups they tested, and Jane said proudly I was now "stronger than the average fireman!" I felt like Marvelous Marvin Hagler after winning his first middleweight crown. It was the first time in my life I'd been demonstrably stronger physically than any person or group. The giddy feeling (like a new kind of high) made me think the unthinkable: maybe I could really cut down permanently on my daily wine consumption.

I began to keep a record of my wine intake and how it affected my heart rate. I discovered that if I drank one or two glasses of wine in an evening my pulse was the same the next morning, but if I had more than two glasses my pulse would be higher than it was before drinking the wine the night before. I tried to keep from drinking more than two (well, sometimes three) glasses in an evening, switching to diet tonic before dinner, and coffee after (in the past I rarely drank coffee because it cut the effect of the wine). I began to enjoy the feeling of sobriety, of mornings without hangovers, and a sense of being able to exercise some kind of control over myself. In this new, clearheaded condition, I began to think about other aspects of my life besides the physical that I hadn't considered for a long time. I began to think again about church.

After my Christmas Eve experience at King's Chapel, I was both intrigued and apprehensive about church, and I didn't get up the nerve to go back again until Easter. I did not have any attacks of shivering or chills in the spring sunshine of that service, so it seemed that, even as a "latecomer" and former avowed atheist, I could safely enter a place regarded as a house of God. Still, the prospect was discomforting. My two initial trips of return had been on major holidays, occasions when "regular" people went to church, simply in observance of tradition. To go back again meant crossing the Boston Common on a non-holiday Sunday morning wearing a suit and tie, a giveaway sign of churchgoing. I did it furtively, as if I were engaged in something that would not be approved of by my peers. I hoped they would all be home doing brunch and the Sunday papers, so I would not be "caught in the act." I recalled the remark of William F. Buckley, Jr., in a television interview that if you mention God more than once at New York dinner parties you aren't invited back.

To my surprise, I recognized neighbors and even some people I considered friends at church, on a "regular" Sunday. I had simply assumed I did not know people who went to church, yet here they were, with intellects intact, worshiping God. Once inside the church myself, I understood the appeal. No doubt my friends and neighbors found, as I did, relief and refreshment in connecting with age-old rituals, reciting psalms and singing hymns. There was a calm reassurance in the stately language of litanies and chants in the Book of Common Prayer (King's Chapel is "Unitarian in theology, Anglican in worship, and Congregational in governance," a historical Boston amalgam that became three centuries old in 1986). I was grateful for the sense of shared reverence, of reaching beyond one's flimsy physical presence, while praying with a whole congregation.

The connection of church and neighborhood reinforced one another, gave depth and dimension to the sense of "home" that I had felt so cut off from in Hollywood. Church was not just an abstraction or a separate enclave of my life but a part of the place where I lived, connected with people I knew and encountered in my daily (not just Sunday) life. I think the deep sense of pleasure and solace of *place* I derived from returning to the neighborhood was—along with my physical improvement— part of the process of calming and reassembling myself that nurtured the desire to go to church.

When I lived on the Hill before, I enjoyed it but took it for granted. This time I appreciated it, plugged myself into its rituals. I bought my first pair of ice skates since childhood and on winter afternoons slid precariously but happily over the frozen pond in the Public Garden. I looked up Steve Olesky, my old neighbor from Myrtle Street, a lawyer who served as president of the Beacon Hill Civic Association (he also turned out to be a member of King's Chapel), and volunteered to cook at their annual pancake breakfast in the spring. When I burned my thumb flipping blueberry pancakes at that event, just as I had in years past, I knew I was really back. And I knew by then that I had managed to resuscitate my novel as well as myself. *(Under the Apple Tree* went back to my Midwestern childhood roots with a new appreciation of "place" and old loyalties.)

Many of us become wanderers, moving from city to city and job to job (as well as marriage to marriage, even family to family) as part of an accepted nomadic life style instead of putting down roots in one place, with one permanent wife or husband and set of children, working for one company—or, as it was more appropriately called in the old days, a "firm." It is little wonder that many of us become psychically disoriented, in need of medical or psychological "treatment," and suffer from a spiritual vacuum where our center should be. My own experience of reconnecting with a place I loved, the significance such an experience can have, was articulated on "The MacNeil/Lehrer NewsHour" one evening by the editor of a small-town newspaper who had left Washington, D.C., to return to his native Minnesota.

"The way to become connected with the world again is to find a place like my prairie—it may be very different—and then become attached to it," said Paul Gruchow. "You can't feel disconnected from a place and passionate about the world. You've got to be tied down somewhere."

In Hollywood I'd been floating, and my need for the signs of the seasons that were lacking in Southern California was a symptom of my general feeling of free fall through time as well as disconnectedness with place. Part of my rehabilitation in coming back to Boston was reconnecting to the cycle of the seasons, not only the sights and sounds and smells (with my eyes closed I could stand on Pinckney Street and know October had come from the scent of fireplace smoke) but also the neighborhood celebrations that mark them. There was the Charles Street Fair at the start of autumn, the carolers in Louisburg Square on Christmas Eve, the flowers that bloom in the window-box competition in spring, the steel-band music from the Joy Street block party in summer.

Once I began going to church, the age-old religious rituals marking the turning of the year deepened and gave a fuller meaning to the cycle of the seasons and my own relation to them. The year was not only divided now into winter, spring, summer, and fall but was marked by the expectation of Advent, leading up to the fulfillment of Christmas, followed by Lent, the solemn prelude to the coming of the dark anguish of Good Friday that is transformed in the glory of Easter. Birth and death and resurrection, beginnings and endings and renewals, were observed and celebrated in ceremonies whose experience made me feel I belonged—not just to a neighborhood and a place, but to a larger order of things, a universal sequence of life and death and rebirth.

This appreciation of "holy days" was a renewal of a feeling I had stifled ever since my angry intellectual dismissal of God and church during college. Although I'd enjoyed the neighborhood festivities of seasons on Beacon Hill, I had maintained a fierce hostility to traditional holidays, which I felt were by nature an offense against all good atheists, especially unmarried or divorced ones without families. I summed up such sentiments in my novel, published in 1973, about the divorced life, *Starting Over*, branding the major winter holiday season of our society as

". . . the most prolonged and dangerous siege of all single people's personal war to survive. The jingly, tinselled specter of it hung just a few days ahead of them, the annual psychic bombardment that every lonely person most feared and dreaded, from the first sign of turkey sales on through the incessant clanging of carols to the last bleary notes of Guy Lombardo playing 'Auld Lang Syne'; the trinity of public trials called Thanksgiving, Christmas and New Year's, that annual punishing gauntlet known gaily as—*The Holidays.*"

Little did I dream that a time would come when I would feel thankful for—of all things—tradition, "home," and the secular holiday that gives us an opportunity to take time out for expressing gratitude. As a child I had always loved Thanksgiving; I thought of the Pilgrims with awe when back at Public School 80 in Indianapolis we sang of them gathered together "on a stern and rockbound coast," and I ate my turkey with a sense of the magic of history, knowing this feast repeated the survival celebration of my own ancestors. Now thankful to be back in Boston, to have found what was beginning to seem like a new home in a church as well as in the old neighborhood, at the turning of autumn into winter my second year of return, I found myself wanting to celebrate the harvest of all I had rediscovered, including the unexpected restoration of body and spirit, the most precious gifts of all.

Though it's not a religious holiday, Thanksgiving is celebrated at King's Chapel, with sheaves symbolic of harvest decorating the altar. I felt a surge of childhood nostalgia as well as current gratitude as I joined the others in singing one of my favorite anthems learned at good old P. S. 80:

"Come, ye thankful people, come,
Raise the song of harvest-home:
All is safely gathered in,
Ere the winter storms begin. . . ."

I thought of the story of the prodigal son I had recently read again after hearing a sermon about it. I was moved especially by the moment the prodigal son knew it was time to go home and so—in that simple and profound summation—"he came to himself." I was reminded of that interior dimension of homecoming when the associate minister, the Reverend Charles Forman, talked about exile in his Thanksgiving homily. Speaking of the universal nature of the harvest story, and especially the Jewish festival of ingathering, from which our harvest stories come, Reverend Forman quoted Psalm 137 describing the anguish of the Jews when Jerusalem had fallen to the Babylonians, the Holy Temple was destroyed, and the people sent into exile: "By the waters of Babylon, there we sat down and wept, when we remembered Zion. On the willows there we hung our harps." But that story of tragedy and despair gave way to another story of faith, just as the Pilgrims' "time of starving" gave way to the feast of Thanksgiving.

I was struck by how each of us lives those stories, and repeats variations of them, in our inner as well as our outer journeys, as the holiday rituals remind us. Reverend Forman closed his remarks on Thanksgiving with a thought that had special significance for me. He asked us to give thanks if our cup was full but added (speaking, I believe, of interior as well as geographic displacement): "If this year your story is one of loss, and you are as an exile in a strange land, remember that even in such a place the Lord's song will yet be sung. In God's good time, even exiles at last come home."

How nice it would be if exiles could end their troubles and live happily ever after simply by coming home. But those are the endings of fairy tales. We aren't told what happened to the prodigal son after his father welcomed him back, but the anger of his jealous older brother does not portend a future of sweetness and light. As fulfilling as it was for me to return to Boston and begin a new phase of life in better physical health, it did not make everything smooth. As the usual trials of life continued, I went to King's Chapel not only for inspiration but for solace, a respite from the all too common afflictions of the human condition, from broken furnaces to broken hearts, from bad dreams to flu and taxes.

I began to appreciate what was meant by the Church as "sanctuary." The word itself took on new resonance for me; when I later heard of the "sanctuary" movement of churches offering shelter to Central American political refugees, I thought of the kind of private refuge that fortunate citizens like myself find in church from the daily assaults of pressures and worries, the psychic guerrilla warfare of everyday life.

Caught in an escalation of panic and confusion in my own professional campaigns (more painful because so clearly brought on by my own blundering), I joined the Church in May of 1982, not wanting to wait until the second Christmas Eve anniversary of my entry, as I had planned. I wanted the immediate sense of safety and refuge implied in belonging, being a member—perhaps like getting a passport and fleeing to a powerful embassy in the midst of some chaotic revolution.

Going to church, even belonging to it, did not solve life's problems—if anything, they seemed to escalate again around that time—but it gave me a sense of living in a larger context, of being part of something greater than what I could see through the tunnel vision of my personal concerns. I now looked forward to Sunday because it *meant* going to church; what once was strange now felt not only natural but essential. Even more remarkably, the practice of regular attendance at Sunday services, which such a short time ago seemed religiously "excessive," no longer seemed enough. Whatever it was I was getting from church on Sunday mornings, I wanted—needed, it felt like —*more.*

I experienced what is a common phenomenon for people who in some way or other begin a journey of the kind I so unexpectedly found myself on—a feeling simply and best described as a "thirst" for spiritual understanding and contact; to put it bluntly, I guess, *for God.* I noticed in the church bulletin an announcement of a Bible-study class in the parish house, and I went one stormy autumn evening to find myself with only the church's young seminarian on hand and one other parishioner.

Rather than being disappointed by the tiny turnout, as I ordinarily would have been, I thought of the words "Where two or three are gathered together in my name, there am I in the midst of them," and I felt an interior glow that the pouring rain outside and occasional claps of thunder only made seem more vital and precious. I don't remember what text we studied that evening, but I can still smell the rain and the coffee and feel the aura of light and warmth.

Later in the season I attended a Bible-study session the minister led for a gathering of about twenty people on the story of Abraham and Isaac, and I came away with a sense of the awesomeness and power of faith, a quality that loomed above me as tremendous and challenging and tangibly real as mountains. The Bible-study classes, which I later, with other parishioners, learned to lead on occasion myself, became a source of power, like tapping into a rich vein.

Bible study was not like examining history but like holding up a mirror to my own life, a mirror in which I sometimes saw things I was trying to keep hidden, even from myself. The first Scripture passage I was assigned to lead was from Luke, about the man who cleans his house of demons, and seven worse ones come. I did not have any trouble relating this to "contemporary life." It sounded unnervingly like an allegory about a man who had stopped drinking and so was enjoying much better health, but took up smoking marijuana to "relax," all the while feeling good and even self-righteous about giving up the booze. It was my own story. I realized, with a shock, how I'd been deceiving myself, how much more "housecleaning" I had to do.

I enrolled in secular courses of "personal growth" and short-term physical and mental therapy on top of my exercise and diet regime, but the organizing element or principle of it all was the spiritual quest whose focus was prayer, meditation, Bible study, and the Church. In the course of five years I was able to give up the alcohol that I had used as regularly and purposely as

daily medicine for twenty-five years, then gave up the marijuana that replaced it, and along the way even threw out the
faithful briar pipe I had clenched and puffed for a quarter of a
century.

I used to worry about which of these addictions I kicked
through "church" and which through secular programs, as if I
had to assign proper "credit," as if it were possible to compartmentalize and isolate the influence of God, like some kind of
vitamin. The one thing I knew about the deepest feeling connected with all my assortment of life-numbing addictions is that
at some point or other they felt as if they were "lifted," taken
away, and instead of having to exercise iron control to resist
them, it simply felt better not to have to do them anymore. The
only concept that seemed to describe such experience was that
of "grace," and the accompanying adjective "amazing" came to
mind along with it.

I was grateful for these changes but before I could feel too
self-righteous about them, or harbor any illusion that they *ipso
facto* made me a "better Christian," I happened to read again
Graham Greene's great novel *The Power and the Glory* and saw
that his "whisky priest" was a far more pure example of faith
and dedication of one's personal life to God in his alcoholic state
than I had ever been in my sober one. My re-encounter with the
fictional priest who gives his own life for others (and therefore
for God, according to Christ's commandments) made me realize that giving up booze or even drugs, or losing weight or
lowering the heartbeat, are not necessarily—or even desirably
—by-products of religious experience. For many people, such
effects may not have anything to do with religion. In this realm
more than any other, each person's quest is his own.

I became fascinated by other people's spiritual experiences
and, thirty years after it was first recommended to me, I read
Thomas Merton's *The Seven Storey Mountain*. I had avoided it
even when the late poet Mark Van Doren, my favorite professor
and Merton's former mentor at Columbia, had spoken of it with

high regard, but now I devoured it. I went on to read everything else of Merton's I could get my hands on, from the socio-
political *Conjectures of a Guilty Bystander* to the mystical *The
Ascent to Truth*. Most meaningful was a slim "meditation" by
Merton called *He Is Risen,* which I found by chance in a New
York bookstore; it said in matter-of-fact prose that Christ "is in
history with us, walking ahead of us to where we are going. . . ."

I thought of those words while walking the brick sidewalks of
Beacon Hill, conceiving of my life for the first time as a "journey" rather than as a battle I was winning or losing at that
moment, on whose immediate crashing outcome the fate of the
universe (e.g., the turbulent one in my own head) depended. I
remembered years ago reading Dorothy Day's column in the
Catholic Worker when I lived in Greenwich Village, and I appreciated now for the first time the sense of the title: "On
Pilgrimage."

I cannot pinpoint any particular time when I suddenly believed in God again. I only know that such belief came to seem
as natural as for all but a few stray moments of twenty-five or
more years before it had been inconceivable. I realized this
while looking at fish.

I had gone with my girl friend to the New England Aquar-
ium, and as we gazed at the astonishingly brilliant colors of
some of the small tropical fish—reds and yellows and oranges
and blues that seemed to be splashed on by some innovative
artistic genius—and watched the amazing lights of the flashlight
fish that blinked on like the beacons of some creature of a sci-fi
epic, I wondered how anyone could think that all this was the
result of some chain of accidental explosions! Yet I realized in
frustration that to try to convince me otherwise five years before would have been hopeless. Was this what they called "conversion"?

The term bothered me because it suggested being "born

again" and, like many of my contemporaries, I had been put off
by the melodramatic nature of that label, as well as the current
political beliefs that seemed to go along with it. Besides, I didn't
feel "reborn." No voice came out of the sky nor did a thunder-
clap strike me on the path through the Boston Common on the
way to King's Chapel. I was relieved when our minister explained that the literal translation of "conversion" in both Hebrew and Greek is not "rebirth" but "turning." That's what my
own experience felt like—as if I'd been walking in one direction
and then, in response to some inner pull, I turned—not even all
the way around, but only at what seemed a slightly different
angle.

I hoped the turning would put me on a straight, solid path
with blue skies above and a warm, benevolent sun shining down
all the time. I certainly enjoyed better health than when I
began to "turn" back in 1980, but the new path I found myself
on seemed often as dangerous and difficult as the one I'd been
following before. Sometimes it didn't even seem like a path at
all. Sometimes I felt like a hapless passenger in the sort of small
airplane they used to show in black and white movies of the
1930s, caught in a thunderstorm, bobbing through the night sky
over jagged mountains without a compass.

I found strength in the hard wisdom of those who had delved
much deeper than I into the spiritual realm, like Henri
Nouwen, the Dutch Roman Catholic theologian who wrote in a
book our minister recommended, called *Reaching Out,* that
". . . it would be just another illusion to believe that reaching
out to God will free us from pain and suffering. Often, indeed, it
will take us where we rather would not go. But we know that
without going there we will not find our life."

I was thrilled to meet Father Nouwen at lunch several years
after I returned to church, through the consideration of my
friend and neighbor James Carroll, the former priest who became a successful novelist. I told Father Nouwen that I had
appreciated his books but that it dismayed me to read of his

anguish in *Cry for Mercy: Prayers from the Genesee;* it made me
wonder with discouragement what chance a neophyte had in
pursuit of the spiritual, when someone as advanced as Father
Nouwen experienced pain and confusion in his relation to God.
(I was neglecting numerous other, even more powerful exam-
ples, the epitome of which was Jesus Christ on the cross.) Father
Nouwen answered sharply that, contrary to what many people
thought, "Christianity is not for getting your life together!"

At the time I was taken aback by that statement and found it
discouraging, but later I came to appreciate it and even to
discover a kind of relief from realizing that my mistakes and
muddles didn't necessarily mean I was a spiritual failure or even
unchristian because I didn't have my life "together" in the way
I thought it should be.

There was a period around four years after I returned to
church that I felt as if finally, with God's help, I was on the right
track in my own journey. Then I had an experience that was
like running head on into a wall. I turned down a lucrative
opportunity to write a movie script because it would have
meant making a series of trips back to Los Angeles. I knew I
never wanted to live there again, but this would have meant
only four or five week-long trips (or so I was assured, though I
feared I might be drawn back into the Hollywood orbit by its
own powerful suction). I prayed intensely, and felt it was not
right to go, but then as soon as I made the decision I fell into
panic, fearing I had unnecessarily rejected money I sorely
needed. Then I questioned my own prayer, and wondered if in
fact I was only reacting to fear, instead of to God's will that I was
trying so hard to discern and follow. Or was I simply a fool to try
to make business decisions based on prayer?

My agony over what I had done and why I had really done it
was made more intense by the question of God in the midst of it
all and the fear that I might be misusing Him for my own self-
justifications. I felt a sort of psychic pain as unrelenting as a
dentist's drill. In the torment I prayed, and there was no relief,

and twice I turned back to my old way of dealing with things, by trying to numb the pain with drugs. Throughout all this I never lost faith in God, never imagined He was not there, but only that His presence was obscured. Then the storm broke, like a fever, and I felt in touch again, and in the light. I was grateful, but I also knew that such storms of confusion and inner torment would come again, perhaps even more violently.

I learned that belief in God did not depend on how well things were going, that faith and prayer and good works did not necessarily have any correlation to earthly reward or even tranquillity, no matter how much I wished they would and thought they should. I believed in God because the gift of faith (if not the gift of understanding) was given me, and I went to church and prayed and meditated to try to be closer to His* presence and, most difficult of all, to discern His will. I knew, as it said in the Book of Common Prayer, that His "service is perfect freedom," and my greatest frustration was in the constant choices of how best to serve.

At a time of difficulty I went to Glastonbury Abbey, a Benedictine monastery only forty minutes or so from Boston, to spend a day and night in private retreat (I had first gone there on a retreat with King's Chapel, and enjoyed returning alone as well, as I did in this instance). I went with about seventeen questions in my head about following God and finding the path He wills us to take. In the chapel bookstore I saw a thin paperback volume called *Abandonment to Divine Providence,* which I bought and took to my room and devoured. It was written by an eighteenth-century Jesuit named Jean-Pierre de Caussade, and it sounded (at least in that new translation) as if it had been written the week before, specifically to answer my questions. I continued to read it from time to time, and always found some new passage that seemed to speak to the urgency of the mo-

---

* Throughout the book I refer to God as "He" and "Him" purely from tradition and familiar usage, but am just as comfortable thinking of God as "She" and "Her," and even more as a divine mystery transcending human gender.

ment. On one of those occasions when I felt again jarred and confused about what to choose I read:

"So we follow our wandering paths, and the very darkness acts as our guide, and our doubts serve to reassure us. The more puzzled Isaac was at not finding a lamb for the sacrifice, the more confidently did Abraham leave all to providence."

In times of anguish it was hard to have the faith of an Abraham, and difficult to be reassured by doubts when I seemed to be walking in darkness. Yet there I was, like everyone else, having emerged from all sorts of crises and heartbreak and traumas, events that seemed to have insured my destruction or at least any chance of ever feeling joyous and fulfilled again, and I had gone on, and felt renewed and hopeful all over again, and the very pits of despair most often seemed to have been entries to the next unexpected, unimaginable (while in the pit) emergence and rebirth.

I did not come to think that "everything works out for the best," certainly not in the earthly, egocentric terms by which we judge the occurrences of our lives, or in the way that the larger events of the tumultuous world of wars and earthquakes, murders and plagues, affect us personally. I was fascinated most by the mystery of it, and of how, to paraphrase William Faulkner, we so often not only endure but prevail.

I began to look at my own life from a different angle when I returned to church, and I got a whole new lens through which to view it when I took a course our minister offered in "religious autobiography." There were only about a dozen people in the class, a small enough group to feel comfortable about getting to know one another and share some of our inner selves by reading aloud brief papers about early "religious experiences" (not necessarily having to do with church or formal religion). One evening each of us went off alone and drew a "road map" of his or her life, showing the personal mountains climbed and deserts crossed, the pits into which we fell and the forests through which we passed, and then we paired off and exchanged "guided tours" of the mazes, detours, and unexpected routes that brought us to where we were that moment—in the parish house of King's Chapel, sharing our religious pilgrimages with others engaged in the same quest.

I was able to discern the spiritual direction of my own "wandering path" and started to write about it in the papers we were asked to read to one another. Because of the intimacy of the group I wrote in a very frank and unguarded manner, not worrying about what would "look good" or cause embarrassment, and I continued what has become this book in the same spirit. It started that night in the class at the parish house when our minister asked us to draw a picture of the house we grew up in, and try to remember what was in it—the furniture, rugs, wallpaper, windows.

I looked inside and saw the beginning.

II
BEGINNING
AND
WANDERING

1. The Light

First there is light. My father is playing the small foot-pedal organ in the living room of our house in Indianapolis and my mother and I are singing along with him that "in the dark streets shineth the everlasting light" and I feel a deep and quiet thrill, a tingling in the skin, for I know this season and its music are sacred and so is the light described in the song and even the light from the lamp outside in our own dark street that shines in the frosted pane of the front-room window.

That was the first memory that came to me when I thought of my childhood feelings about God in the class on religious autobiography nearly half a century later. Christmas was the high point of the year for me as a child, not only because of Santa Claus and the toys and gifts and tree, but because of the sense of something greater, deeper, brighter than everyday life, a kind of magic aura whose mystery I sometimes tried to penetrate by staring at a candle flame or studying the frost formations on the window by the glow of the street lamp reflected on fallen snow. I longed for that time of year and felt instinctively more alive in it, as if the whole earth in that season—culminating in Christmas Eve—had revolved closer to the source of life itself, which I knew from Sunday school was God.

My parents had me baptized and took me to Sunday school at the First Presbyterian Church, because it was Christian and Protestant and conveniently located only two blocks from the drugstore at 16th Street and Central Avenue where my father worked as a pharmacist for my Uncle Crawford Harbison. The minister was the Reverend George Arthur Frantz, a stern and imposing man with a mighty voice who wore black robes with red trimming on Sunday and seemed an appropriate earthly representative of that thunderous biblical God who laid down laws that were written on stone and punished people who didn't obey them. We Sunday school children were spared the forbidding prospect of the Reverend Frantz himself as our teacher, and were thankfully delivered by our parents instead into the gentler arms of his wife Amy.

If George Arthur Frantz appeared to a child's eyes as a human incarnation of the God of wrath, his wife Amy was by the same vision the warm and comforting embodiment of the God of mercy. I remember her in red, a large, round shining apple of a woman, brown hair pulled back in a bun, face scrubbed and glowing, eyes lively and glinting, mouth in a smile that seemed a genuine expression of delight at being a believer in and bearer of the "good news" of Christianity. I can't recall a child ever crying in Amy's Sunday school, or imagine any need for doing so, even for us preschoolers temporarily separated from parents in an era before professional "child care" when such separation was potentially traumatic simply for being so unusual. Children instinctively trusted Amy and were drawn to her, calmed by the sense of love and warmth that seem to spread around her like a comforting blanket.

Grownups, I learned later, considered her a little bit "touched." I'd forgot that expression till this moment—it meant people who were not quite "normal," but acted in a manner that the world around them considered to be slightly bizarre. Maybe it's what Eugene O'Neill meant by *A Touch of the Poet,* though what seems to me appropriate in Amy's case is that she was "touched by God." (I doubt that her critics had anything so impressive in mind, however.)

There was an aura of disapproval of Amy of a condescending

kind, a sort of behind-the-back snickering. I think it must have been partly because of her style—she spoke in a melodic voice and with perfect diction that people I knew then might consider a bit "hoity-toity" or "uppity." But most important of all, she took the lessons of her Christian religion as literal and seemed to apply them in her everyday life—really loving your neighbor as yourself, turning the other cheek, doing unto others as you would have them do unto you. She taught us children those and other radical ideas (I think she got away with it because we were children and the "responsible" adults knew we'd grow out of it, which we did). One of the main lessons I remember from Amy's Sunday school was that God loved everyone regardless of race, creed, or color. I remember it not only because of her words but because of a painting reproduction that hung on the wall of our Sunday school room.

Jesus was holding the children. They were not only white, like me, they came in all colors. Jesus loved them all, you could see that clearly from the picture. And Amy told us so. This was Indianapolis in the 1930s, which only the decade before had been a stronghold of the Ku Klux Klan. In fact, my father used to speak in hushed tones of how the Klan met in the church across from his drugstore and came in afterward for Cokes and ice cream.

There were no real children of other colors in my Sunday school class, but simply to have such a picture displayed and to instruct little kids about equality was radical in those days. It was only a picture, but it made a lasting impression on me. It came again to my mind when I went for the first time to Spanish Harlem, where I wrote my first book a few years after graduating from college. (Even when, as a practicing intellectual atheist, I thought I had put Christianity out of my mind, that picture stayed in it.) Again when I covered the civil rights movement of the fifties and sixties in the South, traveling for *The Nation* magazine to places like the Mississippi delta, Birmingham, and Little Rock, I kept seeing that old Sunday school picture in my head and it meant something not only because of what it showed but because of what Amy had said about it.

In her lilting, pure-toned voice, she told us matter-of-factly that Jesus loved all the children, no matter what color they were, and he wanted us to love them too, and that's what *we* should do, and I believed her (even when I no longer "believed in" Jesus, I believed in Amy and the lesson she had taught us). I believed her more than other adults who told me things, and I sensed that, for the very reason other adults thought her strange, she was one of the only one of them daring to tell us the truth; and that, in fact, was why they thought her "touched" and didn't quite trust her.

When I was five years old we moved from the apartment near my father's drugstore—and the Presbyterian church—to the little half of a house of a kind called a "double" where we lived for the next decade in a neighborhood called Broad Ripple on the north side of town. Going to church and Sunday school now meant getting in the car and making a trip downtown on my father's one day of rest, so we stopped attending on a regular basis, and soon our family churchgoing dwindled to major holidays. Of course we still believed as completely as always in God, Jesus, Christmas, and Santa Claus, just like everyone else in the world we knew, but our formal worship had pretty much stopped. That probably would have marked the end of my childhood religious education, had it not been for Lloyd Harter's rich, eccentric aunt.

Lloyd Harter was a neat guy in my grade at school who was also a fellow member of our new neighborhood Cub Scout group (Den 6 of Pack 90). When Lloyd's family had moved to town a few years before and he entered the second grade he made friends right away, through not only his amiable personality but his colorful family. His beautiful, dark-haired mother was said to be a former model, which in pre-World War II Indianapolis seemed as exotic as having an ex-movie star in our midst. As if that weren't enough, Lloyd announced in class one day that his Uncle Louie was a magician. He pronounced it *"maj*-i-kun," which made us laugh, but no one laughed when Lloyd invited us to a party in his own basement starring Uncle Louie performing magic tricks just for us kids. To make the occasion even more memorable, Uncle Louie taught us home-made magic tricks we could do ourselves with matchsticks and rubber bands.

Lloyd's track record as a provider of quality entertainment was one of the reasons nobody hooted him out of the room when he invited some of us fellow Cubs to join him in what would have otherwise seemed a form of medieval torture for a healthy group of All-American nine-year-old boys: an after-school Bible class at a Baptist church on the other side of town. None of us were goody-goodies or aspiring little angels, least of all Lloyd, and in fact his reputation as a regular fellow helped make the whole thing respectable. (Had the invitation come from someone like the scholarly and sensitive Bill Berner, who was known to read a dictionary under his desk during class and liked lettuce and tomato sandwiches without any meat in them, it might have been dismissed with a general scoff of disdain.)

The idea had come not from Lloyd himself, of course, but from another of his fascinating relatives—a wealthy aunt who wanted her nephew to get some old-time Baptist religious education, and was clever enough to know that the best way of luring him into it was to recruit his buddies to come along with him. She was also clever enough to make the whole prospect not only easier but even *glamorous* by offering to send Lloyd and his friends to the Bible class across town and back home again *in a taxicab.*

I had never been in a taxi, nor did I know anyone who indulged in such luxuries. In our world, people only took taxicabs in movies. But if we signed up for the Bible class, we would get to ride in a taxi twice every week. We knew that the aunt must be rich, in order to afford such an expensive scheme, and certainly eccentric to think it up in the first place, which made the whole thing more intriguing. I doubt we really believed her assurance, passed on via Lloyd, that this Bible class was going to be fun and exciting, but even if it turned out to be dull we had the two-way cab ride to make up for it, so we said yes.

Of course we had to get permission from our parents, and I think at least one boy's folks refused, sharing a feeling of some more moderate Protestants that the Baptists, with their reputation for preaching "hell-fire and damnation," were too "extreme." My own parents were pleased, especially my father, since *his* father had been a Baptist minister in South Carolina and Kentucky. My father had taken us to the Presbyterian church because of its proximity, but it seemed as if fate (or God?) had come up with this totally unexpected means of getting the grandson of the Reverend William Daniel Wakefield to a Baptist church, even if it meant getting him there by taxi!

I never knew my Baptist preacher grandfather, who died when my own father was twelve years old, and most of the stories I heard about him were stern and scary. He was usually invoked by my father to show how tough it was in the old days, and how easy and soft it was for boys like me. If I whined about having to wear a shirt and tie, my father would tell how he had to wear a stiff collar and sit in a front pew in church and pay attention, without fiddling around, or his father would punish him, sometimes by a "whipping" with his belt. If I was not behaving myself during the Christmas season, my father would tell about the year his own father saw to it that he only had sticks and coal in the stocking he hung by the fireplace.

Sometimes the sticks and coal in the stocking story became so blatantly maudlin that my mother and I would get to giggling about it, and in later years my father would tell it with mock meanness, laughing at his own melodrama. Still, my grandfather even in memory was no laughing matter, but a stern man of God who punished the wicked, even his own son. (He obviously bore a striking resemblance to the God of the Bible!) For some reason, though, despite the stories of his wrath, I thought of my grandfather more with awe and fascination than with fear, and was proud of having as an ancestor someone who had held such a grand position as a Baptist minister. He seemed to me not so much a relative as a historical character, like Robert E. Lee or Daniel Webster.

The minister and his wife who taught our Bible school class were not stern or scary in the least. They were a happy, enthusiastic young couple named McCarthy (I don't remember their first names, but as children then we probably only knew them as "Reverend and Mrs. McCarthy"). The class in fact *was* fun and exciting, just as Lloyd Harter's aunt had predicted, not only because of the genuine joy with which the McCarthys delivered their message but also because they taught us by telling stories. They made the Bible stories come alive with their spirited recounting, sometimes by acting out parts, sometimes with homemade "visual aids" like crayon-drawn pictures and maps, sometimes with ingenious recreations of miracles. I remember still the thrill of Mrs. McCarthy demonstrating how the rod of Moses brought water from a stone as she tapped a brown paper bag (arranged to look just like a rock) covering a drinking fountain that Reverend McCarthy hid behind and turned on to spout a tremendous jet of miraculous water!

We not only listened to stories, we sang hymns—not the solemn, stately songs of the Presbyterians but rousing Baptist hymns like "Life Is Just a Mountain Railroad" and "Throw Out the Lifeline." When we sang that last one we stood up and dramatically extended our right arms as if hurling life preservers to drowning souls while we sang at the top of our lungs, "Throw out the lifeline, throw out the lifeline, someone is drifting a-way-ay . . ." We didn't hear a word about hell-fire or damnation but rather were told of the love of Jesus, who seemed in this Baptist view to be a strong, wise, understanding fellow—a kind of divine lifeguard—and at the end of the sessions I was among those who heeded the call to come forward and declare that I believed in this Christ as my savior.

The belief was not a passing fancy that faded when the Bible school ended. I insisted on returning to the Baptist church across town on Sundays, though without the largesse of Lloyd Harter's aunt paying for taxis, it meant two different streetcars and several long walks in a journey that took more than an hour and a half each way. My parents eventually persuaded me to find the closest thing to a Baptist church near home, and I discovered that at the Broad Ripple Christian Church right up near the end of my block they sang the same hymns (I could continue to "Throw Out The Lifeline"!) with *almost* the same fervor, and also practiced baptism by full immersion. I now wanted that kind of baptism myself, feeling instinctively as soon as I heard about it that the discreet sprinkling of drops of water I had received as an infant from the Presbyterians was hardly adequate for the job.

I would have to wait, however, as this church required young people to attend its Sunday school for at least a year and then take a class of study and preparation given by the minister to be sure that the candidate understood and wanted by his own free choice this kind of baptism (like the other Baptists and their offshoots, they did not believe in baptism of infants, but felt that it only counted if a person was old enough to understand the meaning of the act).

At first I went to Sunday school most Sundays, said the Lord's Prayer every night before going to sleep, often hummed, "What a friend I have in Jesus," when walking alone after dark in spooky places or if called to the principal's office for a possible bawling out, but was not a proselytizer or any kind of junior evangelist. I was even slightly embarrassed by the cardboard sign that said "Jesus Saves" in the front-room window of the Neudigates' house on my block, feeling such a show of faith was excessive.

The greatest passion in my life at this time was sports, though

I never was very good at any of them. I played football and baseball with the other kids on the block in the vacant lot next door to the Alexanders' house, went to every basketball and football game and track meet I knew about at nearby Broad Ripple High School, and lay on the living-room floor on Saturday afternoons next to the radio listening to broadcasts of college football games. My favorite book of the time was the biography of Knute Rockne, the legendary coach of Notre Dame, and my favorite movie the one in which Pat O'Brien played the part of Knute Rockne, All-American. Though I had no intention of giving up my Baptist faith to become a Catholic (I thought of it as an exotic religious sect suitable mainly for fanatics and foreigners), I wanted to go to college at Notre Dame, and I wanted to be a football coach when I grew up. Aside from sports, I loved the Cub Scouts and their lore of knot tying, Indians, and the outdoors. I listened to "Jack Armstrong, All-American Boy" on the radio and aspired to the "regular guy" virtues he represented.

I recount these things to put into context the unexpected experience I had around this time. Religion was an important part of my life, but it was not the main focus of my attention. My belief in God did not make me think I was different from other people, but more like the people I admired. Belief in God, I felt, was part of being a good American, appropriate and even necessary for a Cub Scout working his way up to being a Boy Scout. It was in this "normal" ambience that the occurrence took place, and that made it seem all the more surprising—and, in a sense, more "real"—for I knew I was a "regular person" rather than some kind of Holy Joe.

On an ordinary school night I went to bed, turned out the light, said the Lord's Prayer, as I always did and prepared to go to sleep. I lay there only a few moments, not long enough to go to sleep (I was clearly and vividly awake during this whole experience) when I had the sensation that my whole body was filled with light. It was a white light of such brightness and intensity that it seemed almost silver. It was neither hot nor cold, neither burning nor soothing, it was simply *there*, filling every part of my body from my head to my feet. I did not hear any voice, or any sound at all for that matter, but with the light came the understanding that it was Christ. The light was the presence of Christ, and I was not simply in his presence, his presence was in me. The experience lasted for several minutes, long enough for me to be fully aware of what was happening, to know it was "real" and not an illusion or trick of imagination or anything else except what it was—the light that was the presence of Christ infusing my whole being.

The experience was not frightening but reassuring, like a blessing, a gift, and a confirmation all at once. I don't think I told anyone about it, at least not for some years. I didn't need to ask anyone about it, because I so clearly knew what it was, and I didn't want to try to explain to others who, not having had the experience, would not be able to understand. I went on about my life of sports and school and Cub Scouts and friends, and I think the only thing different about me was that I decided that when I grew up I wanted to be a minister instead of a football coach.

I don't remember much about Sunday school at the Broad Ripple Christian Church, not even the identity of the teacher, so it must have been pretty boring. That Baptist Bible class, with the exuberant McCarthys leading us in "Throw Out the Lifeline," was a hard act to follow. My new minister was a kindly, tall, skinny Ichabod Crane sort of man who was painfully shy and lacked the least hint of charisma.

Though I still attended Sunday school sporadically, I began to feel more spiritual refreshment out of doors than in church. In the fields and woods not far from my house, in the burning leaves of autumn and the running streams of spring, I felt close to the source and mystery of things. The perfume of wet clover, the rough hide feel of the bark of oaks, rushes of wind lifting curled red maple leaves off the hard autumn ground in swirling eddies—these and all the million sights, sounds, and smells of nature, from the sweet taste of foxtail grass I chewed as I strolled, to the quick flash of a perch below the surface of a brook, all were revelations and messages of some great creating force, which of course was God.

Sometimes I felt a frustration that I couldn't decipher the message, that I couldn't learn the meaning of it all, of life and earth, simply by trying to communicate with nature: staring, for instance, as hard as I could at a rock with layers of colors, or feeling its smooth cool surface with my fingers and pressing it in my palm as if I could squeeze out an answer. I knew there were secrets in the woods and sometimes I felt I was very close to them, close to understanding, and there was a thrill in sensing such knowledge was *there* if only I could look close enough or be still enough or attuned enough. But there was also a sadness in always coming up short, being stopped just before the moment of revelation, and suspecting that despite all my efforts I would never quite be able to penetrate the veil, to see into the hidden meaning, the very heart of existence itself.

There was a sadness at home around this time, too, of a different kind. It was not the bittersweet sadness of secrets hinted in the woods and fields but rather the stifled, angry ache and clash of a man and woman at war, and not just abstract men and women but the ones who made me and, through God's design, gave me life: mother and father. (Is that why I fleetingly then had the common childhood fantasy I must have been adopted? Do the million kids who go through a phase of such suspicion come to it out of the fear of who they really are, what kind of monster they must surely be, if produced by two such angry opposing warriors as they see at their own supper table?)

For my sake, I know, they muted the pitch of their battle. It sometimes came out in sudden cries from my mother when she sobbed out her sorrow over the ironing board on nights when my father was working the late shift at the drugstore. If men in the great cliché script of marital discontent are supposed to tell

Other Women that their wives don't understand them, to whom could a woman complain (in those housebound days before careers and child care) that her husband didn't understand her, except her own child?

My father, face flushed red and a vein in his temple throbbing, complained about monthly bills with an anger and anguish that even a child could see (perhaps could see better than adults) came from deeper frustrations than department store charges. Around this time my mother developed a terrible, deep-down wrenching cough that erupted in the night and required her to sleep on the living-room couch instead of in my father's bed, while he fell prey to "sick headaches," migraines that kept him home from work in taut, pale-fleshed pain and spasms of vomiting.

Suppertime was too often a period of strained silence, and neither parent complained when I made a habit of turning on the kitchen radio to listen to "The Lone Ranger" while we ate. Our fragile family (I feared for us, felt our vulnerability) ate without conversation as we listened to the melodramatic strains of the masked man's theme song. The famous cry of the legendary masked do-gooder—"Hi Yo, Silver, away!"—and the reassuring grunts of his faithful Indian companion Tonto were welcome substitutes for domestic dialogue in those times of tension.

I loved the order and security of school, the fun and fascination of learning, the calm of the classroom presided over by loving, daytime mothers who never cried, who always seemed to have themselves—as well as their assorted children—under control. My parents were shocked when my teacher told them what a happy boy I was at school, for they saw me as a sorrowful, moping child at home. They were hurt and wanted to help— me, themselves, us—the Wakefields of 6129 Winthrop, within whose white frame half of a house was hid enough explosive emotion to blow the planet off course. (I did not suspect then that similar forces might be contained behind the bushes and porches and walls of the other little houses on the block, but assumed that inside all the rest were panoramas of Norman Rockwell family bliss.)

What to do? Psychiatry was a decade or so down the pike, at least for Middle Western, middle-American, middle-class families like ours. I doubt that our family or friends even knew anyone who sought the help of therapists or professional family counselors if any such existed in the Indianapolis of the 1940s. People like us still took their deepest personal problems to ministers or priests, but my parents no more than I could have revealed anything private to either the minister of their old church or my new one. I suspect we feared that confession of family discontent would cause painful embarrassment for the good Reverend "Crane," while the mere notion of human strife would have seemed so far below our image of the mighty Reverend George Arthur Frantz that we surely trembled at the fear of eliciting not his sympathy but his wrath; or even worse, his disdain.

My mother came up with just the right counselor for us: the reassuringly mortal wife of the Godlike Presbyterian minister, my shining former Sunday school teacher, the round and ample Amy Frantz. My mother and father and I went together to Amy's for breakfast sometimes, and other times for tea. She always served tea, mornings or afternoons, with toast and jam. We never had tea at our house and it seemed very English and special and faintly "upper class," a treat from an older, better world, a world more solid than our own. The comforting aroma of the tea and the sharp tangy scent of fresh-cut lemon, wisps of steam curling up from the newly poured cups, combined in the overall aura of security and grace. I knew that no one could yell or curse in that atmosphere. We were there not to confront but to calm ourselves.

Amy was more our comforter than counselor, and that's what we needed. We needed her love, her care for us not only as individuals but as a family. She did not take sides. Though my mother was the one who had asked for her help, Amy showed just as much affectionate respect for my father. *Ben.* Amy smiled when she said his name. You could see she felt he was a fine fellow, and it helped you to see that too, and helped him see himself that way; it was obvious, the way he warmed and brightened in the beam of her attention. And my mother didn't get itchy and testy as she sometimes did when people showed their appreciation for *him*, since she knew that Amy appreciated *her* just as fully as possible, too. In Amy's presence we were equally loved, not only as individuals but also for what we were to one another—husband, wife, father, mother, son. Amy somehow enabled us to become those things in one another's presence. She helped us accept who we were and who we might better be for each other, and then, even though we'd later lose that sense, we knew it was there, because we had recognized it at Amy's.

Of course none of all of this was said in such a way as I am telling it now, this is my later understanding of what was really happening there in Amy's sunlit living room as we sipped our tea and ate our toast and jam and spoke in halting, broken sentences, never directly confronting painful specific issues. None of them really were "the issue" anyway, but only angry eruptions, like outbreaks of fever or rash, caused by a deeper disharmony, some struggle of will between my parents that I felt caught in the center of, squeezed and jabbed, like an unsuspecting animal in a trap. We brought all our burdens to Amy even though we didn't say them out loud, and she accepted them as she accepted us, and in doing so brought us to some kind of greater acceptance of one another.

Though we didn't call it that, I realize we went to Amy for healing (which of course is why people go to any kind of "counselors," from Freudian analysts to ministers' wives). I believe she was a real healer, not only with her tea and benevolent presence but with prayer. Amy got us to do something that each of us did individually but weren't able to do as a family—pray. Somehow we could do it with Amy's blessing; with her support we could do what we couldn't do at home. We always left Amy's feeling more whole, more connected.

Though my interest in Sunday school had waned at the Broad Ripple Christian Church, I still looked in the woods for answers to the secrets of life and God, as well as in books. I read a child's book of Bible stories and identified with Daniel in the lions' den because of having the same name, and perhaps because I somehow felt I was in a similar situation at home. For a while I tried to use Daniel's method of warding off the lions. I rose early in the morning, went out to the porch, and made the sign of the cross, hoping this would protect me from the threatening passions and fears that seemed to roam inside our own seemingly innocent house, and inside my own outwardly innocent body and mind.

I went to the nearby public library and avidly read books of Indian lore, and was especially fascinated by ones about Indian boys around my own age. The story that most engrossed me told how an Indian boy had to go into the woods alone for several days and nights and find his own name. It was part of his growing up, of eventually achieving his own manhood and becoming a brave. The journey into the woods was an adventure and a test, and during it the boy would see some sign or have some experience that transformed him, gave him his name—like Running Bear, Flying Eagle, Tall Pine. I, too, longed for some sort of adventure that would give me a new, more manly identity, transform me from a weak, vulnerable child into a capable, strong, respected young man. A "brave."

Maybe I thought baptism would do the trick. I had wanted the full-immersion experience after that Baptist Bible class, and that was one of the reasons I joined the nearest neighborhood facsimile. As well as the waiting period of at least a year, I think it was also felt that a young person ought to be at least eleven years old in order to undergo, by his own responsible decision, an experience of such significance, one that would surely affect and perhaps alter the course of his life (not to speak of afterlife, too, right on into eternity). At any rate I remember it was shortly after my eleventh birthday that the sacred dunking I so desired was finally scheduled.

In a child's sense of time a year and a half seems an aeon, and during that waiting period from the high point of accepting Jesus Christ as my personal savior to the doldrums of the Broad Ripple Christian Church Sunday school, the strength of my faith ebbed and flowed. Waking up early on summer mornings to make the sign of the cross on the front porch, à la Daniel in the lions' den, had brought a temporary recharging of spiritual strength, but the autumn air of Indiana put a chill on those personal rituals (for some reason no longer clear to me, it was necessary that the sign be given outdoors, perhaps so God had a clear view of the proceedings).

Christmas was, as always, a time of spiritual recharging for me, with an extra zap that year from being asked to read "The Story of the Other Wise Man" by Henry van Dyke in front of the whole congregation at the adult church service. I still have a memory of standing at the pulpit, my voice sounding clear and assured without my having to worry about it; there was warmth in the air and in the friendly, upturned faces of the neighbors who made up the congregation, and I had that rare, solid sense of knowing I was doing that moment what in all the world I was supposed to be doing.

With the turning of the year the holiday light dimmed down to ordinary days and soon the snow was melting, bleak rain turning hard ground to mud as my own thoughts turned from God to basketball. Even in the sixth grade, I followed the Indiana State high school basketball tournament with awe and wonder, caught up in what the sportswriters I avidly read had appropriately dubbed "Hoosier Hysteria." My first published work appeared in the "Shootin' 'Em and Stoppin' 'Em" column of Indianapolis *News* sports editor William F. Fox, Jr., when he printed a doggerel verse I had written predicting the outcome of the tournament, in which—I now realize—I mixed my religious metaphors with sports (they were almost inseparable in my mind anyway as the highest realms of life):

You'll see that the boys who in glory will reign
Will be those old Archers—South Side of Fort Wayne!

The thrill at seeing not only my words but my name in print far outweighed the literary criticism offered on my work by sports editor Fox when he introduced it. Noting that the team I had enshrined in my verse had been defeated the day before, Mr. Fox wryly commented: "Think how Dan Wakefield must have felt after struggling to write these lines."

I wrote stories for my grade school newspaper, the *Rippler*, read more books about Indians and nature (the "Mother West Wind" stories, and animal books like *The Bears of Blue River* and *Biography of a Grizzly*), and increasingly found more inspiration and feeling of connection with God out of doors than in Sunday school. Now that my "real" baptism was finally near, I didn't much feel in the mood for it, yet hoped it might revive in me the commitment I had felt in the Baptist Bible school class.

I was restless and beginning to experience a new, confusing, yet dizzily exciting feeling when I saw movies like the one where Barbara Stanwyck was a beautiful Indian maiden trying to ward off the advances of a handsome cavalry officer as they wrestled in a haystack. I was troubled at the same time that I was strangely excited by gazing at pictures of Rita Hayworth in *Life* magazine, and when my mother asked who my favorite movie actress was (why did she want to know *that?*) I assured her it was Irene Dunne—a symbol of the pure virtues of hearth and home.

A friend in the Cub Scouts showed me his older brother's *Boy Scout Manual*, where it told about the unsettling feelings boys begin to experience around the time of Scouting, and recommended long walks, cold showers, and something called a "hip bath," which required sitting in a washtub of lukewarm water until the dark urges passed. This chapter in the *Scout Manual* was called "Conservation." My friend and I joked about "hip baths," giggling nervously and secretly fearing for our immortal souls. Perhaps baptism, which was said to wash away sins, would be more effective than a mere hip bath in eliminating lustful feelings. But oh, what delicious feelings! Did I really want them eliminated? I wished I'd been baptized a year and a half before, when things seemed simpler.

A boy on my block named Charles Pettijohn (nicknamed "Chod") signed up to be baptized along with me. I know we received instructions from the minister, but the only thing I remember was that we were to show up for baptism wearing white shirts and white duck pants. Each of us was baptized individually, and we had to walk forward alone from out of the congregation up to the front of the church. There was a kind of a stage, and a deep tank filled with water. The minister was already down there standing in the water up to his waist, and I had to walk down some steps into it to stand beside him.

As I walked down into the water the organist started playing a hymn, and I remembered to my dismay that I had forgotten to tell the minister the hymn I wanted. It had been my right to choose whatever I wanted, and I had been trying to make up my mind between "What a Friend I Have in Jesus" and "Leaning on the Everlasting Arms." (My top favorite was still "Throw Out the Lifeline," but I feared that might seem a contrary message for someone walking down into the baptismal tank, as if I might want to be rescued from baptism, or saved from being "saved".) The hymn the organist was playing at this crucial moment was none of those. In fact, it was one I never would have chosen at all. Damn! They were playing a hymn I really hated for my own baptism. The whole congregation was singing those words that so disturbed me at the very moment I approached my ritual of transformation:

> "Have thine own way, Lord,
> Have thine own way,

Thou art the potter,
I am the clay. . . ."

That wasn't what I had in mind. I wanted to have the Lord on my side, but I wanted to have *my own way*. I wanted God to be a kind of divine bodyguard and right-hand man in helping me achieve everything I wanted in life, defending me against my enemies and making me number one in whatever I chose. Now here I was about to be baptized while the opposite message was being played and sung, which I feared might make it come true!

It was too late to argue. I stood by the Reverend Crane and he pressed a handkerchief over my nose and said, "I baptize you in the name of the Father, the Son, and the Holy Ghost," and then dunked me under the water. When I came up dripping (but otherwise feeling very much the same as before) I turned to climb the steps leading up the other side of the tank, and I saw, awaiting me, a life-sized, cardboard replica of Jesus. It made me feel cheated and sad. On top of the wrong hymn being played, the cardboard Jesus put the finishing touch of disappointment on my long-awaited baptism.

The day itself was gray and humid. After church, Chod Pettijohn and I snuck off to the Vogue Theater and saw a movie called *Bataan* about General MacArthur fighting the Japs. We knew it was not a holy thing to do on the day of our baptism, and we ate a lot of popcorn and felt depressed afterward. That night, it rained.

The words of the hymn kept ringing in my mind, taunting me. "Thou art the potter, I am the clay." It asked God to "mold me" into whatever He wanted, and that didn't seem fair. To hell with it. I stopped going to Sunday school and gave up the idea of being a minister, returning instead to my earlier ambition. I was going to be the football coach of Notre Dame, whether God liked it or not.

Firmly in charge of my own fate, I entered the fury of adolescence.

2. The Unknown Test

> "What if the events of our history are molding us as a sculptor molds his clay, and if it is only in a careful obedience to these molding hands that we can discover our real vocation and become mature people?"
>
> —Henri Nouwen, *Reaching Out*

I was cut from the freshman football team at Broad Ripple High School, a blow that did not bode well for my future career plans as head coach of Notre Dame. I had already begun to secretly accept the painful truth that I was not born to be a sports hero, but I knew that many successful coaches had only been ordinary athletes in their own schooldays. I did not, however, know any cases of coaches who hadn't been able to make the team.

My failure felt like more of a curse because almost all the kids who tried out for freshman football were kept on the squad. There weren't quite enough uniforms and equipment to go around, though, so a few of the most hopeless cases—those too small or skinny or bumblingly uncoordinated—had to be dropped, and I was among the misfits.

I had prayed to be on the team, but I didn't blame God that I didn't make it, and in fact was rather ashamed I had bothered Him with such small-time concerns as freshman football when He had a whole universe to run. I consoled myself by whistling "What a Friend I Have in Jesus," believing the Son of God would understand my plight since he after all had been human himself. I took it on faith that Jesus had been a teenager, assum-

ing the lack of any record of those years was simply to spare him
the ungodly embarrassment that goes with adolescence.

I wished I could have known more, though, about that period
of Jesus' life. Did he go out for the team at Nazareth? Did he
have a pimple? An erection? A crush on a pretty girl? I con-
structed my own theory from the slim evidence available, ad-
miring Jesus' rebelliousness at age twelve in going off without
telling his parents to debate with the wise old men in the Temple, a risk I suspected must also have incurred the ridicule of the
other kids for showing off his intelligence. Luke's report that
after that incident—"Jesus increased in wisdom and in stature,
and in favor with God and man"—made things sound too
smooth to be human for a teenager, but I took comfort in knowing he was later rejected by his people and made to feel an
outcast in his own hometown.

Even before my football fiasco I had felt out of place and
foreign at Broad Ripple, my own neighborhood high school.
This feeling of alienation was all the more upsetting because it
made no sense. All my friends from the eighth-grade graduating class at Public School 80 had gone on to Broad Ripple High.
Ever since I was old enough to find the way, I had crossed the
Monon Railroad track that ran behind my house on the way to
far-off Chicago (which I knew as Carl Sandburg's "city of the big
shoulders" as well as the home of the great pro football team,
the Bears) and walked the mere quarter mile or so to the Broad
Ripple football field, baseball diamond, and basketball court to
cheer on the "Ripple" Rockets. I assumed, as did my parents
and friends, that I would go to high school for four years at
Broad Ripple just as I had gone for eight years to the warm,
friendly elementary school at the top of the block where I lived.

After getting cut from the football team I told my parents I
wanted to transfer to Shortridge—an archrival high school with
a reputation for catering to rich kids and being "social" and
snobby. My old friend Jerry Burton, a regular guy and straight
shooter I'd known since kindergarten, told me it was a great

place, though. The Burtons had moved from my grade school neighborhood closer downtown and Jerry was going to Short-ridge, where he played on the freshman football team, and he assured me that at Shortridge everyone who wanted to play made the team and got to wear a uniform. (Oh, the glory of the uniform, the visible proof you belonged!)

Besides that, Shortridge had its own newspaper, the *Echo*, famous as the first daily high school paper in the country. Maybe I could make something of the writing talent that got me pub-lished in the School #80 *Rippler* and the Indianapolis *News.* Transferring high schools was a pretty big deal and required special permission from the school board, but my parents, see-ing how unhappy I was at Broad Ripple, backed me all the way, and I was able to start to Shortridge almost immediately, in midsemester.

It meant getting up earlier, walking farther than the distance to Broad Ripple just to get a streetcar and later transferring to a bus, but I was happy to make this longer, more elaborate jour-ney. As soon as I got to Shortridge, I felt at home. It was as if the fog lifted and I could see and understand what was happening, even though I had never been in the place before and only knew a few of the two thousand or so students when I started.

I recall even now my sense of relief on entering those long, high-ceilinged halls, and can almost bring back in memory the special smell of the place, a mixture of sweat and perfume, ink and old books, the odors of all high schools then but with its own individual accent, definably different than Broad Ripple. Maybe it was because the girls wore a different kind of perfume, as they wore their bobby sox in a different style; Ripple girls wore the white socks (barelegged or over hose) rolled down to the tops of their saddle shoes, while Shortridge girls wore them pulled straight up on the leg where they reached to about mid-calf, and this single identifying gesture seemed the sign of an en-tirely different social order. Each high school in the city (there were eight in all then) had its own dress code, as each had its own distinctive odor in its halls, and to me the Shortridge scent was headier, sharper, muskier, more redolent of legend than the others.

That sense I had on entering Shortridge of being in the right place, a deep inner feeling of relief and centeredness, of balance in relation to the rest of the world, is something I have experienced in most of the crucial places and times of my life. It is like an interior compass, or maybe a divine divining rod, telling me *here,* or, as Brigham Young put it when he looked on Utah: "This is the place." (I use the term "divine" because with this feeling is a sense of being in tune with the universe, of the larger force or purpose or higher power I identify as God.)

Even though I was glad to be at Shortridge I was lonely there at first, unknown and a nobody (I wish I had known Emily Dickinson's poem that asked "Are you Nobody too?"), but my shaky self-confidence was bolstered by the fact that one night a week I was what we called then a "big dog," my importance confirmed by a uniform with lots of badges, in the Boy Scout troop I had joined at age twelve and where I'd become a leader at age fourteen. The Scouts around that time provided not only my most meaningful social but also spiritual experience, at least of any institutional kind.

I believed in God as much as ever but I felt closer to Him in the Boy Scouts than in church, especially at a magical place seven miles north of the city where Scouts from our area went every summer called Camp Chank-tun-un-gi. There was an outdoor amphitheater with wooden bleachers facing a stage, and the woods behind it served as dramatic backdrop. We gathered there every night at campfire for songs, games, contests, lectures, and theatricals, and on Sunday mornings held services that started by singing at the top of our lungs "Come to the Church in the Wildwood" with the deep-voiced boys chanting in counterpoint "Come—come—come—come . . ." (As grown men, decades later, in Indianapolis or New York City, those who had been there could take up that chant and the sound of it always evoked the scene again for me: the fresh dizzy morning scent of summer woods, and sunlight bursting through deep green foliage with a gold brilliance that made you blink.)

The Scout camp version of "The Church in the Wildwood," beneath the wide sky, seemed closer to God than the stuffy confines of meeting halls and pews, just as the waters of the streams and the old gravel pit where we learned to paddle our canoes were deeper and more mysterious than the bathtub-like baptismal tank behind the pulpit at the Broad Ripple Christian Church. The spiritual sustenance of camp was not limited to the Sunday morning service but came through hundreds of discoveries that lay waiting all around us, from sightings of meadowlarks and flickers during prebreakfast bird-study merit badge hikes, to identification of the bloodroot plant whose stem could be broken open to release a red liquid that we, like the Indians, could smear on our skin for decoration.

Indian lore dramatically permeated the life of the camp, and almost everything had an Indian name (or at least some original Boy Scout leader's imaginative version of an Indian name), from the creek—"Old Tuscarora," to the latrine—"Old Masacoma." Nomenclature was colorful, but not as important as ritual. I was deeply thrilled to find at Camp Chank-tun-un-gi a sort of Hoosier Boy Scout version of those stories I had read in library books about Indian boys going into the woods to prove themselves and discover their new identity as young men.

I was pledged to silence, blindfolded, led into the woods, and left alone with only two matches. This was the beginning of the "Overnight Experience," one of the tests required for gaining the exalted rank whose very name brought awe and mystery to me: *Firecrafter.* It was not just a rank but a kind of unofficial Boy Scout camp fraternity with chapters in several different states throughout the Midwest. I was well on my way to earning the rank of Eagle Scout the following year, but becoming a Firecrafter was more important to me. Eagle was the highest rank in Scouting, an honored and coveted award, but there was nothing secret about it, no ritual mystery or rite of passage, no going into the wilderness to be tested and transformed.

Each candidate for Firecrafter was issued a card that listed the requirements for the rank, the last of which was simply called the "Unknown Test." How could any red-blooded boy resist the challenge? Rumors were rife every year among the rookies that the Unknown Test was some terrible physical trial, like leaping a chasm across a canyon at night, walking through fire in your bare feet, or maybe (more likely) running a gauntlet of veteran campers who would beat your bare behind bloody with shellacked wooden paddles as the college fraternity men did to pledges in their own initiation rites.

I was prepared for the worst when my own time came and along with my fellow "candidates" I was blindfolded and led by a guide to a secret place in the woods called Firecrafter Hill to undergo the final initiation that culminated with the Unknown Test. To my relief and amazement and finally awe, the rigorous secret rites of the mighty, manly Firecrafters involved no trial of the body at all; instead of presenting any physical challenge the ceremonies were in the deepest sense spiritual.

I do not remember the words that were spoken but I remember the three fires and the young men standing solemnly behind them (our leaders, whom we admired and respected), speaking in firm and quiet tones of our responsibilities to our fellow humans and to the earth, and finally and most importantly to God. The Unknown Test had to do with how we fulfilled those responsibilities throughout our entire lifetime, and we would not know whether we had passed until we came at last before the God who made us.

The sense of God invoked that night—of fire and honor, of the mysteries of nature and the fellowship of friends—was the one I tried to keep fixed in my mind as disturbing new thoughts and feelings that had first begun to flicker to life a few years before now seemed to be growing with power enough to overturn heaven and earth.

The adolescent stirrings of sex were like some kind of interior volcano that threatened to explode and tear me apart. The first time I ever masturbated I didn't even know what was happening and was terrified that the throbbing sensation in my penis meant that I had done myself some awful, irreparable damage. Open talk about sex was taboo at that time, and I feared asking my father about it in case it might be something demanding punishment, and feared asking friends out of worry that it might reveal I was different and even "worse" than they were. In spite of my fears and prayers ("God help me!") the deep, delicious urges returned, as sure and powerful as the tides, overwhelming all fears and vows with the undeniable surge of life. These natural impulses were stimulated by hundreds of provocative pictures in movies and magazines as well as by the beautiful girls who were blossoming all around us in their first, full-bodied glory.

The hip baths, hikes, and cold showers recommended by the *Boy Scout Manual* were pitiful defense indeed against the daily assaults of lust. It was very soon clear that, in order to ward off the urges of the flesh by means of the Boy Scouts' recommendations, I would have to spend my entire adolescence sitting in a washbasin of lukewarm water, only emerging at age twenty-one to rush down the aisle with some prearranged bride (how could I woo her from the washbasin?) and directly into the marriage bed.

"Saving yourself for marriage" was in fact the standard procedure urged upon young men and women of my time and place. One of the beloved adult counselors of Camp Chank-tun-un-gi gave me that specific advice when a college-age staff member I shared a cabin with reported me for the un-Scoutlike sin of squeaking bedsprings that were keeping this censorious roommate awake at night, not only by the noise, I bet, but also by the disturbing thoughts such sounds provoked in his own imagination).

Mr. Grey, the adult counselor, a businessman in regulation khaki shorts and knee socks, who looked like Humpty-Dumpty, with fat belly protruding over chicken-thin legs, told me with tears in his eyes that he knew I was basically a good boy despite my weakness, and that someday such problems would be happily resolved when I found "the right girl" and settled down with her in holy matrimony. That was not much consolation to a fifteen-year-old male in Indiana in 1947.

The only advice the Bible had to offer was not to spill my seed on the ground, which I was able to observe only in the technical sense that I never did it outdoors. (I almost nightly spilled my seed in the sheets of my own bed, a matter never discussed with my mother, who regularly changed those same sheets without ever mentioning the incriminating stains.) I wondered if Jesus had been prey to these human urges, or whether he simply "grew in stature and in wisdom" without any such torments. Did the later account of his temptation in the wilderness, which he passed with flying colors, mean that the divinity in him enabled him to ward off all temptations, including the sexual?

I was not about to put such questions to the good Reverend Crane, nor could I imagine addressing them to gentle, motherly Amy Frantz (or any woman, least of all my own mother!). Though Amy was still a loyal friend of our family, her gentle and benign ministrations hardly seemed suited to these unexpected new torments of my own, and my parents' problems had also seemed to escalate around this time. I am only guessing now, as I guessed then, from hints and tears and whispered names overheard from the dark at the top of the stairs, that my mother and father were each guiltily engaged in some sort of extramarital attraction that seemed to last about a year. I never knew how far it went with either of them, but it was far enough to cause fresh pain and perturbation between them.

Then my mother, in her search for answers (she was our

determined Diogenes, looking always for the truth that would save us), discovered Moral Re-armament. This was a movement that was founded by a Dr. Frank Buchman, a kind of middle-class religious revivalism based on adherence to "absolutes" like Honesty and Purity, and "sharing" of failures to live up to these lofty standards in something like early versions of encounter groups.

My mother became so carried away by the hope of this new form of salvation that she got my father to take us—including a friend of mine from the Boy Scouts—to the MRA headquarters on Mackinac Island the summer I was fourteen, for intensive training with the MRA leaders. Their young people were zealous, bright-eyed girls who wore no makeup, and boys with all-American smiles who neither drank, smoked, swore, nor engaged in sex before marriage; and they recruited others in a kind of golly-gee varsity version of Christianity. One of their older youth leaders, a collegiate fellow in his late twenties who still wore his old letter sweater, got me and my Scout friend in a room where he persuaded us to get down on our knees and confess our worst sins, which turned out to be masturbation. I cried in tears of shame and guilt while my buddy assured me later I shouldn't feel so bad about it since "everyone did it." When I got home I resumed my habit, and resented the forced down-on-the-knees confessional. MRA gave me my first bad taste about religion in general, with its piety and prurience in eliciting group confessions of what its leaders conceived to be sexual misconduct. (I think they regarded anything other than intercourse in the missionary position between man and wife as coming under this category.)

The message of sin and guilt I was getting from my middle-class, middle-American sex education was reinforced at school in a class called "Health and Safety." The one day devoted to learning about sex consisted of having all the boys go out of the class and stand giggling and shuffling nervously in the hall while the girls looked at a set of pictures; then the girls left the room to stand in the hall while the boys went in to look at the pictures. The pictures were colored medical photos of people in advanced stages of syphilis, with disease-ravaged skin. This, we learned, was what sex could cause: the sickness unto death that constituted the wages of sin.

We were too "enlightened" to believe that masturbation caused insanity or blindness (that was a few generations in the past) but it was still popular street knowledge that "beating off" caused pimples. My friends and I assured each other we really "knew better than that," but joked about it with such hysteria that we sensed in some way we really did fear it was true. Well, didn't we have personal proof? Sure enough, I was masturbating, and I began to get pimples. First it was just a few, like the other kids. That was disturbing enough. But then somewhere around the summer before my sophomore year in high school the real horror began. The breaking out of my skin began to spread, like a red fury.

It was not just an ordinary case of acne but one of the worst, one of the all-consuming kind, and I feared I in fact might be consumed by it, might not be able to survive its onslaught, not be able to stand to look at myself in the mirror as I had to do every morning in nightmare agony, knowing this was me, my very identity, the way the world saw me—a leper, a mess, plagued by some kind of sickness of the cells of my body, my very self.

"I wish it was anything else, I wish it was something wrong with my arms or legs, some other place, anything else," I choked out to my father one morning when he drove me to school and I had to face the world again with my awful face. It was not just ugly but a sign of my sin, my guilty secret that everyone could see!

Our father, who art in heaven, help me please get rid of this curse, make me whole and clean again, please, God . . .

But God was no more help than the creams and ointments, the vitamins and pills and medications. Sometimes I blamed

Him for this curse that had befallen me, on the grounds that it was the kind of unfair punishment of sin that modern people were beginning to believe was outmoded, and was the very kind of thing that gave God a bad name in our enlightened psychological era. Even if it was not God's punishment, though, but only physical affliction like any other kind of disease, why didn't He answer my prayers? Then sometimes I came to the even worse conclusion that the whole thing was simply my fault, and I had no one to blame but myself. Despite some brief, tormented intervals of agonizing self-control I continued my habit of sexual self-indulgence, so how could I blame God? In the back of my mind I secretly feared the street lore was true, and I was simply causing my own disfigurement by my lack of restraint.

Worried not only about my skin condition but probably even more about the depression it was causing me, my parents found a doctor who was supposed to be a specialist with this problem who might be able to help my case. The doctor gave me some sort of injection, and then asked me, awkwardly (I remember his heavy, uncomfortable breathing), how depressed I was and whether, like some teenagers who suffered from this problem as acutely as I did, I ever felt so badly I thought about suicide. I said no, which was not quite a lie, since even though I sometimes felt I would rather be dead than disfigured I didn't think about how to go about it or make any specific plan for doing it.

After the shots of the specialist failed to have any effect and I sank deeper into despair, my parents with love and desperation told our family doctor they would do anything to help me, but what in the world could they do? He said if they were serious the only thing he knew that might offer any hope was the world-famous Mayo Clinic in Minnesota, and my parents arranged to take me there during our summer vacation after my junior year in high school. We went with the hope and faith of pilgrims to Lourdes.

I sat on an examining table wearing only a white hospital

wrapper while a doctor on the staff of the Mayo Clinic delivered his verdict on my problem to me and my parents in a tone of brusque annoyance.

"People come here expecting miracles," the doctor said, "and we don't have any. You have a bad case of *acne vulgaris* and there simply is not any cure for it. It will get even worse than it is now, and will leave you scarred for life."

Having delivered his prognosis, the doctor turned and left the room.

At the time, I only wanted to die. It was not until I was grown and felt healed and healthy that I wanted to kill the doctor. I am sorry even now that I did not at least find out who he was and seek him out and tell him what he did to a vulnerable sixteen-year-old boy and wreak some measure of revenge for his gratuitous cruelty. It was not until five or six years after his examination, while describing the experience to a psychiatrist, that I learned that *acne vulgaris* was Latin for "common acne." I thought it meant "vulgar," as in the worst, most offensive, most repulsive variety.

Going back home from Mayo's, knowing the long, hot journey had been in vain and the future worse than I thought, I lay in the back seat of my father's green Mercury coupé, not wanting to sit up and show my face at the window. My father had gently persuaded me to put on some of the latest medicine he had brought from his drugstore, a kind that tightened the skin when applied and made my face feel like a stiff, burning mask, but somehow its very discomfort seemed to offer some slim hope of healing and in my desperation, I put the stuff on. Curled up womblike in the back of the car, the rough nap of the seat covers rubbing against the ghastly mask I wore for a face, I pressed my eyes shut and prayed into the dark.

Even though sometimes I felt as though I wanted to die, I knew I was going to live because Aunt Ollie could see into my future; therefore I must have one. Aunt Ollie was famous (or infamous, depending on who you talked to) in our family for being able to foretell the future, as she did one summer after-noon when I was a small child and she telephoned my Grandma Irene (known as "Ireney"), my mother's mother, to ask "Where is Charles?" Charles was Ireney's youngest and favorite child, an "angel child" she called him, and at that moment he was a bright and handsome twenty-one-year-old who was on a vaca-tion at a lake in a place called Three Rivers, Michigan. Grandma Ireney reported his whereabouts to Aunt Ollie and asked her why she wanted to know. "I sense death and water," Aunt Ollie said. That same evening Grandma Ireney got the news that Charles had drowned.

Aunt Ollie was not literally my aunt but a distant cousin on my mother's side of the family, and her actual name was Ollah Toph. She lived alone in a small house north of town that was like a cabin in the woods. When I was a teenager she was in her eighties, a proud and beautiful woman with a thick crown of snow-white hair who carried herself with a special dignity. She wrote verse that appeared in the three local newspapers, the *Star,* the *News,* and the *Times,* and her favorites were collected in a privately published volume of selected poems. Her house was overflowing with books, and in the living room was an old foot-pedal organ, something like (but larger than) the one my father played in our own living room.

As well as being a poet and organist, Aunt Ollie was a clairvoy-ant, and a member of the Spiritualist Church. (In one of her thick, fascinating scrapbooks was a clipping describing a world Spiritualist conference she attended in England, one of whose delegates was Arthur Conan Doyle.) She believed that when people died their souls or spirits went on to a higher plane, that some of them looked after or over us in a role like that of guardian angel, and that sometimes she was able to communi-cate with these souls who benignly hovered around us. These beliefs were part of her religion—as was a belief in God and Jesus Christ, which was expressed in the most sensitive manner in some of her verse—and she was offended by being thought of as a "fortuneteller" or dabbler in the occult. She was a spiritual person in the deepest sense, one of those rare individuals whose beliefs are not compartmentalized or added on certain occasions like an afterthought or a Sunday hat, but rather are part of their being, their way of acting and communicating.

My parents took me to visit Aunt Ollie in those troubled early teenage years, perhaps to offer me some diversion or even "hope" through her special way of seeing things, her faculty that was indeed an "extra perception." Although we knew better than to ever request it (for fear of insulting her), sometimes Aunt Ollie would close her eyes and with a sharp intake of breath describe the presence of a man or woman we could not see at all, standing beside one of us, and indicating something about us by a gesture or expression; from Aunt Ollie's descriptions of these presences, they did not have halos or wings but seemed like ordinary people whom she could see but we could not. ("There is a tall man standing beside you, Danny, wearing a gold watch chain over his vest. . . .")

At other times Aunt Ollie would take one of our hands and with a concentration so intense it indeed seemed trancelike she would speak of our future as she did one time to me, saying, "Danny, you will be close to death through some experience that will interrupt your education, but you will survive it, and complete your education, and then you will cross the ocean— not the Atlantic, but a farther ocean, to a farther land than Europe. . . ." It was of course fascinating and a little spooky, but we had no idea what she was talking about; being close to death and crossing distant oceans sounded as romantic as reading *The Arabian Nights* or *The Seven Wonders of the World* as we sat in that little house in the woods north of Indianapolis in 1947.

Sometimes Aunt Ollie would just play the organ or recite some of her verse, and that was fine too—being in her presence was itself a calming, restoring experience, like being in a special kind of sanctuary outside of ordinary time, away from the jangle and clash of daily life. Of course we were most enthralled when Aunt Ollie went into one of her trancelike states and spoke to us of other times, or communicated one of those "presences" of another being. I never saw one of those spirits or "angels" myself. No matter how hard I concentrated I couldn't catch a glimpse, but I believed Aunt Ollie really saw what she told us she saw, and I knew she really could "see" in a way that we could not.

I was comforted as well as intrigued by Aunt Ollie's concept of guardian angels; I already knew that life was full of adversity, that dark forces whispering of death and surrender operated within us as well as the more obvious enemies without (from Hitler's legions to snobby kids and unfair teachers in high school) and I wanted all the help I could get. Besides, there was something about it that made sense to me. What about the "close calls" we all experienced, the brushes with harm we seemed to be pulled back from at the last moment, like the time I was pounding a tent pole into the ground with the head of my Scout ax and the blade came back up and struck me right across the bridge of the nose, leaving a scar but stopping a hair short of serious injury? Or what about those times of panic when for no apparent reason a sudden sense of calm would come, like the soft impression of a touch of reassurance, yet no one was there— like that stormy day in Lake Michigan when we all swam out too far and there was an undertow, and I settled down from breathless thrashing and swam back to shore.

Perhaps it was all chance or a meaningless series of haphazard happenings that might go either way—after all, my Uncle Charles did drown and no saving "presence" or even Aunt Ollie's prescience saved him—yet in the midst of my own unknowing, the idea of guardian angels struck a chord of response and welcome in me.

There were other guardian angels in my life then whom I couldn't recognize as such because they were, like me, of flesh and blood. Aunt Ollie's term for her other-worldly visitors also fit some of those people we all are blessed with who are not only friends but whose presence seems to touch us in some deep way, whose reaching out is special and saving, bringing some essential new dimension to our lives. Sometimes they are older people—teachers, counselors, and mentors—who take an extra interest in us; sometimes, growing up, there are kids our own age who teach us some of the most valuable lessons, or extend the steadiest hand or most meaningful word or deed of reassurance.

My first day at Camp Chank-tun-un-gi I was so nervous and "green" that I couldn't even perform the simple task of unrolling my brand-new official Boy Scout sleeping bag on the upper bunk assigned me. As I fumbled with simple knots and zippers, in walked Jack Hickman, leader of the Hawk Patrol of my own Troop 90, who was a year older than I was and already a respected veteran of a whole summer at camp.

I was terrified that he would not only laugh at me but would spread the word that I was such a dumb rookie I couldn't get my sleeping bag unrolled. Instead, he quietly helped me get the damn bag properly laid out in official fashion on my top bunk, ready for inspection. Even more amazing, when I stammered out my embarrassed thanks, instead of bawling me out or making fun of me, he said with the staunch sympathy of a comrade: "That's okay—these sleeping bags are pretty tricky." I learned from Jack, to my surprise and relief, that to be a "Big Man" you did not have to ridicule the ineptitude of others; that respect and understanding and even *gentleness* were not signs of weakness but might in fact be indications of confidence and strength. (I also felt then that I had a friend for life, and I was right.)

I heard from my parents, teachers, and all other adult authority figures that perseverance and hard work and dedication and faith (in yourself as well as God) could overcome obstacles and make your dreams come true, but I saw it actually happen by watching Jack. Like me, he was not very big or physically strong or athletically able and, like me, he longed to be a football hero or at least a player on the team who wore a uniform and sometimes got into the game and maybe even helped win it. Unlike me, he was determined to make his dream come true.

Realizing his physical limitations, Jack decided the only way he could make the team was to become something very rare in those days—a specialist. He decided to become a placekicker, an expert who would trot onto the field to kick the extra point or a field goal with such methodical skill that his reliability would become indispensable to the team. He practiced after school, after the team had finished working out and gone home, on the empty football field at Broad Ripple High School, and I am proud to say I was his assistant, the guy who placed the ball on the ground at the right angle and held it steady with my fingertip when he kicked.

I was still in grade school while Jack was a freshman at Broad Ripple when he set out to master this art, and I was honored to be a part of it, happy to join him in the lowering dark on those autumn afternoons and then into winter, even sometimes when snow was on the ground (as it might be in crucial games, and one had to be able to kick accurately in all weather conditions) and through the muddy days of spring and the heat of summer until Jack became so good at the art of "splitting the uprights" that in fact he made the team as a placekicker. He went on to be the varsity extra point and field goal expert not only for Broad Ripple High School but later for Wabash College, earning the adulatory nickname "Golden Toes" and setting a record for consistency.

Serving as the ball-holder for Jack's placekicking practice was the closest I came to glory on the gridiron. I never even went out for the team that everyone could play on when I got to Shortridge High School, using the excuse that the season was already more than half over then anyway and I would be too far behind in knowing the plays, but I think secretly I was afraid of getting hurt, something so shameful in its unmanliness I would never have admitted it even to myself.

In one last desperate grasp at the success in sports that seemed so essential to happiness, I tried to emulate Jack's dedication by sneaking over to the deserted track around the football field at Broad Ripple under cover of dusk and practicing the mile run. The conventional wisdom of coaches and even most high school principals of the time was that any red-blooded American boy could be good at sports if he only tried, and even those who were frail or badly coordinated could succeed with guts and determination in track, especially the distance events, since all you had to do was grit your teeth and run. So I ran. I even bought a stopwatch.

I ran my heart out and somehow struggled to the finish of four laps of the quarter-mile track at Broad Ripple and pressed the timer button on my brand-new official stopwatch, only to find I had run the mile in the shockingly slow pace of seven minutes and two seconds, surely a record for leisurely pacing, even for that era. Most healthy grandmothers could have run it in less. Undeterred, I prayed for strength and dedication, practiced harder, and ran the mile again a few weeks later. This time I did it in seven minutes flat. Though in fact I had improved my time from 7:02 to 7:00, my failure to break the seven-minute mile turned me finally from running to writing about other people running.

Instead of going out for the football team at Shortridge, I tried out for the famous daily paper, the *Echo,* and after proving myself by reporting with accuracy (and what I hoped was style) such lackluster events as the monthly meeting of the Stamp Club, I made the staff. In Room 240, the offices of the legendary school paper, complete with a semicircular copydesk like the regulation kind used in real newsrooms, I felt as naturally at home as I had felt awkwardly out of place on the oval cinder track where I tried to push myself to accomplish what simply wasn't in me to achieve. In the office of the *Echo*, my stringy arms and flat feet were no deterrent at all to doing a good job. Instead of being barked at by an angry coach, I was quietly and gently corrected and shown approval at the appropriate times by Miss Jean Grubb, a wry, wise woman who served as the faculty sponsor for the *Echo* and at some point coined the nickname that described my eager activities for the paper: "Scoop, Jr."

Soon I was not only covering football, basketball, and track for the *Echo*, but my diligence got me a coveted job as sports "stringer" for the Indianapolis *Star*. My boss was one of the sportswriter idols whose prose I avidly read every day in the morning paper, a sharply eloquent observer of the glorious high school and college athletic scene in the Indiana of the 1940s. He was a neat, thin, wiry man with a quickness of mind and gesture, and his name fit his breezy manner of casual wit and style: Corky Lamm.

It was my job (though I would have paid for the honor and pleasure of doing it) to act as host and assistant when Corky came to cover a big game for the *Star* at our home field or court, supplying him with names and numbers, background and anecdotes about our players and coaches, scurrying up and down the sidelines with him during the games, keeping stats and acting as his "spotter." Sometimes he offered me a ride home after the game, and I got to talk with him.

At first we just talked about sports and newspapers, and what I enjoyed most was that Corky talked to me like an adult. As he drove me home from a game one afternoon I questioned him about some tactic of his boss that did not seem correct sports-editorial behavior and Corky gleefully slapped the steering wheel and said in appreciation: "Out of the mouths of babes!"

It was a light, cloudless afternoon, and we were driving over the bridge across Fall Creek toward the Marott Hotel. It was a cold day at the end of the football season. The trees were bare, and Corky had on a pair of black gloves with wool lining that made a kind of thud when his hand hit the steering wheel. I was so proud that Corky approved of my viewpoint that the moment itself became fixed in my memory.

He became my mentor and friend. He in turn trusted and confided in me. In my hero-worshipful innocence I was shocked to learn that this bright and caring man with the beautiful, loving wife and two small sons and a daughter, this man of enormous energy and talent (he also took and developed his own photographs and drew sketches and cartoons for the paper as well as writing), had suffered his own setbacks and disappointments.

After a brilliant college career at DePauw, in Greencastle, this small-town boy from Indiana stormed the very gates of New York, the pinnacle of his profession, where the greats like Grantland Rice and Ring Lardner had gone and sealed their fame. And he was rebuffed. He told me how he made the rounds with his sketches and clippings and photos from his college paper, but the best job he could land was a clerical position with one of the giant insurance companies, and they stuck him in some anonymous cubbyhole. He already had the wife and they planned soon to have the children. After six months he came back home to Indiana.

Things had not even gone all that smoothly at the *Star*, where he was passed over for the sports editorship in favor of the flashier guy who was now his boss. He still had hopes of being "discovered" and called to some high position in a major city of the East, but even though some of his stories and photos won national honors, he was never summoned on from Indiana. His early dream faded, leaving a tinge of disappointment, an aura that was almost invisible. I imagined only I could see it, and was honored that Corky had let down his customary snappy, happy-go-lucky way with me to allow that glimpse. I was also sobered by it, for it gave me my first real sense of how tough and wrong-headed life could be, even for the good guys. And I knew there were none better than Corky.

The sports department of the *Star*, where I went to deliver my stories, was a kind of mecca for me, made thrilling by the staccato beat of the wire service teletype machines and the casual, irreverent talk of the sportswriters, who let me into their world as if I were an equal instead of just a kid. Bob Collins, a former Cathedral High School athlete, who was younger than Corky, also became a friend and mentor, later turning me on to some of my first novels outside the classroom, talking with me about books he loaned me by Budd Schulberg and Kenneth Roberts. (When I recently read the autobiography *Boston Boy* by my old Greenwich Village friend Nat Hentoff, the jazz critic and social observer, I had a sense of recognition when he described getting to know the jazz musicians at the old Savoy Café as a teenager and how, unlike the other adults he had known, including his own father, they talked to him "with remarkable openness . . . about loneliness, failure, women, death, and such things." The *Star* sports department was my Savoy Café, the sportswriters my jazzmen.)

By writing about the guys who were running, passing, catching, blocking, and kicking I got to know them, and by getting my name in the school paper in stories about the athletes' exploits, other kids got to know who I was, and soon, instead of feeling like a lonely outcast, I had a lot of friends. They accepted me somehow (to my own amazement) in spite of my ravaged complexion, and even pretty girls who were actually popular went out on dates with me and some of them even let me kiss them (one of them, with graceful self-appointed responsibility and patient tactfulness, showed me *how* to kiss) and I knew the dizzying ups and downs of falling in love, and the heated passions of parking and backseat petting, which was about as far as most of us went in the tame teenage climate of the forties, though a few famously precocious ones did "go all the way." Many of the boys as well as girls (for we were not designated men and women yet) still believed as I did that it was actually sinful to "do it" ("the big deed" or "the dirty deed" we most often called it) before being married, or unless (at least) with the person you were absolutely sure you were going to marry.

The deprivation was made easier by my deep guilt and fear, as well as the earliest inside report from a close friend who came by my house one memorable Sunday morning after a big party the night before, insisted I get out of bed and take a walk with him, in the course of which he confided "Well, Wake, I gotta tell ya—I did the big deed last night." I grabbed him and demanded he immediately reveal what it was like, in every detail, and he stopped and shook his head and said with a sense of mystery and awe, "Well, I gotta tell ya—it's not what it's cracked up to be." (I am glad to note that in later life that pal went on to a happy and lasting marriage with a highly satisfactory sex life, but I am also grateful that at the time he was so honest about his first awkward experience—a glowing account would have been too much for me to bear.)

Like most teenagers, we traveled in packs, and nothing in my life to that point made me feel so proud and part of things as being "one of the boys" of my own great gang. We giggled and punched and sang and screamed and piled into one another's jalopies, circling the drive-ins like sharks before nosing into a slot at the Ron-D-Vu for french-fried onion rings and a chance to talk to the fabulous girls who ran in their own herds, feminine reflections of our own need and panic and joy. They were not just our loves but our counterparts and comrades on the teenage journey. We tentatively groped with words and feelings and thoughts as well as hungry mouths and seeking hands to connect, to know, to relate in our fumbling ways those ineffable messages burning inside us, to say somehow to one another—and in so doing to discover for ourselves—who we were.

Of all the gang, I confided most in Harpie (there was a calmness about him and a sense of trust that I think made him everyone's favorite confidant), and he was the only one of my high school friends I dared introduce to Aunt Ollie. I knew she would sense his own sincerity as a seeker, not simply some ordinary teenager wanting her to play fortuneteller. In turn, I knew Harpie would treat her with the proper respect, that he would appreciate the spiritual nature of her gifts, and I was right on both counts. I don't remember any particular thing she told him, but I remember sitting in Aunt Ollie's living room with Harpie and afterward driving with him as we quietly pondered the mystery of it all—not just of Aunt Ollie's powers to seemingly penetrate the veil of our visible world, but the deep and limitless mystery of why we were here and where we were going.

Harpie was our great driver, a natural person with a car, and driving with him was a kind of meditation. It was what he did to think, and you, too, were able to think when Harpie was driving. You could relax because you didn't have to worry about him doing anything crazy or stupid behind the wheel, and you could sit back and let yourself be lulled by the hum of the motor and the bright, white eyes of other cars passing in the dark. After being at Aunt Ollie's with Harpie one night I remember driving with him even farther out north of town where only occasional lights, like distant beacons, shone from lone farmhouses scattered over that dear, flat land, and I had a feeling of acceptance and protection, of it being all right that we were really in the dark, not knowing where we were headed. I sensed the peace that sometimes comes from being aware of what we don't know, and being beside a friend.

Harpie was the only friend to whom I showed the book I was reading on the lives of the great philosophers, the only one I knew would not laugh at my search for some answer to the meaning of it all, some explanation for the suffering we each seemed doomed to undergo. Staring in the mirror every morning at my red, swollen face and trying to shave the ravaged skin was a daily hell that prayer did not cure and Jesus did not heal and God in what seemed His cruel wisdom did not relieve, and I was no more comforted by reading the Book of Job than Job was by his well-meaning comforters. So I had turned to seek other answers to the meaning of life and adopted some high school version of agnosticism with Tennyson's *In Memoriam* from the great philosophers book that I still remember:

> I can but trust that good shall fall
> At last far off, at last to all—
> So runs my dream—but what am I?
> An infant crying in the night,
> An infant crying for the light,
> And with no language but a cry.

But I did have more language than a cry, I had the language of prayer, and even with my doubts I continued to pray, and I know that sacred language was crucial to my own survival of the onslaught of adolescence. Life was like a close-up, in which every detail was enlarged. All was raw and open, there was nothing you could hide. Everything was moving and growing and changing, not just around you but in and on and of you. There were no drugs in my day and my gang didn't even drink much, so I wasn't under any peer pressure to escape in that way. My parents didn't drink, except for a "nip" or cocktail at Christmas and I knew they didn't approve of it, so I abstained through high school, having only a few sips from a can of beer that tasted sour and sudsy. Even without artificial stimulants, the highs and lows of that era seemed so extreme that the time of life itself, with its happy hysterics and gut-wrenching sobs, was like some extended acid trip. I have no trouble understanding why teenagers drink and take drugs and some even commit suicide, especially when they are given no faith or belief in anything beyond the moment or greater than their own immediate angst.

At my high school graduation ceremony in the vast space of the Indianapolis Coliseum, I stood before my assembled classmates and their families and delivered with ringing tones a valedictory I had composed with great care and believed was stunningly original, beginning with the observation that "Tonight, we have reached a milestone in our lives. . . ." The graduation address was given at Shortridge not by the number one academic student but by the winner of a speaking competition, and I was proud to have beat out my friendly rival Richard Lugar for the opportunity. This squared the score of our oratorical competition that had begun a few years before when I came in second to his first-place performance in the Indianapolis I Speak for Democracy Contest sponsored by the American Legion. I did not feel badly about beating Lugar for this honor since he had won many other graduation awards and I knew as did all of our classmates that he was someday going to be President of the United States and would get to make all the speeches he wanted (he came close to being the Republican candidate for Vice-President in 1984 and distinguished himself as chairman of the Senate Foreign Relations Committee after that election year).

I had finished my high school career in a blaze of teenage glory that included being editor of the 1950 Shortridge *Annual* (an elected post as a class officer), editor of the Thursday edition of the *Echo,* author of the weekly column "Sportlite" (a rival to Lugar's "Shooting the Works"), member of the prestigious Club 30 of popular senior boys who planned the graduation dance. I had placed third in the "Bluebelle-Uglyman" popularity contest (the only non-athlete in memory to finish in the top three), had a date with a beautiful girl for the grad dance and, happiest of all, I was enjoying a sort of remission of the acne, which had calmed in the months before graduation.

I might have thought all this good fortune meant God was on my side again, as He had been when I was a little kid, but I think my feeling was more one of *self*-confidence; that these triumphs showed I could mold my own fate (without troublesome intervention from God) as I headed for a glorious college career at the journalism school of chic Northwestern University. I vaguely had in mind going on to a career as a successful sports columnist for the Chicago *Tribune,* winning a glamorous and popular sorority girl for a wife (a cheerleader who wrote poetry on the side), and moving to a sumptuous home in the suburbs in that popular Tudor style of the time that reminded me of miniature castles.

That wasn't how things worked out. At the beginning of the fall semester I was curled in a womblike position in the back seat of my parents' car as they drove me home from Northwestern in defeat before I had even attended a class. I had gone through fraternity rush week without being offered a single invitation to join. My face had flared up again during the summer and I felt it was the reason for this across-the-board rejection, that I was branded by my skin as an outcast, and all the triumphs of high school were only a kind of illusion that counted for nothing and had made this defeat even more painful for being so unexpected. Fraternities were of major social significance at this time and place, the ultimate symbol of belonging, and all my friends had either pledged before even getting to college or were planning to do so as soon as they arrived on campus; it was unthinkable that any of "our gang" would not be sought after and included in the ranks of collegiate "Greek" eminence.

At the end of high school I had thought I was one of the elect, one of the in-group of life who was destined to look down benignly on the less fortunate as I climbed my way to success. But something had gone wrong. Instead of a bright collegiate future I saw only a blank wall, or worse, a mirror reflecting the awful image of myself as one who was marked as damaged goods, doomed to be an outcast. I prayed to God for help, but all I thought I could hear was mocking silence.

3. Another Kind of Baptism

It was one of those drafty rooming houses off campus, with ice-cold linoleum floors and creaky windows. Mail that consisted mostly of bills and advertisements, much of it to addressees who had long ago moved, spilled like fallen leaves from the bottom post of the stairway landing. The place had an air of anonymity as well as of impermanence, and might have been a student rooming house on the fringe of any big university in the country. It happened to be in Bloomington, Indiana, where I had fled to try to recoup my forces and get on with college education after the fiasco of fraternity rejection at Northwestern. I had never thought about going to school at Indiana University, but in the circumstances it suited my needs for reassurance and acceptance: it was only an hour from home in Indianapolis, and I was able to share a room with Jerry Burton, my old friend all the way from kindergarten through high school.

Most of my high school friends were shocked by my rejection at Northwestern, and supportive of my retreat to Bloomington. A few, however, confirmed my own guilty fear that I had taken the coward's way in failing to stick it out. Dick Lugar, who himself was not chosen in the freshman fraternity rush at Denison, told me in language left over from his sports column, "It's easy, of course, to fall back to the shadow of your own goalposts." He had chosen the manlier course of remaining at Denison, proving himself, and later being invited to join the prestigious Betas (demonstrating character worthy of a future President of the United States).

My friend from the Boy Scouts, Jack Hickman, had a year before taken a similar courageous stand, staying on at Wabash after getting no bids during rush week, and then being later pledged by one of the top houses on campus. Though Jack became a loyal fraternity man, his father was deeply embittered by the system. I will never forget the sound of his fury as Dr. Hickman drove me once to visit Jack at Wabash and recalled his son's rejection in rush week: "Did they think my boy *smelled bad?*" (The protective love that sounded in "my boy" and the rage of *"smelled bad"* were so intense, and so accentuated by their juxtaposition, I can still hear the words, and they make me shiver.) Jack, at any rate, did not scorn my own retreat to Bloomington, but urged me to try out for the student newspaper and think about joining a fraternity later on.

After my Northwestern experience, I understood the outsiders' complaint that fraternities were discriminatory and harmful, but as soon as I was asked I joined one. My friend and roommate Jerry was asked to pledge the same house, and we joined our high school buddy Bails at Kappa Sig, enduring the indignities and physical punishments of hazing and Hell Week, including middle-of-the-night rousings from sleep for "lineups" in which we were loudly berated and then had our asses beat black and blue, and sometimes literally bloody, by boozy upperclassmen, which was standard "Greek" procedure in those days.

Formal initiation was a serious rite in which you had to put on a suit and tie, swear belief in the Bible "and all its parts," and listen to the usually rowdy upperclassmen read a solemn passage about the ancient roots of the brotherhood, which seemed, at least to my own ears, a nonsensical hodgepodge of history and myth having something to do with, of all things, the Italian Renaissance. I think that even Romulus and Remus were cited, though I can't remember if they were supposed to have founded the Kappa Sigma fraternity as well as the city of Rome. None of it seemed to have any real connection with this assembly of Hoosier good-old-boys, most of whom were from farms and small towns in Indiana. The whole thing seemed embarrassing and childish to me compared to the initiation rites of the Firecrafters at Camp Chank-tun-un-gi.

I was grateful to the guys who had accepted me, yet ironically I felt more alien now that I was literally "in" a fraternity than I had before, and I moved out of the house at the first opportunity. I took an apartment off campus with Reggie, a fellow from my pledge class who shared my own general sense of uneasiness with the frat house as well as my new passion for reading and books—not just books assigned in classes but novels and poetry you read just for pleasure and intellectual stimulation, a concept regarded by many of our "brothers" with suspicion and even hostility. We avidly read F. Scott Fitzgerald and once I was "caught" with a copy of *This Side of Paradise* under my arm at the frat house, where one of the more neanderthal brothers yanked it away, held it up like a dirty sock, and asked accusingly, "You really like that stuff, don't ya?"

Reading seemed the most "real" part of my life in my brief time at IU, a time that I sensed was a kind of interim period, a purgatory I had to pass through. I remember a feeling of emptiness, of wind rushing through the wide streets and past the limestone buildings, making a hollow, echoing sound. The young men and women all around, dressed as college students, made the scene even more unreal to me, like the landscape of one of those science fiction novels where things only appear to be normal but are really, if you look close enough, the illusions of an alien planet. I knew this was not the way other people saw or experienced this place and time, and sometimes I felt frightened, as one who finds himself alone in a foreign place is frightened, and I was often depressed.

I prayed. I prayed the Lord's Prayer and the Twenty-third Psalm, and I prayed from a set of small cards with Scripture passages on them that my mother had given me when I went down to Bloomington. The cards came in a small plastic case that looked something like a miniature recipe box, and the idea was to pull out one of the cards every day for the inspiration and/or guidance of the message. It was rather like opening fortune cookies, and I guess I used it that way, but the scriptural passages in fact had a power that often provided a feeling of renewed strength and hope. The one I remember that refreshed and consoled me in a special way was Isaiah 40:31: "But they that wait upon the Lord shall renew their strength; they shall mount up with wings as eagles; they shall run, and not be weary; and they shall walk, and not faint." Maybe this message gave me hope that I would not only rise up out of my state of depression but fly from this alien place to one where my interior "divining rod" told me I was supposed to be.

There was another quotation that sustained me during that time, though it wasn't from Scripture. It was a quote from Abraham Lincoln that was carved in wood in the beautiful university bookstore, and it struck me so deeply I got goose bumps whenever I repeated it in my mind: "I will study and get ready, and maybe the chance will come." In that same bookstore, beneath those words, I discovered Sinclair Lewis and bought the Modern Library edition of *Arrowsmith*. I was awed that a man's life, in the fullness of its private as well as its public course, could be told in a book. That type of book, the novel, created with the kind of compassion and understanding of humanity the author displayed, seemed to me not only miraculous but as close to "sacred" as a secular book could be. I wondered if I would ever dare aspire to that kind of creation myself, which seemed to me the highest thing a writer could achieve.

I studied freshman lit with an English professor named Pratt who had a pipe and an Eastern accent. He was a courtly, thoughtful man who spoke with nostalgia of his undergraduate days at Dartmouth, and made *The Iliad* and *The Odyssey* come alive in the limestone halls of Indiana. I wrote so voluminously on the final exam, rushing to the front of the room for extra blue books, that one of my frat brothers in the class razzed me later about my eager-beaver attack on the final—behavior unbecoming a fraternity man. I didn't care. This professor, this class, these books, had released something in me, some powerful response that rushed out with tremendous energy and relief, bringing my mind and spirit to life in a way that was new to me and that seemed as necessary, once experienced, as food and drink. It *was* food and drink. The newfound hunger fueled my writing of that final exam.

The autumn of my sophomore year I took English composition with a young instructor whose name I have forgotten (I remember the elbow patches on his sweaters, and the intense enthusiasm he exuded when he talked about books) but to whom I'm eternally grateful because he asked me the question that gave voice to a growing inner feeling of my own: *"What are you doing here?"* He felt I had talent as a writer and would benefit from seeing something of the world farther than sixty miles from the home where I was born and had lived all my nineteen years. If my parents were sending me to college, couldn't they send me to some place in the West or East, where I'd never been and would learn all sorts of new things besides what I studied in books? He invited me to his apartment for tea with him and his wife and showed me how to underline passages in books and make comments in the margin that, instead of "devaluing" the pages, added to the pleasure of reading and made them your own, and he loaned me his treasured copy of Sherwood Anderson's *A Story Teller's Story*. I think of him now as one of those earthly "guardian angels" who suddenly appear in your life out of nowhere, offering a kind of confirming reassurance and appreciation, and serving as a guide to the next point in your journey.

This supportive graduate student instructor didn't tell me where to go, but simply said I ought to move on, that it was time to try my wings ("they shall mount up with wings as eagles"). It was shortly after that conversation that I read an essay assigned in another English course called "Education by Books." It told how the "great books" concept of education had begun at St. John's and was used in a modified form at Columbia College, the undergraduate school of Columbia University in New York City. The essay made reading sound as thrilling as I was learning to experience it myself, and it spoke with a kind of clarity and power that was new to me, making me want to know more about the author. His name was Mark Van Doren, and he was identified in the volume of essays as a poet who taught English at Columbia.

I can still recall the way those words looked on the page, for in some way that was as clear to me as it is unexplainable they were not only telling me who Mark Van Doren was, they were telling me I was going to study with him. I stared at the words a long time, enthralled, and I knew I was going to finish college at Columbia. The only thing I knew about Columbia until that moment was that its football team was called the Lions, and the coach was Lou Little. I didn't know anyone who was there or had ever been there, nor did I know anyone in all of New York City. I would have to persuade my parents to send me to this place they knew less about than I did, if my father could (and would) afford the higher costs of tuition as well as travel. Besides all that, I knew that getting accepted was really not feasible, for I hadn't even taken the college boards that were required for entry to an Ivy League school.

Still, I knew that somehow or other that was where I was going. I got copies of my transcripts from IU, made an appointment with the admissions office at Columbia, and took a train to New York City just before the Christmas holiday. The train ride itself was as thrilling as the ones described by Scott Fitzgerald of his own college days; it was a real rite of passage, formalized by a dinner in the dining car with the parents of my favorite high school girl friend, who were going to visit their eldest son at

Yale, and graciously bought me my first whiskey sour as a token of good luck and celebration for my journey.

I hoped to persuade the admissions officer to let me transfer to Columbia for my last two years of college. He looked at my grades, noted I was from Indiana (the geographic point was in my favor since Columbia traditionally was topheavy with New Yorkers), and said he thought it would make more sense if I started to Columbia the following month, when the spring semester began, rather than wait until the fall. I felt dizzy with gratitude and excitement. Columbia was not just another college to me, and a new beginning, it was also an opening to the great world of literature and books, art and ideas, in the very capital of all such thought and enterprise. I had studied and got ready, and the chance had come.

There were concrete and brick, congestion of crowds and traffic. I had not only come to Columbia, I had come to New York City. The subway rumbled to a stop at 116th and Broadway, heart of the uncollegiate-looking campus where I lived in a dormitory with an elevator run by a uniformed operator, and a lobby that had the look of an anonymous hotel. I ate breakfast at a drugstore on Amsterdam Avenue where students pressed up to the counter with old people from the neighborhood, drinking coffee and eating delicious things that looked like doughnuts with icing but were called French crullers, and at night I crowded into a booth at the V & T Pizzeria farther up the street and consumed my favorite new food, lasagna. Everything was wonderfully foreign to me, even the smell of the place. It wasn't worse, or better, just different—more exotic, sharp, complex, heady. With my eyes closed, I could take a deep breath and know that I was not in Indiana.

My ears as well as my nose and eyes told me I was far from home. I not only heard foreign languages—Italian, Greek, German, Yiddish—spoken in full or in phrases on the streets and subways, in groceries and delis and drugstores and bookshops, I heard my own native tongue rendered in accents I knew only from movies I had seen with New York "characters" or ones I considered "upper class" or "English." Most shocking of all, my own accent—the slow Indiana slurry kind of drawl that I had always regarded as "normal" speech—was regarded as a novelty and cause for amusement. My new classmates—most of them native New Yorkers—would gather round in good-natured jibing and ask me to say certain words or phrases whose pronunciation would send them into gales of laughter. "Hey, Wakefield, say 'Mozart,' " one would gleefully request, and I would accentuate my own natural rendering of *"Mose-art,"* slowing it even more for the laughs, playing my own sort of Hoosier version of Bojangles to ingratiate myself with the crowd. Even when I was loneliest—and at first there were times I was achingly lonely—I loved the place, for I had that deep, gut sense that for all its strangeness and unfamiliarity, for all the discomfort of feeling sometimes like an alien, this was precisely where I should be.

It was another kind of baptism. I was not dunked in water but rather immersed in a new kind of world, not only of sights and sounds and smells and rhythms (the pace of all aspects of life was quicker, like the way of talking), but also of thoughts and ideas, books and poems and paintings, music and art. The Columbia College catalogue used to boast that New York City was "our laboratory" and certainly I got a rich part of my education by boarding the IRT (I soon learned that only outsiders, hicks from the hinterlands, called it "the subway") and discovering the cultural treasures of Manhattan.

An assignment from an art appreciation course sent me to the Metropolitan, and friends from Furnald Hall (the hotel-like dormitory) took me in hand when they heard I had never been to the Museum of Modern Art. They opened my eyes to Picasso's *Guernica* and a whole new way of looking at the world. Mike Naver, a classmate and new friend from *Spectator* (I had joined the staff of the Columbia daily newspaper and immediately met kindred spirits) who was born and grew up in New York, took me on a Saturday afternoon to buy standing-room tickets for *Don Giovanni* at the Met and I came out overwhelmed, awed, awakened, unnerved, feeling at once pulverized and energized by seeing and hearing an opera for the first time.

The impact of my cultural immersion can be measured by the distance I had come in less than four years. As a sixteen-year-old junior in high school, I had turned in an English paper on "My Favorites," reporting that "my favorite book is *A City for Lincoln*" a fictional drama of high school basketball in a small town in Indiana by John R. Tunis, the beloved author of sports books for boys. My favorite poems were Kipling's "If" and "Gunga Din." Summing up my appreciation of the arts, I said, "I believe that music, like poetry, expresses the highest emotion of man. My favorite songs of a serious nature are 'Clair de Lune,' and 'Serenade' from *The Student Prince*. On the lighter side, 'I'm Always Chasing Rainbows,' 'Shine,' 'Back in Your Own Backyard,' and 'On the Sunny Side of the Street' rank tops with me." At Columbia, I had the feeling that most of my classmates at that age had been reading Proust in the original French, playing Bach on the harpsichord, and reciting "The Waste Land" from memory.

My year and a half at Indiana University had fortunately served as a kind of prep school for Columbia, acquainting me at least with Homer and Sophocles and some of the basic ideas of the heritage I hadn't even known was my own. (Before freshman lit at IU, I would have guessed that "Western civilization" meant the settlement of Texas by the cowboys, and that its key figure was Davy Crockett.) At Columbia the "Education by Books" concept I had first read about in Mark Van Doren's essay was incorporated in the curriculum with two required years of Contemporary Civilization that gave us a survey of the development of our culture's ideas from Plato and Aristotle to Nietzsche and Kant, and on to Marx and Freud.

I don't remember reading the specific Nietzschean pronouncement that "God is dead," though I certainly got the drift of that idea's currency in our time through the course of my classes in Contemporary Civilization (or CC as it was known in student shorthand). My CC course that covered the beginning of the modern era was taught by a tough-minded professor of philosophy who enjoyed jousting with students and took particular pleasure in puncturing undergraduate preconceptions. I don't remember what we were reading or how the subject came up, but I recall with special clarity an exchange during class between this professor and a student on the subject of God.

I can see the student still in a seat in front and to the right of me in the classroom, hunched low in his chair (perhaps that's why he seemed a physically small fellow), saying in a somewhat high, tentative voice:

"But I thought Jesus *was* God."

The professor leaned forward over his desk. He was a big-chested man with a large head of gray-black hair and massive matching eyebrows set over deep brown eyes behind heavy horn-rimmed glasses. With his deep voice and powerful, glowering visage, he might himself have served as a personification of God—the Old Testament Yahweh, or perhaps even Zeus, ready to release a kind of intellectual thunderbolt. He smiled as he clasped his thick hands on the desk in front of him and focused his full attention on the student. I braced myself, cringing at what seemed the intellectual equivalent of an elephant about to trample a fly. I noticed other students either bracing themselves as I was or smiling with a kind of condescending pity at their naive classmate, or simply looking out the window or over the head of the professor in what seemed an effort to avoid awareness of what was going on.

"Oh, no," the professor said with obvious relish. "You are only talking about the belief of *one* minority of people during *one* brief period in the history of the human race."

The student sank lower in his seat and did not reply. I can't remember any further details of the class. What was so important about it? There was nothing in what the professor said that could have shocked or surprised me by then. After all, I had already advanced to the study of the forces molding the modern era. By studying the civilization of the West I became conscious of the fact that there was also a whole other tradition of civilization in the East; I was aware of Buddha and Mohammed as well as Christ, I knew the names of the gods of the Greeks and Romans, had read some Margaret Mead and Ruth Benedict on primitive cultures and their worship, and knew of the native American Indians' Great Spirit from my Boy Scout lore. I had learned at Columbia that not all atheists were Communists (in Indiana in the 1950s, that was a widely held impression) and that in fact some of the smartest people in the world no longer believed in God, much less Jesus (as a divine rather than historical figure). I gathered that most intellectuals (including most of my professors) agreed that science, along with Marx and Freud, had proved that Nietzsche was right, or at least that God was not so much "dead" as nonexistent (religion having been found to be an "illusion" by Freud, an "opiate" according to Marx) and certainly not a factor in modern life for up-to-date, educated people.

Perhaps the memory of the CC class has stayed so vividly in my mind after more than thirty years because it symbolized a turning point in my own relationship to God. I was not so much shocked or even surprised by the professor's reply (he seemed only to be stating what I regarded as common knowledge then, albeit with an almost sensuous pleasure) as I was by the naiveté of such a question being posed not only by a college student but by a *Columbia* man! I was embarrassed for the guy, as if he had committed some blatant social gaffe, and my embarrassment was no doubt so acute because I realized that only a year or so before I might still have been so benighted as to say the same thing myself! The notion that an intellectual might claim to be a Christian regardless of that religion's place in the polls or in world history, and despite the fact that no religion of any kind was felt to be valid in the "enlightened" modern Freudian-Marxist-scientific view, seemed to me unthinkable. So perhaps that memory is so vivid not because it was the moment I lost my Christian faith but because it was then that I first *realized* I had lost it.

I cannot mark the day or even exactly the year that I consciously decided I had stopped being an inactive or "passive Christian" (one who didn't go to church and prayed only in automatic reaction to immediate crisis, as in *Dear God, please don't let that car crash into me!),* and became an actively practicing intellectual agnostic: one who took pride in explaining to others that because of recently acquired knowledge he now knew too much to be able to know any longer whether there was a God. (The clear implication of the latter stand was that the possibility of the existence of God was extremely unlikely but ought to be kept open in a broad-minded spirit of objectivity since the converse could not be proved by the scientific method. I was not yet an atheist who believed with certainty, like Marx and Freud, that there was no God.)

I cannot even "blame" Columbia for my defection from faith (though my parents and some of my Indiana relatives did), for I knew it began at least as far back as Bloomington, when Reggie, my off-campus roommate, who was a bright, sophisticated skeptic, turned me on to F. Scott Fitzgerald. He loved to recite that romantic author's famous dictum on the twenties as the time when a new generation found "all Gods dead, all wars fought." I always felt a guilty, exciting tingle of response to that dramatic declaration as we sat up late drinking bourbon, smoking Pall Malls, and, like secret Hoosier subversives, poking fun at Midwestern provincialism (which Reggie felt was based on churchgoing piety).

Or maybe my first withdrawal from the faith I grew up with went back to high school, after the Mayo Clinic visit, and the poem in the great philosophers book about not being able to know if there was a God ("I can but trust that good shall fall . . ."). Maybe it began with the erosion of childhood faith when I asked every day and night that the acne be taken away and woke to find it still my skin, my identity, my very self. The Book of Job was no comfort, nor for a teenager is any promise that has to do with "later" when all of existence seems to teeter on *now*.

I suspect another reason that the CC class was so highly charged that it stayed fresh in my memory for more than thirty years was that it had to do not just with God but with Jesus. This made it personal. God was in some sense an abstraction, the greatest of all forces or puzzles or curses or fantasies depending on what you believed, but Jesus was a particular, historical person as well as a divine force whose presence had powerfully made itself manifest to me as a boy. When in adolescence I focused my search for understanding on that fellow sufferer Job, and raged with him against God, I somehow kept Jesus out of it. After my childhood experience of the light that I understood as Christ, to directly deny Jesus would have been to deny some basic sense of my inner self, the one that people couldn't see, the one that still existed despite the outer scourge of the skin. Jesus had not been an abstraction to me but the inner light, the life force itself, the heart of the matter.

If the CC class symbolized a shift in my belief system, the greatest and most disturbing assault on my feeling for Jesus (and my connection with Christianity) was not coming from atheistic Columbia professors but from popular Christian ministers of the day who were trying to make Jesus relevant to the spirit of the fifties by turning him into a glad-handing kind of Rotarian businessman, a spiritual version of the current symbol of conformity, the Man in the Gray Flannel Suit. The most successful of these purveyors of country club Christianity was Norman Vincent Peale, whose *Power of Positive Thinking* had become a national best-seller and a byword of middle America. For a budding intellectual, fired with the discovery of Kafka and Dostoevsky, who was seeing the works of O'Neill and Chekhov performed in Greenwich Village and finding insights into the human condition in contemporary writers like Salinger and Carson McCullers, this kind of bland, conformist Christianity not only seemed superficial but downright offensive. It seemed to embody all the cliché hypocrisies that I so despised in middle American culture (with the special intensity of one who had once so staunchly adhered to them), and made Jesus a kind of representative spokesman of such values.

I recently reread *The Power of Positive Thinking* to see specifically what so angered me about Peale's message, as well as to ponder on what had made it so overwhelmingly popular that in 1953 it outsold every book—both fiction and nonfiction—except the Bible. I suspect its tremendous success was due in part to some of the very things that enraged me, which included the author's assurance that religion was a "scientific" method of making one's life rosier (the Bible contains "techniques" and "formulas," Dr. Peale wrote, that "may be said to form an exact science") and also that its application for solving one's problems was easy. Dr. Peale made it seem so with his assortment of hints for happiness such as "10 simple, workable rules," "7 simple steps," and "magic words." I knew from my own struggles and those of my parents that religion, no more than anything else, offered easy or surefire ("scientific") or magic solutions to problems.

I was not nearly so upset by the Reverend Billy Graham, another of the pop preachers of the fifties religious revival, for he seemed to be sticking to the "old-time religion" of traditional evangelists (perhaps like my own Baptist minister grandfather) rather than trying to hoke up his message with fashionable gimmickry.

Such a negative reaction to the power of positive thinking was considered subversive by my family and some of my friends and neighbors back home in Indiana, many of whom sincerely feared for the safety of my immortal soul. After my first year at Columbia I wrote a letter to the Indianapolis *Star* decrying the fact as reported in the New York *Times* (my new "hometown" newspaper) that *Robin Hood* had been banned from local schools on the grounds of its hidden message of Communism—its hero stole from the rich to give to the poor. I also decried the nationally famous incident (covered by Edward R. Murrow on "See It Now") of the refusal of the Indianapolis War Memorial Commission to allow a newly formed chapter of the American Civil Liberties Union to hold its first meeting on its premises. Not only I but also my parents received many phone calls and letters expressing anger and sadness at my being subverted by Columbia, the gist of which was summed up in a letter to the *Star* in reply to mine, saying I was an example of what happened to our fine young people when they went off to school in the East. (That letter was not signed, and a friend of mine from high school who was then at DePauw University in Greencastle, Indiana, wrote in my defense and said my views were also held by some people who stayed home to go to college.)

In the wake of rumors leading to acute concerns about my political, moral, and spiritual well-being, a friend of my parents who was the father of one of my Boy Scout buddies back home arrived in New York on business and invited me to have lunch with him that Sunday at Luchow's, the famous old German restaurant that was his favorite in New York. After I accepted, Mr. Martin said he first wanted me to go to church with him, and then we'd proceed to dine. The invitation was obviously a package deal, and as I knew Mr. Martin was a kind of emissary of my parents (if not all Indianapolis) it was an offer I couldn't refuse. Mr. Martin said he knew I would be as thrilled as he to attend the service of New York's famous Marble Collegiate Church, whose pastor was the Reverend Norman Vincent Peale.

I don't remember the words of the sermon, except that they conveyed in appropriately cheerful tones the message of "togetherness" and positive thinking that the Reverend Peale had made popular. I remember the vastness of the church and the huge crowd of worshipers (there was not an empty pew) at that shrine of 1950s upbeat conformity and assurance. I remember the smile and the gleaming white teeth of the famous pastor. I remember thinking when we got to Luchow's that the only way to redeem this depressing experience was to eat as much as I could, and I downed the most extensive and expensive pigsknucklesauerbratenschnitzelstuff topped with dark beer and Black Forest cake for dessert, glad that the lederhosened band oompah-pah-ing around the tables rendered conversation if not impossible at least unnecessary. Afterward I repaired to the dorm where I shucked off my suit and tie, hurried to the bathroom, and promptly threw up the entire feast, feeling weak but blessedly purged not only of the guilty banquet but also the image of Jesus as the Man in the Gray Flannel suit purveying the power of positive thinking to a civilization of salesmen. *(Sinclair Lewis,* I summoned in fevered imagination, *thou shouldst be living at this hour!)*

I recounted my visit to the Marble Collegiate Church and Luchow's (and the ensuing results) to my friends in the dorm as they sat around enthralled by such bizarre adventures. As far as I could tell, most of my classmates only went to religious services as academic observers rather than participants, on field trips for sociology or anthropology courses, gathering "material" on the rites and behavior of the worshipers with the respectful but detached attention of a Margaret Mead at some Samoan puberty ceremony.

Most of my new friends at Columbia were Jews who were not "religious" except for going home to observe Jewish holidays with their families. They were not otherwise involved in religious issues or concerns (except of the academic kind) but were not in any way intolerant of my Christian background or hostile to religious expressions of any kind. My two most antireligious friends at Columbia were an Englishman who grew up in the Anglican Church, and a New York "lapsed Catholic" of Italian heritage. My only student friend who was openly and comfortably religious was a Jew, and he was regarded with general respect if sometimes genuine curiosity by his agnostic/atheistic peers of all backgrounds, who sometimes asked him theological questions since he seemed to be the only one interested enough in God to know the answer. His own response to my distress over the Norman Vincent Peale adventure was to suggest I go to some other Christian church that I might find more intellectually acceptable. I appreciated his intent but I didn't do it; partly because I was developing a hostility to religion and especially contemporary Christianity, and partly, I suspect, because another side of me didn't want to be disillusioned any further, especially in regard to Jesus.

What saved Jesus for me at college was not going out to hear the sermons of any minister but attending classes taught by Mark Van Doren.

The man whose written words and whose very name on the page had first drawn me to Columbia assured me by his teaching and his presence that I had made the right choice, bizarre as it seemed at the time. When I first came to visit the college and told that beneficent admissions officer that Van Doren's essay had sparked my desire to attend Columbia, he arranged for me to take the professor's popular course on poetry during my first semester, as a kind of elective plum among a diet of required potatoes (like Contemporary Civilization). Far deeper than academically, the course was the most important single part of my transplantation.

In the midst of the confusion of adjusting to a new place and new people and ideas and manners, Van Doren's class twice a week was a focus and refreshment, as emotionally calming (centering, I would say now) as it was intellectually stimulating. I had never seen a picture of Mark Van Doren but he looked exactly as I thought he should. His hair then was gray and his face had the "craggy" look of wisdom and experience one associated with greatness. I remember him as a tall man, yet I think it was not that his height was especially great but that he carried himself with such erectness that he gave that impression. Everything about him was straight, plain, open. He spoke slowly, thoughtfully, sometimes rubbing his chin in reflection. His eyes were lively with wit and curiosity and his wry humor would sometimes unexpectedly evoke from us a kind of happy laughter unusual for college classrooms. He reminded me of Lincoln, and in fact he was also from Illinois. His accent was wonderfully familiar to me, as was his manner, and his references to growing up in Illinois (right next door to Indiana!) made me feel relieved and justified. Filled with elation after the first class, I said to one of my new classmates, "Hey, Van Doren's great, huh?" and this native New Yorker shrugged and said, "I dunno, he's a little too Midwestuhn," and I blurted out, "Yes, that's it!"

Many of my classmates from New York were just as enthralled by Van Doren as we outlanders were, though some students of all geographic groups preferred the more polished, urbane style of Lionel Trilling (undergraduates who majored in English were roughly divided into those who idolized Van Doren and those who idolized Trilling). Before the end of that first semester I worked up the nerve to go in and introduce myself to Van Doren during his office hours, and found him the most accessible, warm, and gracious of men. He immediately made me—a mere transfer student from a state university—feel welcome, important, interesting, as he chatted with me about our mutual Midwestern backgrounds and about poetry. More than that, he made me feel safe, with a sense that nothing unfair or evil could befall me at this new and imposing university as long as such as man was on the faculty.

Though I never got to know him beyond such office visits, and the treasured comments he wrote on my papers (he graded and wrote personal critiques of every student paper for each of his popular classes), Van Doren was certainly a guardian angel of my time at Columbia, as he was for so many years for so many students. He used to speak fondly and respectfully in class of one of those students in particular, the Trappist monk Thomas

Merton, who had written some kind of religious autobiography
called *The Seven Storey Mountain.* Though I usually followed all
Van Doren's literary leads, I stubbornly resisted Merton's book.
The true story of a Columbia student who wanted to be a writer
but turned out to be a monk living in a monastery in Kentucky
simply made me too uncomfortable. When I finally read *The
Seven Storey Mountain* more than a quarter century later, I
found that Van Doren had served as a spiritual as well as an
intellectual guide for Merton:

"Mark, I know, is no stranger to the order of grace, but con-
sidering his work as teacher merely as a mission on the natural
level—I can see that Providence was using him as an instru-
ment more directly than he realized. As far as I can see, the
influence of Mark's sober and sincere intellect, and his manner
of dealing with his subject with perfect honesty and objectivity
and without evasions, was remotely preparing my mind to re-
ceive the good seed of scholastic philosophy."

Merton also felt that Van Doren's example of clarity of mind
helped him see through the allure of the Communism that
exercised an intellectual popularity on the campus in the 1930s.
As I look back at my own experience as a student in the 1950s, I
think the most important thing I received from the rich gift of
Van Doren's teaching was something I would have least expected to gain from an English professor at Columbia: a new,
adult respect for Jesus.

One of my most rewarding courses (and there were a number
of them in the amazingly rich curriculum and gifted faculty of
Columbia in the fifties) was Van Doren's "The Narrative Art."
Our texts for the course were *The Odyssey* and *The Iliad,* the
Bible, *The Divine Comedy, Don Quixote,* and Kafka's *The Trial*
and *The Castle.* Van Doren's lectures on the New Testament
marked the first time I had ever heard someone other than a
Christian minister speak to an audience about Jesus. I don't
know what I expected—perhaps a debunking—but what I
heard was a description and appreciation of Jesus as given in the

text, without regard to theological or historical speculation or interpretation. As with all the books we read, Van Doren honored the story, took it on its own terms, and helped us to absorb and understand it, to look at it fresh, not through the eyes of other interpreters, but with our own vision.

I remember his telling us that many people had an erroneous impression of Jesus, imparted by American Sunday schools, as a sort of "wispy figure who floated around Jerusalem in something like a nightshirt" and was a soft, effeminate character, one who was always sympathetic and comforting. That was simply not the Jesus of the Scriptures, Van Doren pointed out. I can still hear the deep, clear timbre of his voice as he said that in fact "Jesus was the sternest of men," one who denied his own mother in public in the name of his mission, who demanded that his disciples give up all to follow him, not even stopping to bury their dead. He was not a "popular" man or one who sought to be "liked" by winning the approval of the crowds or promising success or riches (in fact he told the rich man he would have to give up those riches that were the most important thing to him, or his chances of getting into heaven were those of a camel passing through the eye of a needle).

Van Doren's portrayal of Jesus made such a powerful impression on me that I quoted my college lecture notes from his class in an article called "Slick-Paper Christianity" that I wrote for *The Nation* two years after graduation. The occasion of the article was the publication of a new Methodist magazine called *Together* that celebrated the fifties religious ethos of "togetherness" (one big smiling Norman Rockwell happy family of the kind mine was not) and summed up what seemed to me the parochial, fraternity-like smugness of that kind of faith with the selection of an All-American football team made up entirely of Methodists! The magazine also had a feature on the changing perception of Christ through the ages, that led from the agonized countenance of the man on the cross to a beardless, rosy-cheeked smiling fellow painted recently by a contemporary artist from Ohio. I thought the painting embodied the approved, bland characteristics of the Jesus of the fifties religious revival. Against that image I proudly quoted my esteemed Columbia professor on Jesus:

" 'He was not,' Van Doren said, 'an easy man to follow. He was certainly not like our ministers now who try to be "one of the crowd" and take a drink at a cocktail party to prove it, or tell an off-color joke. That seems to be their approach today.' The Professor paused for a moment, and then he said 'Maybe that's why we hate them so much.' "

What a relief—he did too!

Though I might and did dismiss the divinity of Jesus (along with any other kind of divinity) as I moved into my agnostic/atheist position as an enlightened college man, after Van Doren's class I could never again dismiss or demean the power and perception and courage of the man Jesus of Nazareth—not the one who was air-brushed and softened for an affluent society by the pop preachers of the fifties, but the one whose story was told in the books of Matthew, Mark, Luke, and John.

At the time, though, I was far more absorbed in the books of Sinclair Lewis, Thomas Wolfe, F. Scott Fitzgerald, and Ernest Hemingway. None of those were assigned in any classes, for Columbia's faculty believed, as Van Doren explained to us, that students who studied the classics of their literary heritage did not need lectures on contemporary fiction, since they were sure to discover that on their own and spend whatever free time on it they wished. It was true. For those enthralled with literature, reading great books does not numb or even satisfy the need for reading further, but rather stokes the desire for more. After reading Dante, Shakespeare, and Dostoevsky for class, then books like *Babbitt* and *Look Homeward, Angel, The Great Gatsby* and *A Farewell to Arms,* indeed became, intellectually, a pleasant and rewarding kind of light entertainment.

On summer vacation I returned to Indianapolis to work on the sports desk of the *Star*, and over coffee or beer breaks discussed books with Corky Lamm and Bob Collins, who introduced me to exciting current fiction and also loaned me a fascinating biography of the colorful former mayor of Boston, James Michael Curley, called *The Purple Shamrock*. (I could not have dreamed then that I would someday live in Boston and sit on a bench by the statue of Curley in the waterfront park; or in 1965 meet in the office of the *Atlantic Monthly* Edwin O'Connor, whose fictional version of Curley's career had become the best-selling novel and popular movie *The Last Hurrah*.)

The following summer I landed a job away from home on the Grand Rapids *Press* in Michigan, where a new set of newspaper mentors of the same mold as Corky and Collins, people of great wit and intellect and generous kindness to bumbling new reporters, nurtured my confidence as well as my craft. The pinnacle of my summer at the *Press* came when I was able to use some of my new literary lore to jazz up a garden-page feature on a woman who grew rosebushes from her own rosebush plants. The lead to my story was "A rosebush is a rosebush is a rosebush in the garden of Mrs. Henry Jones of 3217 Elm Street." The managing editor himself, a legendary character straight from the pages of Ben Hecht named M. M. Kesterson (we all knew the initials stood for Montmorency Maximillian), came out of his office on one of his rare trips to the newsroom, shook my hand, and said, "You are the first person to get Gertrude Stein into the Grand Rapids *Press*."

Despite all kinds of hangups and fears, I seemed to be gaining in confidence and knowledge and was eagerly looking forward to returning to my senior year at Columbia when my life took a different turn that might have abruptly ended it altogether. I literally ran into a stone wall, when a friend totaled my father's new four-door Mercury sedan as we drove to Chicago.

Following the Indianapolis wedding of my first friend to get married, I agreed with two other buddies of the groom that it would be a great idea to drive up to Chicago for the weekend, starting at once. It was early in the morning and I was half asleep in between the other two guys when the friend who was driving went straight into the concrete retaining wall of an S-curve. The crash came and then the sirens. There were lights and screams and shouted orders. The driver was unconscious, while the friend next to the passenger door was bleeding from cuts and had a broken jaw. I was sore and scared and disoriented, but I seemed to be basically okay. When I was taken into Emergency they asked if I had any complaints and I said my shoulder hurt. They X-rayed my shoulder, said there was nothing wrong, and put me in a bed.

"Your son was very lucky, heh-heh," the nervous doctor told my parents, who had rushed up from Indianapolis to my bedside the next day. "Just the broken thumb, which I've set, and beyond that, some bruises, otherwise he's just shaken up. You can probably take him home today."

I said I felt awful; my back hurt terribly. It felt like it was on fire. The doctor made his nervous laugh again. "Probably just due to sleeping in a strange bed," he assured me, then scooted off. My parents questioned me further and I said I knew there was something wrong with my back. I was really in pain. They went out and talked to another doctor, and some new people came in and took X rays. My parents stayed by my bedside and chatted and we all worried about the driver, who had a concussion and wasn't conscious yet. Then suddenly doctors and orderlies came running in with pulleys and sandbags, shouting at me, "Don't move!" They put me in traction and explained that I had a broken and dislocated fifth cervical vertebra; in layman's terms, a broken neck. I was later told that if I had jerked my neck around during that time before I was put in traction I could have been killed, or paralyzed from the waist down for the rest of my life. I thanked the God I no longer believed in, and prayed that my buddy would regain consciousness. He did, and came out of it all right. The other guy went home with only the broken jaw and was soon fine.

I lay flat on my back in a hospital bed with my chin pulled back by a strap that attached me to weights which provided the saving mechanism of "traction." I was told I would have to remain in that semi-immobile state for three months. There was plenty of time to puzzle over the meaning of life, time, God, and the universe. After my initial reflex thanking of God for being spared from death or lifelong paralysis, I resumed my collegiate agnostic skepticism, questioning why I should thank the God who got me into this mess in the first place—by some reasoning I can no longer recall, I managed to blame the accident on the God whose existence I questioned. (There was no way I was going to let Him win.)

My time of confinement loomed ahead like a hunk of eternity, yet I wasn't at all miserable. Life in my fixed position was made not only tolerable but often pleasant by the tender, loving care of those people whose work could legitimately entitle them to be called "professional guardian angels"—the nurses. They changed my bedpans and fed and bathed and massaged me and told me jokes and stories and inquired about my pains and my hopes and dreams with solicitous interest, and kept me emotionally as well as physically alive. I fell in love with two of them and spent hours spinning fantasies of getting married and coming home to each one (never at the same time, for my imagination was still strictly Midwest puritan).

The nervous doctor set my broken thumb, and when the cast was removed it was pointing the wrong way—it looked as if I was perpetually hitchhiking. Again the doctor laughed awkwardly and said it looked like we'd have to break it again. I said I'd prefer to wait till I got home to Indianapolis for that particular experience. (It was broken again then and still did not come out right, but I said since I wasn't going to play the violin I would stick with the odd-looking thumb, which I still have today.)

My parents brought me refracting glasses so I could set a book on my chest and see the pages from my prone position. Out of all the world's literature I chose to read the Greek tragedies, trying to glean from these ancient dramas the key to human beings' relations with one another and with the gods (whom I could deal with more easily at the time than with God). I attributed wisdom to the Greeks more profound than that found in the Bible, and brooded over the meaning of the inevitability of human suffering and tragedy. I also thought of Aunt Ollie, and remembered her words back in high school: "Danny, you will be close to death through some experience that will interrupt your education . . . and then you will cross the ocean—not the Atlantic, but a farther ocean, to a farther land than Europe. . . ."

Well, the first part of her prediction had come true. Did the second part mean I would go off to some exotic place like India or China? The East held no attraction for me, and the rest of Aunt Ollie's message remained as puzzling as the riddle of the Sphinx. In the meantime I had to go on a far more threatening journey before I could return to Columbia and complete my interrupted education. I had to go back home to Indianapolis in a body cast.

At the end of the three months of traction I was put in a plaster cast that came up over my head and down to my waist, with holes cut out for my face and my stomach. Knowing that I was supposed to fully recover from the vertebra injury, and hopefully return to Columbia the following spring semester in a neck brace, what I most feared was that the plaster cast that covered all but the front of my face would probably make my skin even worse since I wouldn't even be able to wash it until the cast came off.

The other terror was that I had to go home and live with my parents again—partly helpless, like a child, in the condition I had fought so hard to escape from. I would be dependent on their care, just when I felt I had emancipated myself from it once and for all, and when I was most at war with them over every important issue in life: God, sex, politics, people, music, art, literature; you name it, my parents and I disagreed. And now I would be their captive.

It never occurred to me how hard the situation must have been for *them;* having their angry young son at home, half invalid, raging and railing at them, making fun of their beliefs, being sarcastic and snide and combative. We had our first television set and I sat with my mother and father in the den and they insisted on watching (to torture me, I thought) their favorite program, Bishop Fulton J. Sheen, the first of the successful TV preachers. I regarded him as the Catholic version of Norman Vincent Peale, though I had to admit (to myself, not my parents) that he seemed smarter and less offensively country-clubby than the popular Protestant. Still, Bishop Sheen's eyes glowed with what looked to me like a kind of madness of faith, which I chalked up to Catholicism and fanaticism. I made cracks as he talked, and hooted and jeered one night when he recited a poem called "The Hound of Heaven," and preached his whole message about it. The poem recounted in gaudy (but annoyingly memorable) language the experience of the narrator in trying to turn from God and run away from all that was holy, but the "hound of heaven" relentlessly pursued and at last caught up with him, restoring his belief. Bishop Sheen's eyes beamed with fervor as he spoke of what he said was this common phenomenon of a man trying to flee from his faith, only to have the heavenly force eventually catch him again before the end. Some of the lines struck me with a specially haunting kind of discomfort:

> I fled Him, down the nights and down the days; . . .
> I fled Him, down the adamantine ways
> Of my own soul. . . .

I laughed louder, shivering underneath. At the same time that I was mocking "The Hound of Heaven" I had the awful suspicion, somewhere back in the remote recesses of my consciousness, that this heavenly "hound" was someday going to get me too! The singsong verses kept running through my mind for a long time after, taunting my intellectually secure agnosticism and troubling my sleep. I longed to get back to Columbia, where I'd feel safe and my new unbelief would not be threatened.

4. Substitution: Freud for God

The cast was coming off. The bones were healed. I'd be fitted with a neck brace that supported my chin in an upright position for another three months, but I'd no longer be wrapped like a mummy from head to waist. I'd be able to scratch anywhere on my back with my own hand instead of frantically straightening a metal coat hanger into an impromptu poking device, agonizingly guiding it to the point of some unbearable itch. (This method was sternly forbidden by the doctors as dangerous, for it could have caused a wound of its own, but an unreachable itch leads you to risk any danger; the house was soon strewn with twisted coat hangers.) I'd be able to take a shower again, get dressed without help, be free to resume my life and my interrupted education, and return to New York for the start of the spring semester at Columbia.

All of this was wonderful, cause for celebration, but behind it I had a terrible fear: what would my face look like after three months of being encased in plaster, the skin unwashed and unable to breathe? The part of my face I could see looked remarkably well, but perhaps that was because it was the only part I could get at, and I scrubbed it with devoted intensity. But it was only the "front" part, the lower forehead and area around the eyes and nose and mouth. I could not get at my cheeks or even my chin, the skin of which might be consumed by the ravages of so long a confinement. My chest and back, where the acne also had spread and seared me, was of course not as sensitive an area to me as my face, yet the inflammations there sickened me as well, making me feel this was like a disease that was devouring all of me. I was embarrassed to be seen in a bathing suit or to find myself in any situation that involved taking my shirt off in public, and all this blemished skin of the chest and back was also confined under the plaster of the cast, and subject to the effects of no soap and water or air for three months. Would it also worsen there?

My parents went with me to the hospital for the removal of the cast. The experience was something like a birth, literally emerging from an old shell, but I wasn't sure what would come forth. After the cast was taken off I was bathed and given a shave and a haircut and then I was handed a mirror. My parents had looked on with concern, and they kept assuring me I looked fine (they were the only ones I had told of my fears about my skin), but I knew they would say that no matter how horribly the plaster encasement had affected my already blemished exterior. I braced myself as I took the mirror in my hand, closed my eyes for a moment and muttered a basic, blunt, desperate prayer that I tried to keep as short as possible (and thus less hypocritical for an unbeliever): *Please, God.*

I opened my eyes and blinked and looked again. My skin was clear.

What happened? Was this a miracle? Had I not read and been told (and once believed) the many miracles of healing performed by Jesus? Didn't I know that millions of Christians alive today believed that, though Jesus was no longer with us in the flesh, he (or his "spirit" or "the Holy Spirit" acting through him) still performed such miracles, like the ones in the Bible stories? Did he not say, "I have come to give sight to the blind and set free the prisoners . . ."? Such thoughts flashed through my mind but I pushed them away, reasoning that they had no application to my experience since I was no longer a believing Christian.

I made a cursory thanks to God, touching all bases just in case, and then began to search for the "real reason" (one I could believe as a practicing agnostic intellectual) for my amazing dermatological recovery, which even surprised the doctor and nurses who took off the cast, as well as my grateful parents. In a sense, the clear skin was a more dramatic recovery than the one from the broken neck; it seemed as if both those "miracles" had saved my life. I was almost as curious as I was thankful. There had to be a "rational" explanation. I couldn't wait to return to New York, where I could talk about it with the one person I felt was most likely to help me solve the riddle of the unexpected cure.

Back in high school Aunt Ollie had seen in my future "a man who will help you, a man who is sitting behind a desk." I knew this was he. I knew it the first time I went to his office. As soon as I was back in New York I went to see him, anxious to have him help me understand the real nature of the "miracle." After I sat down he leaned across his desk and peered at me.

"Your skin looks clear," he said.

"Yes," I said. "And the incredible thing is, it was supposed to be worse because of being covered up in the cast for three months."

He nodded.

"So why do you think it got better?" I asked eagerly.

He took out a cigarette, lit it, and blew a stream of smoke. Then he looked at me with a slight smile.

"What do *you* think?" he asked.

He was my first psychiatrist.

My parents had found Dr. Ernest for me by calling the Menninger Clinic (they always went to the top to seek help for any of my problems) and asking them to recommend a good psychiatrist in New York City for their son, a student at Columbia.

During my second year there (the early spring before the car crash at the end of the summer of '53) I had fallen into a trough of depression, perhaps a letdown after the initial excitement and challenge of a different kind of college life had begun to wear off. Perhaps it was because the new life, free from home, was not altogether new after all, for I still carried with me the burdens that had plagued me in the past—the acne that still flared then and tormented me and, along with it, an unrelenting sexual frustration relieved mainly by masturbation, whose momentary ecstatic release was followed by feelings of shame, guilt, and sadness.

I had seen Dr. Ernest every other week, and I felt those visits had helped me pull out of the numbing spell of that extended depression. Looking back three decades later, I would say now I believe Dr. Ernest helped me first of all because I liked and trusted him. He was a fairly young man (I would guess in his middle thirties) who had recently completed his training at the Menninger Clinic and started his own private practice in an office in the neighborhood preferred by his colleagues in the American Psychoanalytic Association, the fashionable Upper East Side of Manhattan. I liked him because he was quiet and thoughtful and intelligent and he seemed to like and be interested in *me*. I also sensed, as I think any patient instinctively can about a therapist, that he was essentially *kind*. I trusted him enough that I sometimes showed him short stories I had written and I was elated when he expressed his appreciation, for his praise was never overly lavish or condescending, but spare and direct.

Sometimes he used a story as the occasion for probing my own feelings ("Why do you think the character behaved that way?") and sometimes he simply indicated his admiration of a piece: "It makes a neat point."

Another reason I think the therapy "worked" or was helpful in getting me out of that depression was that Dr. Ernest gave me his full attention for the course of the fifty-minute hour I spent with him every other week or so. When I saw one of the great plays that so eloquently spoke of and for that era, Arthur Miller's *Death of a Salesman,* the famous line that most stuck with me (as it has with so many others who have appreciated the drama over the years) was Willie Loman's wife's desperate plea, "Attention must be paid!" I knew it was true not just for down-on-their-luck salesmen but for all of us, even brand-new Columbia intellectuals with inflated notions of their own knowledge that sometimes made them feel superior to the parents who paid for their education, and the friends and home they had left behind (whether in the Bronx or Indianapolis).

Of course I as well as most other people received attention from my parents (no doubt I got more because of being an only child) and a great amount from teachers and from friends, but there was something specially powerful about the undivided *professional* attention of the therapist who watched you and listened with the special focus of one who might find in your words or even your body language clues to your behavior, and so studied them with the total interest of a spy trying to break a code. What a luxury, to be so attended!

I had written to Dr. Ernest from the hospital and looked forward to seeing him when I returned, in hopes of solving the riddle of the miraculous healing, and in the process learning more about myself. I believed this would help free me from my old problems and make me a whole person in the new enlightened age of science, of which psychiatry was simply the branch dealing with mental and emotional problems.

When during that first visit to his office after my return Dr. Ernest tossed my question back at me about the cause of my seemingly (for I felt I must intellectually qualify it now) miraculous skin cure, I was both thrilled and frustrated. Obviously it was frustrating not to have someone simply give you the answer to your question (especially when you suspected he really knew). On the other hand, the process of psychiatric therapy was still fresh enough for me to find it exciting, and to feel honored as well as challenged by the doctor's implied belief that I *could* know the answer myself, that it was buried somewhere deep below in the detritus of the unconscious. (I imagined the unconscious as a vast garbage dump which one had to dig down into through disgusting refuse, to find the small gemlike nuggets of truth hidden underneath.)

When Dr. Ernest put my own question to me, I realized after a bit of reflection that in fact I did know "the right answer." It was something I had naturally been thinking about quite a bit.

"I suppose," I said, "my skin might have cleared up because being in the cast was a kind of punishment, and maybe if the acne was unconscious self-punishment for masturbation and all my sexual fantasies and stuff, then I didn't need to be punished in that way any more since the new punishment of being in traction and then the cast and now the neck brace served that purpose."

What a good student I was! Dr. Ernest did not give me a grade, or in fact even tell me directly whether I was right or wrong, but I knew by the way he nodded and blew his next smoke ring that he approved of my answer. I felt like a prize patient.

It is little wonder that a frustrated twenty-one-year-old male of the 1950s found credibility and solace in a view of life that held sexual behavior to be a key factor in understanding and ameliorating the human condition. Since puberty, sex had been the most powerful, puzzling, and elusive aspect of my experience. I was still a virgin, and even though my society recognized me legally as a man, an adult, my sex life consisted primarily of masturbation and fantasies, supplemented by heavy petting in the back seats of cars during summer vacations, and back at Columbia, even less satisfying good-night grapples in front of girls' dorms and on darkened dance floors.

The Columbia College of the 1950s was all male, and the most titillating event of a sexual nature during my time there occurred when my first-semester roommate, a prep school grad regarded as a wild and reckless kind of guy, succeeded in smuggling a Barnard girl (as such were known then) into our room in the dormitory. She was dressed in a sweater and slacks, and had removed her makeup and tucked her hair up under a faded blue workman's cap she pulled down low on her forehead. In this amazing "disguise" she was able to get past the sleepy scrutiny of the aged Negro (as such were known then) elevator operator in Hartley Hall and onto the fifth floor of the dorm and into our room. Once in the room, she perched on the upper bunk bed and sat there smiling mischievously as the word spread through our hall of the exciting, illegal, unprecedented presence of a real live Barnard girl in one of the rooms. Some of the bolder Columbia men (as such were known then) came all the way into the room and stared and even talked with her, exchanging a few nervous words or phrases, while many simply peeked in the door, gaping wide-eyed at the exotic alien visitor. There was no suggestion that any further activity might take place; the daring girl didn't even remove her cap, and was quietly smuggled out the way she had come about an hour later. This event was regarded as a major sexual caper in the life of the dormitory—in fact it's the only one I heard of during my time at Columbia.

Of course there were "panty raids" on Barnard, in which Columbia men cast off their veneer of sophisticated intellectualism and joined their bawdy collegiate brethren across the country in that peculiar rite that so summed up the sexual atmosphere of the fifties, gathering in gangs below the windows of women's dorms and howling like starving hyenas for the favor of the females' tossing down their underpants to symbolically satisfy the lust that society said was supposed to wait for marriage to be consummated. (No wonder Jack Kerouac and his Columbia cohorts of a few years earlier had rebelled against society!)

There were no females in our classes at Columbia College, and Barnard students were symbolically enclosed behind the great green fence that made it seem as sacrosanct as a convent. There were "mixers" and dances at which Columbia men were able to meet females from Barnard and other colleges, but it was generally felt that girls who would come to such events would be desperate and undesirable, while showing up at one ourselves would reveal that we were male counterparts of the same sad category. It was a Catch-22 for all concerned. I did not know any classmates who had any sort of intimate relations with college women until our senior year, and then only a few. They were young men from New York City who seemed to me paragons of worldly finesse, like suave bachelors in a Cary Grant movie of Manhattan night life. Several of the guys I knew went to prostitutes around our Morningside Heights neighborhood, and once I phoned and made an appointment with one who was highly recommended (she was said to be not ugly, and kind enough not to ridicule inexperience) but after I walked around her block between Broadway and Riverside Drive enough times to get up the courage (I think it was about eight hundred times, with a few stops for beers at the West End Bar & Grille) the woman was busy with her next customer. She whispered through the door to come back later, but I fled in relief and disappointment, never to return.

Sometimes I conveniently blamed my all-male college for my lack of sexual experience, though I knew down deep that had I been the only male in the dorm at Barnard, or even what I excitedly believed to be the freer and more erotic feminine lair of Sarah Lawrence, I would still have been virginal. It was not till the year after graduation, with a girl I knew from home, that I finally, with a great deal of bourbon, managed (at least technically) to relieve myself of the stigma of virginity, in a seedy hotel room on upper Broadway not far from my old dorm.

Columbia College gave me the best education in literature I can conceive. My own time there coincided with the last years of a golden age of the English Department, with the brilliant literary essayist Lionel Trilling and the fine raconteur, drama critic, and nature writer Joseph Wood Krutch joining Mark Van Doren as classroom teachers of the most rewarding and provocative undergraduate courses imaginable. When it came to sex education, however, I might as well have been at the most benighted Boondocks U. The best excuse I can think of for the lamentable (and only in retrospect laughable) sex education supplied by the undergraduate facility of the world-renowned Columbia University was that it was in tune with the frightened spirit of the fifties.

I remember with dismay the entire content of the sexual information taught me at Columbia. It was a course with a title (and approach) like my high school "Health and Safety" class, taught by an assistant coach of one of the college athletic teams who had a Ph.D. in physical education (he wanted us to call him "Doctor" rather than "Coach"). The man I'll call Dr. Denton showed us movies of the birth of a baby and explained the sexual dynamics of marriage by recounting the following anecdote. "If you put a bean in a jar for every time a couple has sexual intercourse during their first year of marriage, and if you take out a bean for every time they have sexual intercourse during the remainder of their married life, you will never take all the beans out of the jar." A stunning and gloomy prospect indeed.

Dr. D. also gave us advice on more immediate sexual problems. He warned us against reading the Sunday New York *Times Magazine,* on the grounds that the numerous ads for brassieres, women's panties and stockings, with their photographs of attractive ladies clad only in such flimsy garments, promoted lustful thoughts that could stimulate young men like ourselves to engage in the unhealthy practice of masturbation. This was taught in an undergraduate class at Columbia University in New York City in 1953.

The sexually repressive tenor of the times certainly must have reinforced my own fears and frustrations. It was little wonder that the whole subject of sex came to seem an overriding subject of concern and significance, not only for me but for many young people raised with the same cultural and educational experiences.

A worldview that sought to explain and improve human behavior through an understanding of the unconscious, most especially repressed sexual drives, could not have been more suitable for the times, especially in America, where Freud and his theories and therapeutic practices caught on with far greater acceptance than in his own Europe. The popular fascination with Freud spread rapidly throughout the culture, even into the hinterlands, and I did not have to wait to get to New York and Columbia to hear about it.

The recognition that sex was a driving force of humankind, that it not only caused psychological problems but might provide answers to such problems, was an idea already seeping through the culture by the time of my growing up. The news of this radical notion, and the identity of its principal exponent had even made its way across the Atlantic to the landlocked Indiana of the 1940s. (My fellow Shortridge High School graduate Kurt Vonnegut has noted that we all were proud to learn in grade school that "Indianapolis is the largest city in the world not on a navigable waterway," not realizing till later this explained why not much news was coming in.)

I have a clear memory of lying on my dining-room floor one afternoon reading the latest issue of *Life* magazine. Late sunlight came through the window and spread on the floor in a sort of pool, making the rug there warm and bright. I was reading an article about a European doctor with a white beard who believed that human behavior could be explained by sex. The idea must somehow have clicked in my understanding even then, or perhaps it was so memorable because it was shocking (the word "sex" was not even used in polite society in those days, at least not in middle-class Indianapolis). The article said that the man who had come up with this revolutionary idea was named

Sigmund Freud. I recall wondering how to pronounce such an odd name and settling on "Frood." Perhaps the distant memory is so clear because it now has the sense of a foretelling, a foreshadowing of what was to become for a while a major theme in my life.

At Columbia I read excerpts from the basic works of Freud in my Contemporary Civilization class, and on my own bought a paperback of *The Psychopathology of Everyday Life* and borrowed *Civilization and Its Discontents* from my friend Malcolm Barbour, a classmate from England who shared my passion for writing fiction and smoking little cigars called Between the Acts that came in neat tin boxes with red and gold lettering. The little cigars made us feel more worldly as we puffed and discussed the meaning of life, literature, sex, and *Civilization and Its Discontents*. (I know I borrowed the book from Barbour, for I found to my surprise recently when I pulled the copy from my bookshelf and read it again that his name was written on the flyleaf.) I was not only reading Freudian theory in my free time as well as in class, and discussing it with friends as well as teachers, I was "putting it into practice" by being in therapy with Dr. Ernest, whose affiliation with the New York Psychoanalytic Association indicated that he was in the camp of orthodox Freudianism. To add to these dimensions, I received an insightful lesson in the contemporary cultural and literary influence of Freudian thought in Mark Van Doren's magnificent course on the narrative art.

Van Doren departed from our assigned reading one day to speak about a remarkable short story that had just been published by a Columbia undergraduate in *New World Writing,* one of the leading literary journals of the time. The author was Ivan Gold, a student I knew then slightly from my creative writing class, who was to become a lifelong friend. Ivan was also taking the narrative art course and was sitting just a few rows from me the day Van Doren praised and discussed his story, "A Change of Air." For those who had not yet read their classmates' story,

Van Doren summarized the plot: "Bobbie Bedmer," a pretty young girl who lives in a poor neighborhood in the Bronx, volunteers to provide sex for the entire membership of a teen-age boys' gang, is traumatized by the experience, goes away to a mental hospital, has psychiatric treatment with a therapist, and returns to the old neighborhood a different person. She politely refuses to engage in sex with the boys who assume she is still a wild, promiscuous girl who will do it any time. They reluctantly come to accept the fact that she has changed.

Professor Van Doren began thoughtfully to question us about the meaning of such a story. As Merton observed of Van Doren's teaching method, "Most of the time he asked questions. His questions were very good, and if you tried to answer them intelligently, you found yourself saying excellent things that you did not know you knew, and that you had not, in fact, known before. He had 'educed' them from you by his question. His classes were literally 'education'—they brought things out of you, they made your mind produce its own explicit ideas."

Van Doren asked us to think about what was different about this story from similar kinds of literature of the past. What was the story about? Well, it was about how a person (the girl of the story) had changed. She had started out as a promiscuous girl who had sex with all the guys in the gang. Then she went away. And what happened when she went away? She was treated by a psychiatrist. When the boys find this out, they accept the change, though they are disappointed. And what has changed her? What force that we don't really see, but is behind the action of the story, produces this change of personality that not only the boys in the old neighborhood but we as readers believe in? Psychiatry. And what was the power described in literature that used to produce such change in people? What was the force that produced change in the lives of characters in Homer, and the Bible, and Dante? Why, it was God, or the gods, wasn't it? Would readers today be likely to believe a story about a girl who changed her behavior because of God? Would such a story seem to belong to another time than ours? What is the equivalent in our own society for the power that once was exerted in life and in people's understanding of life? Why, it was psychiatry. In our own time and culture, psychiatry was replacing God as the factor people believed brought about transformation in human lives.

As so often happened, I emerged from Van Doren's class excited by new ways of seeing things, of connections that were there all along but that I hadn't noticed. I went to my room and looked at my notes from his class and made notes of my own to try to absorb fully what I had learned, and to try to understand it with the kind of clarity he demonstrated in his own thinking. Van Doren had not said he personally believed in psychiatry now instead of God, he had got us to see that this major shift in thinking about the world had occurred in our culture, so that as readers we now accepted—as did the boys in the gang in Ivan's story—that a young woman had been not only changed but "cured" of a kind of behavior that was destructive to her. He had also pointed out that a story about such a change or healing that was effected by God or religion would have not been as believable—if believed at all—by those boys in the story, or by us as contemporary readers. He had "educed" from us, through examining a brilliant fiction by one of our own peers, the perception of one of the great shifts—like the movement of mammoth ice floes or whole continents in a sort of slow earthquake—in modern man's understanding of himself and his world.

It was like a substitution in one of the sports events I had written about since high school, when a star player is no longer effective and a substitute charges off the bench to take his place and perhaps himself becomes the star. A key position could not remain empty; just as you could not have the starting fullback leave the game without replacing him, you could not have a universe without God to explain and alter people's behavior in it. If God was dead, as pronounced by Nietzsche and later popularized by Scott Fitzgerald and the "lost generation" of the twenties—who made nihilism nearly as romantic as moonlight and champagne—then something had to replace Him and the force He represented, religion. It seemed clear that psychiatry had replaced religion as the new, educated, scientific way of understanding the world, and though it didn't have a God, its creator Sigmund Freud with his white beard looked enough like a representation of Him to seem a kind of stand-in figure for the deity in modern men's imaginations (or at least in *mine*).

My own disillusionment with the pap commercialization of Christianity by its pop preachers of the fifties, combined with my growing agnostic/atheistic unbeliefs, made it easier for me to agree with Freud when I read again in *Civilization and Its Discontents* his scornful dismissal of religion: "The whole thing is so patently infantile, so incongruous with reality, that to one whose attitude to humanity is friendly it is painful to think that the great majority of mortals will never be able to rise above this view of life. It is even more humiliating to discover what a large number of those alive today, who must see that this religion is not tenable, yet try to defend it inch by inch, as if with a series of pitiful rearguard actions."

I shared Freud's sense of distress and incredulity when I read that in spite of all the enlightenment in my own time there was a "religious revival" on many college campuses as well as among the populace as a whole. (Was antireligious "enlightenment" largely a phenomenon of Eastern colleges and New York City intellectuals?) A poll showed that an astounding ninety-four percent of Americans in 1954 still believed in God! How was it then that Freud and his psychiatric methods were far more widely accepted in America than in his own Europe? Did positive-thinking Americans believe they could have it all? Did they think religion and psychiatry, God and Freud both, could solve their problems and explain their world? Well, I was one staunch new unbelieving intellectual who didn't think you could have it both ways.

It was clear to me that the way of truth was with Freud and

psychiatry. I not only believed religion was invalid, I began through my own interpretation of Freudian theory to blame religion for many of my ills. I was through with God and against religion. All of that represented the dead past, the dark ages of superstition.

I had dismissed God but what was I to do about Jesus, whom I once declared as my personal savior, and who kept hanging around my consciousness? What was I to do about interpreting the childhood experience of his presence in that great interior "light"? I could still not honestly tell myself that was something negative or false; it remained one of the most real and powerful of my life experiences. Fortunately for my peace of mind, I found a way of explaining it by reading William James's *The Varieties of Religious Experience.* I was relieved to find in this great book that many people had had experiences similar to mine with a sacred or mystical kind of "light":

"There is one form of sensory automatism which possibly deserves special notice on account of its frequency. I refer to hallucinatory or pseudo-hallucinatory luminous phenomena, *photisms,* to use the term of the psychologists. Saint Paul's blinding heavenly vision seems to have been a phenomenon of this sort; so does Constantine's cross in the sky. The last case but one which I quoted mentions floods of light and glory. Henry Alline mentions a light, about whose externality he seems uncertain. Colonel Gardiner sees a blazing light. President Finney [the revival preacher Charles G. Finney, from his *Memoirs]* writes:

" 'All at once the glory of God shone upon and round about me in a manner almost marvelous. . . . A light perfectly ineffable shone in my soul, that almost prostrated me on the ground. . . . This light seemed like the brightness of the sun in every direction. It was too intense for the eyes. . . . I think I knew something then, by actual experience, of that light that prostrated Paul on the way to Damascus. It was surely a light such as I could not have endured long.'

"Such reports of photisms are indeed far from uncommon. . . ."

What a relief! I was not crazy, or doomed to some religious irrationality, stuck with Jesus in some spiritual time warp I couldn't shake, for now I could deal with the experience of his "presence" as an interior light in a psychological way. I had simply experienced a hallucinatory or pseudo-hallucinatory experience called a photism. The fact that James did not share Freud's acrimonious view of religion but rather treated the subject with respect and significance made his explanation, buttressed by much firsthand testimony, all the more credible. With my Jesus-as-light experience "explained away," then, the last obstacle to my full embrace of atheism was removed, and I was free to form my own personal view of a universe without a God.

My new approach was summed up by one of my most dashing new heroes, the journalist John Reed, who after covering Pancho Villa as a newspaper correspondent (and then writing his account of the revolution as the book *Insurgent Mexico*) went to Russia to cover the revolution and wrote the classic firsthand account of it, *Ten Days That Shook the World*. He died in Russia and was buried in the wall of the Kremlin.

I had no romantic illusions about Communism, much less any desire to be buried in the Soviet Union, but I admired Reed's brilliant brand of personal journalism, and I loved the youthful idealism of the life he led—a life so glamorous it was later enacted on the screen by Warren Beatty in the movie *Reds*. I wrote in a journal I kept in college a quote from an essay by Reed called "Almost Thirty" that served as a new sort of "scripture" for me. Reed said:

"In thinking it over, I find little in my thirty years that I can hold onto. I haven't found any God and don't want one; faith is only another word for finding oneself. . . ."

It was a creed tailor-made for me and many of my young intellectual cohorts of the fifties. We were not interested in saving our souls (if such unscientific nonsubstances could even be taken seriously) but in "finding ourselves." We would not be content to remain a "lost generation" like the disillusioned literary heroes of the twenties, but with the new tools provided by the theories of Freud would analyze ourselves or be analyzed into the sort of personal discoveries that would free us and make us whole. (I wonder now if the implied promise of Freudian therapy—that understanding of the past could eliminate neurosis—was just as simplistically optimistic as Peale's positive thinking.)

Unlike the young intellectuals of the thirties, whose particular dream of earthly salvation through Marxist revolution lay shattered in the gulags of Stalin's Soviet Union, we would not be duped by political answers for curing the human condition. My aspiring writer friends and I would recite in this regard a favorite creed from one of our sacred Hemingway scriptures, *Death in the Afternoon:* "Let those who want to save the world if you can get to see it clear and as a whole." All this was exhilarating, and by the time I wrote the John Reed quote in my journal, the pieces of my own new outlook on life—a sort of atheistic Freudian optimism spiced with a gloomy strain of Hemingway bravado—had begun to fit together.

Then something happened, right around this time, that didn't fit. I was working on a short story to submit to my creative writing class. (I also had begun submitting what I thought were my better stories to national magazines, and my classmate Malcolm Barbour and I compared rejection slips, glorying in the rare scrawled comment of encouragement over the cold printed forms.) In my senior year I had given up my enjoyable work on *Spectator,* the Columbia College newspaper, with its immediate rewards of publication and by-line credit as well as the bracing camaraderie of common cause with the staff, in order to devote most of my time to writing fiction. The conscious commitment to this as my main effort for the remainder of college not only meant sacrificing *"Spec"* but also slighting the rest of my courses to concentrate as fully as possible on the fiction writing that had become my love and passion.

I struggled at it with all my might, feeling most of the time like a sculptor hacking at a huge slab of stone with a rusty old Boy Scout knife. Every so often I got a phrase or sentence just right, and sometimes whole paragraphs, and the hope from those small triumphs (if they even were, for sometimes my instructor didn't think so) kept me going, but most of the time it felt like salt-mines work, or slogging through mud in an endless foot soldiers' war of dogged attrition. Then one night in the dorm, as I worked away after dinner with the usual grinding application, something seemed to take over without my even being aware of it at first. Words and sentences began to move forward in more of a flow, and it seemed I could perceive the next thought and situation before I got to it, as if the story were laying itself out in front of me and all I had to do was keep writing to catch up with it. The two or three pages I started with grew to eight, ten, eleven pages (usually my longest stories were five or six pages) and came to a natural conclusion, an ending that seemed to tie everything together and come from the very movement of the story. When I looked up from my desk it was dawn.

I had no idea I had been at it so long, and instead of being exhausted I felt a kind of lightness, as if I had been cleaned and purged, emptied in a fulfilling way, like giving birth. I experienced a natural high, a sense of acute aliveness and elation. Through the window I could see the tops of tall buildings and slashes of brilliant color swatched in the sky. The wonder of being in New York came over me, a circumstance I had come to take for granted. But now I realized anew that New York was a place I had only dreamed about in childhood from movies and the Saturday morning radio program "Grand Central Station" and now by some great good fortune I was living in the midst of it, as if blown there in a miraculous dream. ("We're not in Kansas, Toto!") Along with this, in a feeling like "my cup runneth over," came the deep satisfaction of having just written, at least for once in my life, with a sense of power and ease that made me feel I "had it in me"—the ability to create stories, that most mysterious and marvelous of gifts. Without any other thought I got down on my knees and gave thanks to God, in prayer.

This spontaneous act of prayer did not renew my belief in God but seemed to be a kind of intellectual aberration. I couldn't fit it into my new world outlook so I simply set it aside, in a mental corner, where I didn't have to think about it, and went on with my brave new atheistic vision. If my acne and my sexual hangups had been aggravated, as I now believed, according to good scientific Freudian theory, by religious teachings of guilt and sin and punishment, then I wanted to deny, to wipe out, the God who had caused me such pain and torment. I would have my revenge by not believing in Him. So there. It was easy. He did not exist. I could breathe much easier. I could forget the Ten Commandments and follow the code of my new prophet Hemingway, who said, "What is moral is what you feel good after." (As a matter of fact, if I had taken that to heart, I would not have got as drunk as badly and as often as I did in the years to come, nor would I have gone to bed with women in whom I had no interest except through desperate efforts at affirmation of manhood and satisfaction of need.)

But now that I had eliminated God, there was a void. I had filled the ethical hole with snippets of sayings from my literary heroes, but this still left other gaps. Ever since childhood I had prayed, to God and to Jesus Christ. I kept finding myself praying automatically at certain times, and it bothered me. I did not want to be a hypocrite, and I feared above all things falling into that despised category of human that Salinger's hero (who was also the hero of me and my friends) Holden Caulfield referred to as a phony. Still, the words and cadences of prayers kept coming back to me, invading my mind, against my will. Even if it was only force of habit, it bothered me and made me feel guilty for not being true to my atheism (not only religion had the power to produce guilt, I discovered). The most annoyingly persistent prayer of all that kept coming back into my mind was the Lord's Prayer, no doubt because it was the one learned so early and repeated most often on every occasion calling for prayer. I fought it, but still it kept penetrating my consciousness, "saying itself" to me against my will. How could I stop it?

Because of the semester I had lost from being in the hospital and the body cast, I returned for my final term at Columbia in the fall of 1954 instead of graduating with my class that June. Since I felt I should really be out in the world now instead of confined in a college dorm, I persuaded my parents and Columbia to let me live off campus, and found a basement apartment on West 77th Street that rented for fifty-five dollars a month. It was one dank room with a refrigerator and a stove with two burners on top, a cotlike bed, and a straight-backed chair. There were no windows, but a shaft of dim sunlight filtered down through a grating in the sidewalk. I loved the place. It was my first home of my own. The landlady was a haglike, toothless, harelipped woman who lived upstairs, and out of the goodness of a heart (or soul or spirit) that must have been as beautiful as her physical appearance was appalling, she took a motherly interest in me, and at least once a week snuck down to my den, took away my sheets and socks and underwear and returned them washed and ironed. Talk about a guardian angel for one's first foray into the world!

It was in that cellar room, staying up late as I pored over my books and sometimes as a weekend treat sipped Chianti from a straw-encased bottle, that I found the solution to my paradox about the prayer that I couldn't stop automatically praying. As with so many other of my questions and concerns of the time, I came upon the answer in the work of Ernest Hemingway, who indeed served as "Papa" for many of us young literary intellectuals of the fifties. I loved his short stories, and one that became an immediate favorite, as philosophy (in fact my own theology) as well as literature, was "A Clean, Well-Lighted Place."

The setting is a small bar in Spain, where the two bartenders discuss the only customer left in the place late at night, an old man who had tried to commit suicide by hanging himself the week before, but was cut down by his niece. The younger bartender wants to close up the place and get home to his wife, but the older bartender wants to stay open because he knows the old man needs to drink in such a clean, well-lighted place. He knows the old man feels a "nothing" that he feels himself, and a litany runs through his mind that I adopted at once as my own all-purpose prayer.

At night, when I couldn't keep my eyes open over my books any longer, I would get under the covers between the cold sheets and turn off the light in that windowless room, and in my honesty as an atheist intellectual, I would say the prayer I had learned from Hemingway's story. Sometimes as I lay there late at night the off-key singing or arguments of drunks going home from bars on Broadway came down from the street, and I pulled the pillow over my head and recited the cadenced words that satisfied the old habitual need for prayer but did not betray my brave new unbelief:

"Our nada who art in nada, nada be thy name. Thy kingdom nada. Thy will be nada in nada as it is in nada. Give us this nada our daily nada and nada us our nada as we nada our nadas and nada us not into nada but deliver us from nada; pues nada. Hail nothing full of nothing, nothing is with thee."

I added my own "Amen."

5. Pilgrimage

I pressed against the rail of the ship, waving to friends on shore, watching them recede along with the storybook skyline of my new, adult, adopted home—Manhattan. I was not only saying goodbye to New York for an indefinite, extended period, leaving behind my only earthly goods (a treasured collection of well-marked books) with trusted friends, I was departing from America for the first time in my life. Armed with a new portable typewriter, a knapsack bestowed on me by friends at a going-away party ending at dawn, and two changes of clothes, I was on my way to follow in the footsteps of my literary heroes of the twenties who had left home to see the world and learn about life —not by reading about it in academic courses but by living it— in Paris, Barcelona, London, and Rome. In fact, I was going them a few steps further. The ship I had boarded that frozen January morning in 1956 was the SS *Israel,* bound for a port I had never heard of a few years before: Haifa.

In the year minus a month since finishing my work at Columbia I had published several pieces in *The Nation,* including an essay called "Yeats and the Younger Generation" in which I excoriated my peers for taking the safe way out and "Sailing to Byzantium." I used the great poem of Yeats (which I had studied in Lionel Trilling's course and memorized along with "The Second Coming") as a symbol of the conservative, gray-flannel, no-risk life, a straight and narrow path down which aspiring writers fled to academe, sacrificing (as I saw it through the prism of my youthfully pure idealism) the raw, gutsy stuff of experience for the cool, bloodless tomb of security.

"The academy, not the world," I wrote, "is being chosen as the province of the youngest writers today in what is reported to be a constantly growing procession to graduate schools of English." I found that trend as depressing as the upsurge of religious interest on college campuses, both of which seemed to me a means of cowardly escape from—as opposed to courageous encounter with—"the world," or what I might also have termed "real life." I quoted a Princeton Ph.D. candidate with literary aspirations who told me that "teaching is the only way to write and make a living these days. It's impossible now to just take off and roam around and spend your time writing." I answered in my essay: "But it has always been impossible. It was just as impossible when Hemingway lived on potatoes in Paris. The difference today is that the young are so willing to accept the impossibility." Well, I was one young person who wasn't going to accept it, and in order to back up my words—and again avoid the stigma of falling into the hellish circle of Holden Caulfield's "phonies"—I had got myself a ticket on a Zim Lines ship to Israel by means of a small advance against articles to be written for *The Nation*.

And how in the world had I picked Israel, of all places? My "kissin' cousin" Katherine from Kentucky wrote to wish me well but said she wasn't even sure she knew how to pronounce the place where I was going, much less find it on the map. Her father, my Uncle Jim (brother of my paternal grandfather, the Baptist preacher, and my favorite relative because of his colorful life as a bookie in Louisville and of his eloquent, biblical-rhythmic storytelling) wondered why Danny had lit out for Israel, noting that "it's down around Lexington, but there's nothing much goes on there." A good deal of this confusion, I think, was due to the fact that the new state of Israel was still only eight years old and was not a big subject of conversation or news coverage in the Bible Belt regions of America. Had I said I was going to the Holy Land, or perhaps even Palestine, I am sure there would have been not only recognition but awed approval. I would hardly have approved of such a pilgrimage myself, however.

The very idea of a trek to pay homage or even to learn about the birthplace of some of the world's great religions—including the one I had been brought up with and believed in myself until so recently—would have seemed ludicrous to me. If someone had suggested that the remotest influence of a spiritual nature had anything to do with my journey, I would have answered with sharp indignation that my inspiration for going to Israel came not from the Bible but from an autobiographical book by Arthur Koestler called *Arrow in the Blue.*

I knew about Koestler from his novel *Darkness at Noon*—this became a big hit in postwar America as a realistic fictional document of the evils of Communism. Koestler was an intellectual who had looked for salvation through the Party and found instead betrayal and despair (his *The God That Failed* summed up the deep spiritual appeal and disillusionment that Marxism held for so many seekers of his own generation). The first professional theater I ever saw was the play based on Koestler's novel starring Edward G. Robinson that came to Indianapolis while I was a student at IU, and it moved me deeply. Koestler's brand of intellectual anti-Communism based on hard experience was as appealing to me as the red-baiting smear tactics of McCarthy and his cohorts were appalling. I'm sure Koestler was a significant influence on many young American as well as European intellectuals trying to find their own answers to the big questions of their time. Shortly after finishing college I found in a used bookstore a volume recounting his early years as a student and then free-lance journalist who went to Palestine in the 1920s to work on one of the pioneer Zionist settlements called a kibbutz. I bought the book at once and carried it home like a treasure.

At the time I was living in a rooming house in Princeton, New Jersey, working as the only reporter on "New Jersey's Oldest Weekly," the *Packet*, which had just been bought by Barney Kilgore, a local resident who also happened to be the renowned young publisher (he was in his forties, though I regarded him then as a venerable patriarch) of the *Wall Street Journal*. After pounding the pavements of New York in search of a job without even getting past the outer receptionists of the city's dailies and wire services, I got an interview with Kilgore himself through a mutual Indiana connection. My wise and popular history teacher from Shortridge High School, Dorothy Peterson, had gone to college at DePauw, in Greencastle, Indiana, with Kilgore, a loyal Hoosier who was partial to other home-state products. ("You're from Indiana, you'll do all right here," he told me in his famous alfalfa accent. "These New York fellas don't always do so good.")

Kilgore read my clippings from the Indianapolis *Star* and the Grand Rapids *Press* (including my Gertrude Stein feature-story lead) and hired me, not for the *Journal*, but for the small weekly he had just bought in Princeton, where he lived and from which he commuted to his office in New York. He was a generous, smart, ink-in-the-blood newspaperman and I was grateful to him for the job, but I felt trapped in sleepy suburbia while the excitement and glamor of the world lay less than an hour away but out of reach.

I lived between walls of flocked wallpaper in Mrs. Mulford's rooming house in Princeton, where the big excitement of the day was catching a glimpse of our world-famous neighbor Albert Einstein, who lived a few blocks down on Mercer Street, taking one of his strolls. I interviewed local politicians, chased fires, covered sewage hearings and university lectures, and wondered what I was doing in Princeton as I went home to read of Koestler's daring adventures as a young journalist in the Middle East. I had no way of knowing I would soon be in the exotic places I was reading about, working on kibbutzim like

Koestler and writing about Israel, going to a Bedouin encampment outside of Beersheba and sharing the same traditional meal described by T. E. Lawrence in another book I was reading at the time, *The Seven Pillars of Wisdom.* Least of all could I have dreamed that all this would become possible because of a review I wrote in the Princeton *Packet* of a book by a local resident.

My contemporary journalistic idol was Murray Kempton, who wrote an iconoclastic, brash, stylish, bracing, witty, altogether wondrous column three days a week in the New York *Post.* I got hooked on it at Columbia, and savoring it over lunch was one of the high points of any day in New York, another reason it was the greatest place in the world to live. I learned after I got to Princeton that Kempton lived there with his wife and young children, and I hoped I might see him on the street one day, like Einstein, and maybe even get his autograph.

It so happened that Kempton's first book was published a few months after I started working in Princeton, and I used the "local angle" as an excuse to write a full-page review of it for the *Packet,* justifying the piece by establishing the author's residence in the lead: "Murray Kempton of Edgerstoune Road has written a book that was published this week called *Part of Our Time: Some Monuments and Ruins of the Nineteen Thirties."* That Saturday Kempton called my rooming house to thank me for the review, saying I had really "dug the book," and explaining he was using that currently popular slang word in its meaning of "understand" rather than simply "like." I was overwhelmed that he would deign to acknowledge an unknown reviewer for the local weekly, and when he invited me to come by for a beer sometime, I was on his doorstep in a few hours.

Murray Kempton must have been in his mid-thirties then, a reddish-haired youthful-looking wise man with a pipe and horn-rimmed glasses and a bit of a Baltimore drawl, a man who not only knew about but was comfortably familiar with more subjects under the sun than anyone I have ever met before or since.

He spoke as intimately of the early life of Proust or the leaders of the October Revolution as he did of Willie Mays's batting stance, and graciously assumed that you knew everything he did, which left you not only mentally absorbed but exhausted. His talk was not brilliant for the sake of showing off his erudition —Murray is the least pretentious man I know and has about him a genuine and almost stunning kind of humility—but rather he ranged through references from different times and subjects in a manner that was as entertaining as it was illuminating, and with a sense of the interconnection of all things. He took pleasure in a world so filled with incredible ironies, contradictions, and epiphanies. He also listened carefully to what you had to say yourself (it seemed piddling beside the torrent of his own wit and eloquence) and honored it with his attention and his appreciation. He was as good in person as his prose was to read, and I was overwhelmed both by his learning and by his kindness.

Murray was one of several men whose generous spirits were as large as their considerable talent who allowed me to adopt them as combination mentor/father figures. My good luck in earthly "guardian angels" that began with Amy Frantz and gave me Corky Lamm in adolescence blessed my life in early youth with Kempton and the Columbia sociology professor and author C. Wright Mills. It was Kempton who gave significance to my restless exile in Princeton, and Mills who brought me out of it back to my beloved New York.

Mills was a seeming giant of a man, in broad-shouldered bulk and stature as well as humor and intellect. He was more the pure intellectual than Murray Kempton, a Ph.D. and scholar who was nonetheless impatient with the plodding and petty ways of academia, which he delighted in taunting for its pomposity. Unlike Murray, whose deep streak of Southern gentility led him to clothe his iconoclasm in Brooks Brothers tweed and cordovan, the flamboyant Mills roared into Columbia on his BMW motorcycle, looking like a rebel guerrilla in his work boots and flannel shirts and corduroys (in the 1950s, Ivy League professors were simply not *seen* in such outfits), with canvas bags full of books strapped around him and hanging from his shoulders like supplies for some sort of forced march or strategic attack on the bastions of conformity. Mills also could laugh at all this, as he did one night at his house, showing off his new motorcycle helmet and banging it against the wall to prove its strength in comic cavorting that had his friends and neighbors, the novelist Harvey Swados and his wife Bette, in tears of laughter.

I had admired Mills's iconoclastic critical study of American society in the fifties, *White Collar,* and got permission to take his seminar at Columbia on liberalism, in which we studied heavyweight modern social thinkers like Karl Mannheim, Max Weber, Ortega y Gasset. I wrote a paper comparing Ortega's *The Rise of the Masses* to the message I found in Hemingway's short story "Banal Story," and the offbeat juxtaposition caught Mills's imagination. He called me into his office, asked about my interests and ambitions, became an inspiring friend and guide. He had predicted I would soon get bored with "the small-town stuff" of the Princeton weekly newspaper job, and six months later wrote me to say he had got a grant for a new book and could hire me for part-time work as a research assistant. I gave a month's notice to Barney Kilgore and started packing.

I could make my own hours while working for Mills in the library and so was able to write my own stories and articles that I sent out in neat 9 × 12 manila envelopes that seemed to bounce off the editorial desks of the nation's leading magazines and return to my own mailbox with the speed and predictability of boomerangs. With my fellow aspiring writer-reporter-film-director-artist-producer young comrades from the hinterlands I happily lived on hope, communal spaghetti, and ninety-eight-cent bottles of Chianti. (The jobs of the floating gang of us living at the time in two apartments next door to one another on West 92nd Street included night-shift copy boy for the United Press, stagehand for Max Liebman's television variety show, and office

temp typist for a ballet company.) We adopted Kempton's *Part of Our Time* as our Bible, referring to it as "The Good Book," and reading aloud passages about the rebels of the thirties, like Sam Levenger, who as a boy built a raft to ride down the Mississippi that sank three feet off shore, and became a poet and idealistic volunteer for the Lincoln Brigade who died while fighting the Fascist forces in Spain. High on our own dreams and the heady sense of freedom we felt from release from our parents and their God, we recited Kempton's elegant prose like scripture to guide the conduct of our brave new lives in the capital of the world:

"There were new endeavors and fresh disasters, for they are the way of life; and the art of life is to save enough of yourself from each disaster to be able to begin again in something like your old image."

Such wisdom was especially thrilling because not one of us had yet experienced anything that might remotely resemble a personal disaster. The far more worldly-wise women our own age we invited to one of our "blasts" referred to us with affectionate condescension that was all too correct as "a fun bunch of boys." (Some of them were already having secret martinis with suave married men who were their bosses at work, leading to the sort of experience we had read about in John O'Hara novels.)

Though I still considered fiction to be the highest (and almost *holiest*) form of creation—and the novel the grail—reading Murray Kempton (as well as knowing him), John Reed, and the non-fiction work of Arthur Koestler had given me a new respect for journalism, had shown me that reporting could also be a form of art, rather than simply a preparation and training ground for fictional creation, as Hemingway had used it in his apprenticeship on the Kansas City *Star*. I longed to be unleashed myself on some of the big stories that were changing our own time, and when I read about the trial of two white men in the Mississippi delta for the murder of a Negro boy from

Chicago named Emmett Till for the crime of whistling at a white woman, I felt a deep gut desire to go there and write about it.

I had not had anything published in any national magazine or newspaper, and none of the local ones I had worked for were about to send me to Mississippi to cover that story. Who, in fact, would entrust an unknown young writer with such an assignment, and why should they? In desperation one night, bolstered by a few bourbons, I called up Murray Kempton and asked if he knew of any way I could get to write that story. He said he had been asked to do it for *The Nation,* but he was going down on assignment for his own paper, the New York *Post,* and didn't feel he could write it for both publications. He would call *The Nation* and tell them they ought to send *me* to do it!

They did, purely on Murray's urging. (When I say they "sent me" I mean they gave me press credentials and forty dollars to cover the round-trip bus fare from New York to Sumner, Mississippi.) I was in heaven. It was, as I had read somewhere in John Reed on the brink of a similar big assignment, like "being on the edge of a beautiful dream" to have such an opportunity.

The story itself was right out of Faulkner, a tragedy of the present day, whose narrative was told in the tumbledown court-house of that tiny town that became world-infamous overnight. When the trial was over I wrote all weekend around the clock to finish the story I had to send on Monday morning straight to the magazine's printer in order for it to be published in the next issue (otherwise it would be too dated and they wouldn't use it). I focused in some total way I had never done before, and just in time to make the deadline I got to a Western Union office and filed the story. Its essence was summed up in the first line: "The crowds are gone and this Delta town is back to its silent, solid life that is based on cotton and the proposition that a whole race of men was created to pick it."

The Nation published it just as I filed it. They were pleased (and no doubt pleasantly surprised that this unknown had turned in usable copy). I was asked to come into the office and discuss other possible assignments. The editor was the well-known and highly respected liberal journalist Carey McWilliams, and though he was always perfectly polite to me in the seven or so years I wrote for his magazine, I never felt quite comfortable with him. There was simply no rapport. Fortunately for me, the magazine had just acquired a new publisher in George Kirstein, whose brother Lincoln was the noted patron of the arts. George was a big, rugged, pipe-smoking, blunt-spoken man I immediately took a liking to, maybe because I believed he really liked my writing (he *told* me so) and wanted to get me contributing to the magazine on a regular basis.

Miraculously, I was making a sparse but joyous bohemian living in New York by writing and doing research, and yet I felt restless, worried that I wasn't doing enough, learning enough, risking enough to really become a writer, to follow the true calling of my heroes, to absorb enough experience to someday write that novel, to plumb the depths and scale the heights that were offered by life to the daring instead of playing it safe and drifting into a job in corporate journalism or advertising, or some safe teaching position or graduate degree program. I heard Murray Kempton remark, in one of his complex soliloquies on the relationship of the recent Teamsters Union election to the novels of Ford Madox Ford, that the trouble with some of his friends who were trying to write and failing to say anything worth hearing was that "nothing had ever happened to them."

I suddenly feared that if I didn't take some kind of immediate and drastic action I might become one of those gray, listless people to whom nothing had ever happened. At my age, after all, Hemingway was in Paris writing *The Sun Also Rises,* and Arthur Koestler was working on a kibbutz in Palestine and writing about the Middle East. Well, I couldn't just go somewhere and write a novel like *The Sun Also Rises*—in fact my attempts at fiction then seemed stunted and frustrating—but at least I could go to the Middle East and work on a kibbutz, couldn't I? I was reading about the dramatic events in the new state of Israel, of threats of war and skirmishes with their hostile Arab neighbors. Didn't I need to know about war, see death if I wanted to learn about life? I went to George Kirstein and asked if *The Nation* would send me to Israel—or at least give me the equivalent of that bus fare to Mississippi in order for me to get there and stay a few months in return for my writing a series of articles. He sighed, smiled, shook his head, stoked his pipe, nodded, and agreed.

I shared a cabin with seven other men on the SS *Israel* and was vastly relieved to learn that I was not quite the youngest or greenest member of the group. There was a crew-cut young student from CCNY whose parents were sending him to Israel in hopes of his gaining some appreciation of his roots (and thus perhaps not give his family such a hard time, I gathered) and he was in a near constant state of openmouthed excitement. When the captain made an announcement that we were passing the coast of Africa, the student was the first to press his nose to the porthole, and he called back to the rest of us in a thrilling tone of awe: "The Dark Continent!"

It was only then, after my laughter subsided with that of the others, that I remembered Aunt Ollie's prediction:

"Danny, you will be close to death through some experience that will interrupt your education, but you will survive it, and complete your education, and then you will cross the ocean— not the Atlantic, but a farther ocean, to a farther land than Europe. . . ."

What she foretold was now happening. Aunt Ollie's glimpse into the future was accurate enough to make me wonder if I was really in charge of my own fate. Had all this been determined back when I was a kid in Indianapolis, or even before? Was it all just chance and superstition?

More disturbing to me at the time was the question of

whether all this had anything to do with "God." Was I going
crazy or losing my Columbia-educated intellect to even think of
such a thing? Was this in some way really a pilgrimage to the
Holy Land, and was I being led there in some mysterious way
that was beyond my understanding? What force or chance or
circumstance was taking me to Jerusalem and Nazareth—
places I had read about in the Bible, places where Jesus himself
had walked and preached? Was I really being led there by
Arthur Koestler, or might it in some way have some insiduous
connection to Matthew, Mark, Luke, and John? I trembled, and
went to the ship's bar, trying to look casual as I slapped down
some change and in my deepest, most self-assured and manly
voice ordered a beer.

If there ever was an "innocent abroad" it was me in Jerusalem at age twenty-three with my knapsack and typewriter,
romantic ideas of journalistic derring-do, two hundred dollars
in American Express traveler's checks, and a Hebrew vocabu-
lary of roughly a dozen words I had learned on the boat. God or
no God, I was surely there "on faith," both mine and *Nation*
publisher George Kirstein's. Just before I left he had told me
while pacing behind his desk and puffing his briar, "It sounds
like you'll get into trouble, but I guess that's what you want."
That wasn't quite how I saw it, but I knew what he meant. I
wanted to put myself at risk, to test my courage and integrity, to
expose myself to the kind of life-or-death experience I could
learn from in the Hemingway school of hard knocks journalism.
I wanted to know what it felt like to face death, for I thought the
experience would make me a better writer, and I jumped at the
first opportunity to get myself shot at.
I didn't want to be killed or even hit by a bullet, but I wanted
to know what it was like to be exposed to enemy gunfire. That
was the ostensible lure that drew me to the Sea of Galilee,
where Israeli fishing boats were being fired on from Syrian gun
emplacements on the northeastern side of the shore. If I could

somehow get out in one of those fishing boats, I could write an article based on a firsthand experience in a war that was no less real for as yet being unofficial and undeclared.

It is hardly surprising that, looking back on that experience more than thirty years later, it seems like a dream, yet one of my most distinct memories of that time in Galilee was that I had the sense of it feeling like a dream while it was happening. Part of that impression I can naturally attribute to being in a legendary place, a place I had heard described in stories Amy Frantz told me before I was old enough to read, and whose landscape of hills, sky, and sea, of dusty streets and white stone houses I had looked at in colored pictures in Bibles before I could read the words. *Galilee.* The name itself was magic, calling forth even for a non-believer images of Jesus and his disciples, men who really did walk and go fishing there and for better or worse change the whole course of the history of the world.

I learned when I went to the town of Tiberias that the body of water it looked upon was known as Lake Tiberias by Arabs and Lake Kinneret by Jews, but I could not truly think of it by any other than the Christian name I had learned to call it since my own first consciousness. I, Dan Wakefield, of Indianapolis, Indiana, was standing on the shores of the Sea of Galilee. I could not help thinking of the hymn "I Walked Today Where Jesus Walked" and remembering that, according to the stories in the New Testament, he not only walked these roads and fields, he walked on this water. I had seen a picture of him performing the feat in a Sunday school pamphlet, and as a child I was so entranced by the story, and found it so literally believable, that I tried to do it myself. Luckily, my attempt was made in a city park children's wading pool with water only a few feet deep.

Now here I was at the edge of the real waters of Galilee, with no desire to try walking across, but only the wish to get on one of the fishing boats as a passenger, which under the circumstances seemed as if it would also require a miracle. I didn't know a soul in this place, and I didn't speak any of the languages. In my innocence, and a kind of naive journalistic faith, I simply went down to the water's edge where the fishermen had gathered to load up their boats, and stood there hoping to find someone who would let a young American stranger come along for the ride.

A rough but friendly-looking man with a big mustache and a gold tooth told me I could come with him and his Palestinian crew. He said his name was Nasim, and later explained he had learned to speak English while serving with the British Army in Palestine during World War II. He pointed across to the distant shore and said with a broad smile that we would go over there where the Syrians were, because the fish were there too. Just before the boats began to pull out at four o'clock in the afternoon, Nasim asked me if I liked to fish. One of his crewmen had not shown up, and I could take over his duties with the oars and the nets. I would be not just a passenger but a fisherman, on Galilee.

Our long blue wooden boat with the number 107 had an outboard motor that we used to get across the expanse of water. That was cut off a few hours later, when we reported to the armored gray police launch of the Israeli Navy that was there to protect the boats that were fishing near the Syrian side of the shore. Soon, the night took on an ancient aura. Although we fished for a while a hundred yards or so from where the Syrians had fired on the fishing boats a few nights before, I could not see the guns, and I felt no fear of them. All I could see of the Syrian camp were two small orange lights in the hills, and all I heard was an owl calling.

Earlier, before the darkness had come, I had talked not only with Nasim but with a young boy in our boat named Ali who had learned English "in school and the movies" and asked me about Audie Murphy and the Hollywood stars, and told of his dreams of someday going to Paris and America. Nasim declared proudly that this was the only boat on the lake with anyone who spoke English, and it had not just one but two people who could do so

—and now three, counting me! The other crewman, an older man called Abraham, feeling left out, began singing in Arabic and the others, smiling, joined in. But after dark, after we had eaten the sausages on the big hunks of crusty bread, the talk and singing ceased, and thoughts of America and Paris and movies soon came to seem as remote and unreal as the Syrian guns.

Nasim pushed an oar into my hands. It was not shaped and smoothed like the oars I had held back home, but was simply a long, rough heavy piece of wood that was larger at one end. There was no oarlock or any sort of metal fixture, the crude oar was simply attached to the boat with rope that fitted over wooden pegs. Abraham manned the other oar while Nasim and Ali laid the nets in the black water. The sound of wooden mallets being pounded on the bottoms of boats to attract the fish came like some kind of tribal incantation across the sea. Nasim gave quiet commands of forward and back and we moved with them, pulling, then pushing the heavy oars, Ali and Nasim lifting and laying the nets again. Sometimes I heard the sudden thrash of a fish and saw the silver shape flash in the dark in Nasim's hands, and then we pulled on to another spot, moving in a slow, rhythmic cycle, like the very tides, like the earth itself, as always, forever, in the long dream of life, and the time I had read about in childhood stories of the Sea of Galilee was as real as the time of that night and that water I moved across in the dark.

Back on Tiberias' shore in the morning the fish from the night's catch were loaded into boxes and carried on an old man's donkey cart some fifty yards up the dirt road to the market while the nets were hung out to dry. Nasim picked two fish from our catch and invited me to come with him. He took the fish to a small shop with an open door where the owner cooked them for us over a charcoal fire and served them with bread and glasses of hot tea for our breakfast.

I went to my room in a small pension near the harbor and wrote in a kind of trance, only taking time out to buy an orange and a chocolate bar in the afternoon, and finished the story that night. I never saw Nasim again, except in my mind's eye more than thirty years later when I read the twenty-first chapter of the Book of John. It is a story of Jesus appearing to the disciples after his crucifixion. Peter has taken some of the disciples fishing on the Sea of Galilee, and having caught nothing, they see a figure on the shore, and he tells them to cast the net on the right side of the boat. They do, and when it comes up filled with fish, one of the disciples says, "It is the Lord." Peter is so distraught that he jumps overboard, and the others take the boat with the nets full of fish on to land. In the words of the Jerusalem Bible the story continues like this:

"As soon as they came ashore they saw that there was some bread there, and a charcoal fire with fish cooking on it. Jesus said, 'Bring some of the fish you have just caught.' Simon Peter went aboard and dragged the net to the shore, full of big fish, one hundred and fifty-three of them; and in spite of there being so many the net was not broken. Jesus said to them, 'Come and have breakfast.' None of the disciples was bold enough to ask, 'Who are you?'; they knew quite well it was the Lord. Jesus then stepped forward, took the bread and gave it to them, and the same with the fish."

Reading that passage in the King's Chapel parish house on Beacon Street in Boston three decades later, I thought of the breakfast I had with Nasim, with the fish we had caught in the same Sea of Galilee where Peter and those disciples fished, in the same kind of boat, casting the same kind of net, the fish cooked over the same kind of charcoal fire. I wondered who Nasim was; where he had come from and where he had gone. I remembered he taught me a phrase in Arabic I had long forgotten and it came again to my lips: *"Allah hoo Akbar."* It means "God is great," Nasim told me.

It was half a lifetime later that I found in the Bible that kind of spiritual illumination of my own experiences in the land that serves as the setting of its stories. While I was actually there I rigorously guarded myself against making any such connections or allowing the unfolding drama of my pilgrimage to take on any meaning beyond the strictly secular and journalistic. I can look back now at the self I was then and trace this defensive action by reading the letters I wrote at the time to a girl friend in New York who thoughtfully saved them and gave them back to me years later for the kind of backward look I am now taking.

Having made my headquarters at a wonderfully cheap and hospitable pension in Jerusalem called the Hotel Himmelfarb, I wrote to the friend I'll call Sally on the eve of a trip to the Negev Desert: "I am going to the South armed with Martin Buber, the Bible, and *Rebellion in Palestine*. The Bible is of course strictly for literary purposes—and besides, I was able to buy it for the equivalent of 25 cents from the Evangelical Bible Shop. A real bargain center."

The King James Bible whose purchase I justified as a bargain to be used only for "literary purposes" I took home and kept among my books through the years, rationalizing its continued presence as a "souvenir" of my Israel adventure. It was there on the shelf in my house in Hollywood that awful spring morning when I woke with a scream and reached in desperation for a Bible, with a need that was not at all literary. The flyleaf bore the stamp of the Evangelical Bible Shop, Jerusalem.

On another foray into legendary biblical countryside (my bargain Bible served as a kind of historical guidebook) I found myself sitting in a makeshift shed at Sodom, by the Dead Sea, waiting to hitch a ride on a truck that passed through twice a week taking supplies to kibbutz Ein Geddi. From that sunblasted landscape that looked indeed as if it had suffered the wrath of God I wrote one of my aerogram letters to Sally with a Sodom dateline, reporting: "I read Ecclesiastes this afternoon and it is too bad how I can't get enthused about any of The Bible but I can't. Eccles. is probably the best, but for Godsake it's not so goddam good after that Hemingway paragraph 'The sun also riseth and setteth in the west. . . .'"

By "Hemingway paragraph" I meant the quote from Ecclesiastes my literary prophet-hero had used as an epigraph for his famous first novel and the source of its title, *The Sun Also Rises*. Hemingway's citation of the text had not only made it a familiar part of the intellectual lingo of our time, it had given it a kind of contemporary literary legitimacy that made it seem acceptable to me aside from—or in spite of—its religious significance.

In my letters to Sally I was constantly proving to her (and myself) that my sojourn in the Holy Land and visits to religious sites was in no way corrupting the purity or zeal of my unbelief. I wrote her from Jerusalem, "The other day I visited Mount Zion and what is supposed to be the room of the last supper, though I doubt it. There weren't any bread crumbs on the floor. And a woman was moaning and kissing the wall. In the words of Holden Caulfield, old Jesus would have puked."

I still maintained my seemingly odd and stubborn insistence on keeping Jesus somehow separated from my antireligious wrath, though I made it clear in my dispatches that this respect for whomever I meant by "Jesus" did not in any way ameliorate my antagonism to the religion named after him. For good measure, I asked her to "please read my favorite religious story, 'A Clean, Well-Lighted Place.' "

I approved of something Sally wrote indicating an interest in mysticism, and assured her, "By the way, I too am a mystic, and have an Aunt Ollah who is a spiritualist, or did I tell you that? Anyway I was glad to hear of your own inclination that way, and perhaps that is the answer for Sean [we had fantasized what we would tell a child about God and called the imaginary offspring Sean]: 'Sean old Horse, this church stuff is for the birds, but if you and Billy Brown wanted to go out to Aunt Ollah's some day . . .' " That sort of thing would clearly be approved, probably applauded; I was no doubt envisioning these two imaginary boys, "Sean" and his pal "Billy Brown," in the image of me and Harpie, as questing teenage friends. That was fine. A little dabbling in mysticism, keeping an open mind about such things, was acceptable as healthy intellectual curiosity. But I made the narrow limits of my tolerance clear as I ended one letter to Sally with the tongue-in-cheek but basically bedrock instructions: "Don't get grey hair or married or converted to Catholicism. . . ."

I see now between the lines of my letters from Israel an almost constant, unconscious battle of a kind that must go on within many young people whose new intellectual faith in a Godless universe is at war with their earlier and sometimes deeper religious beliefs and impulses. Even though expressed with consciously sophisticated irony, the old forms of thought and prayer kept breaking through my accounts of experience in Israel, as when I wrote to Sally about the adventure on Galilee:

"The fishermen were wonderful people too and that night was really a tremendous thing. I had just before that been in Tel Aviv at a cheesy imitation-American nightclub that a native had proudly taken me to, and was quite depressed. Then there was this little boat and happy guys with great hunks of bread and work to do. God save us all from the grey flannel suit and deliver us into life. Amen."

I also have a sense, looking back, of being drawn or pulled physically in what seems now an uncanny manner to certain places and experiences familiar to me from the Bible stories of my childhood. Maybe it was some kind of unconscious "acting out" or repetition of some of the stories of Jesus I had read and heard, while on another, conscious level I was simply behaving as a journalist, a reporter trying to get the best story and do his job.

Like any conscientious reporter, I wanted to get "the other side of the story" in the continuing conflict between the new state of Israel and her hostile Arab neighbors. In pursuit of that I wanted to cross over into Jordan, yet none of the Arab nations would allow foreigners to cross their borders from Israel—or even to enter from any other point if they had an Israeli visa stamped in their passports. At that time Jerusalem was divided by the armistice lines of Israel's 1948 War of Independence, and the "Old City" section that contained the principal religious shrines of Christians, Moslems, and Jews was in Jordanian territory. While I could not go there as a journalist or tourist, "religious pilgrims" were allowed to enter through the Mandelbaum Gate for the major holidays of their faith, and I was told that this opportunity would be possible for Christians during the days from Good Friday to Easter. At first I laughed (nervously) at the very idea. Me, the enlightened atheistic Columbia graduate and *Nation* correspondent, a "religious pilgrim"? On the other hand, how else could I get into Jordan to interview Arabs and see the other side of the story in the Middle East? I described my plan of action—and my discomfort about the guise I had to assume—in a letter to Sally: "If all goes well I will be in the Jordan sector of Jerusalem for Easter. I have made application to pass through the gates, on grounds of being a religious pilgrim. Hee Haw. I had to lie something awful. The nice lady at the consulate said 'What religion are you?' I flashed back 'Protestant.' 'What denomination?' she said. I shuffled my feet for a while and said 'duh, uh, Baptist.' I don't know why, unless it was that my grandfather was a Baptist minister in Kentucky and my Uncle Jim who is a bookie in Louisville is a good Baptist. Anyway I had to go to the Baptist minister in Jerusalem, a young fellow from South Carolina who 'felt called to this part of the world.' That is mean and I shouldn't scoff. But that's what he said. So he asked me which church I belonged to and I said 'The 34th Street Baptist Church' and now I have a letter to that effect."

The day after I got into Jordan I got into trouble. I had gone to an Arab village called Beht Safafa that was well known at the time for being divided down the middle by the armistice line, with half the residents in Israel and the other half in Jordan. I thought the human drama that was surely involved in life in "the divided village" would make a surefire feature story, maybe the kind I could sell to the *Saturday Evening Post* for enough money to take me to Europe on the way back home to New York. I was wandering around the village looking for someone who spoke English when I was picked up by two soldiers of the Arab Legion, the army of the kingdom of Jordan. They took me to their commanding officer, who spoke to me in friendly English until I said I had come over from Israel.

"No!" he said.

I had given the wrong answer, yet it was the only one I knew.

"You have come from occupied territory," he explained as he slammed his fist on his desk. The nation of Israel was not recognized, and its very name was not spoken here. The officer told me I would have to see the military governor in Bethlehem, and then he stopped smiling or speaking in English. The trouble George Kirstein had predicted was now upon me.

O little town of Bethlehem, all I saw of you was the dank office of your chain-smoking military governor. He sent me to Arab Legion headquarters in Jerusalem under armed guard. There I repeated the story about only being a religious pilgrim, which naturally made no sense to my questioners since there was nothing religious to see in the village of Beht Safafa, and tourists were not usually found snooping around the border of the enemy country. I was too naive and frightened and dumb to simply say I was trying to write a story, for I feared that coming into Jordan under the false pretense of religious pilgrimage might land me in jail (though not as surely as their suspicion that I was a spy!). My passport said my occupation was "researcher," since that was the last job I had held, with C. Wright Mills, and I had been too shy or self-deprecatory to identify myself as a writer or journalist when I applied for the passport. My questioners asked if I was one of those people trying to make peace between the Jews and Arabs—a free-lance do-gooder or crackpot in other words. They couldn't figure me out and I was too terrified to help them. They told me I could go back and stay the night at my pension but they kept my passport and said I had to report back to them the next morning and they would determine my fate. I might not be allowed to go back through the Mandel-baum Gate but might be shipped instead to Cyprus. I didn't have enough money even to get back from there to Israel.

In a state of acute anxiety I went back to my pension, where the real religious pilgrims were preparing for Easter in the Holy Land. In my room I looked at my notebook and realized that I had all kinds of notes from interviews I'd done the day before with political people, and that this would be even more proof of the Arab Legion's suspicion that I was some kind of spy. I went out to try to throw away my notes, but everywhere I looked it seemed I saw an Arab Legionnaire. I feared I was being followed. I went back to my room and held the notes over the toilet bowl while I put a match to them, but the flame burned my hand and I dropped the wad of notes into the bowl. Now they were soggy wet and even more incriminating since it was obvious I had tried to get rid of them. I knew that later—if I ever escaped and the sun rose on me in some familiar friendly land again—I would laugh about this, but in the meantime I felt I had no alternative but to get rid of the notes the only way I could imagine doing it without a trace of damning evidence. I ate the notes. I sat up all night, wadding the paper into small pellets and swallowing them. As the bells rang out for Easter morn, I made my way not to church but to Arab Legion head-quarters. I was again questioned by the authorities, but thankfully the correlation of my experience with the passion narrative ceased, for I was released by the authorities and told to get back into Israel before nightfall. I was all too happy to comply.

I felt the full glory of a personal "resurrection" into freedom that Easter day I returned from Jordan into what they called "occupied territory" and what I now thought of as home. The non-grand Hotel Himmelfarb had come to feel especially homelike, and in fact the family who owned and ran this rickety hostel in a kind of alley off Zion Square provided me with a personal kind of hospitality and security altogether unknown to the high-level correspondents who stayed at the proud Hotel

King David. The proprietors were a Latvian Jewish couple whose daughter spoke a lilting, singsong English and served me tea and leftover cake in the kitchen (it was sometimes my main meal of the day) and asked about who I had met and what I had seen and learned in my travels around the countryside.

There was a colorful cast of residents who came and went, people from all parts of the world with all kinds of experience. I wrote to Sally, "The Himmelfarb is a joy. . . . A fellow down the hall invited me to his room to see his books, which are literally stacked to the ceiling, and letters he has received from J. B. Rhine [the ESP researcher at Duke University]. This fellow, one Fred Steingart, leaned across the table, his brow wrinkled, and asked 'What is thought? We know what electricity is, but what is thought? How does it move? How can we measure it?' "

I felt I was living in a Koestler novel, and nothing could have thrilled me more—except perhaps to write a novel of my own. "All day I have been reading A. Koestler, *The Age of Longing,*" I wrote to Sally. "A very fine thing I think and probably one reason why my fictionitis is crackling again." I reported in this same letter that Fred Steingart, who generously loaned me books and gave me oranges out of the big mesh sack he kept in his room, had also offered me the use of a small house he had in a farming village an hour or so from Jerusalem as a place to write: "I have in mind to do a bit of fiction writing now by means of going down to F. Steingart's free literary hostel, as for one thing I feel kind of stale about the writing of these other bits [I was trying to do free-lance features to supplement my *Nation* payments, and published a few in the English-language newspaper the Jerusalem *Post]* and maybe this will be a help. Tho I don't know what the hell it will produce in itself. . . ."

What I hoped it would produce was what I referred to as "the tuffest of all the tangled ideas in my head—the midwest novel. I don't see it as anything soon, but the funny thing is, of all the things I want to do, or even *must* do—that is the most important. I don't have confidence enuff in my future to be even sure it will ever be done. But it has to be battled and tried and someday even if in 20 years, set down." It turned out to be a little bit sooner—my first novel, that Midwest coming-of-age story, was published fourteen years later as *Going All the Way*.

After those occasional bouts with fiction writing I would return to my exploration of the country in search of subjects for the *Nation* pieces. My aim was to report Israel through firsthand observation rather than pundit rhetorical assessments, though I did take appropriate journalistic pride in publishing the first foreign press interview with Golda Meir after she became Foreign Minister, thanks to a real "guardian angel" in the Israel Government Press Office named Yakov Aviad. That urbane and gracefully generous man not only set up interviews for me but also took me to his family's home for dinners, and on one occasion loaned me enough money to survive on till my next *Nation* check came through.

I was not intentionally seeking any sort of spiritual subject matter or experience at the time—far from it—and least of all trying to "walk where Jesus walked" either literally or metaphorically, but now it seemed chance or fate or something deeper kept bringing me to such experience. I went to Sde Boker, a kibbutz in the most remote and isolated part of the Negev, twenty miles south of Beersheba, simply because it seemed that such a "desert outpost" habitually under attack from *fedayeen* infiltrators and raids from roving Bedouins would make a dramatic story. Whenever I went to a kibbutz I offered to work in return for their hospitality of food and shelter, but I had no idea that at Sde Boker I'd be given the job of shepherd. I didn't even know they had sheep there until I was told that one of the young men who worked at the sheep camp was taking a week's vacation in Tel Aviv and they needed someone to fill in.

The sheep camp was even more isolated and remote than the main settlement at Sde Boker, and consisted only of a truck converted into a bunkhouse for four people, and pens for the flocks of sheep. We set out each morning before dawn to herd the sheep to the grazing land three miles beyond the camp. I was told to assist Yahiel, one of the young former students turned shepherd, with the main flock. Instead of the shepherd's crook I had envisioned, I was given a bag of egg salad sandwiches and a rifle. A young woman tending the sheep had been killed by Bedouins a few years before, and now all the shepherds were armed. Yahiel showed me how to shoot the rifle and built a fire to make coffee for breakfast once we got to the grazing land an hour or so after dawn.

The sheep kept rambling off in all directions, quickly moving out of sight, and we took turns running to get them, shouting and shooing them back to the main flock. I had always thought being a shepherd was easy—a restful, meditative kind of work—but from my week-long stint I learned that looking after a flock of sheep was demanding, frustrating work, the kind that meant you could almost never rest and must always be alert to keep track of the strays wandering off to danger.

I had always imagined Jesus as the shepherd of the Twenty-third Psalm ("The Lord is my shepherd") though I don't think he ever really worked as a conventional shepherd. He was a shepherd in the metaphorical sense that he was a fisherman: "Follow me," he said to the fishermen Simon and Andrew in the first chapter of Mark, "and I will make you into fishers of men." From my own experience in the Negev, it seems obvious that being a shepherd of men must be the same kind of difficult task as tending those unheeding, wandering sheep, a task requiring almost supernatural patience and caring and love.

There was little sense of romance in what turned out to be the hot, dusty, tiring work of a shepherd, but at night when we took the flock home, timing our arrival back at camp just as darkness fell, an oil lamp cast a special glow in the bunk-truck where Haya, a young woman with dark hair in a long braid, was cooking dinner over the oil burner that served as a stove, and the table was set with pink thistles she had picked in the desert. Before we sat down to the meal we washed off the caked dust of the day by stripping off all our clothes and opening a valve in the pipeline that ran through the Negev from Beersheba to Eilat. In a jet of ice-cold water we danced and whooped as we rubbed off the dust and stared up at the million stars that burned in the clear night sky of the desert. In those intense moments I had the thrilling sense I had been brought out of Indiana by some special chance or fate or guiding force known long ago (as Aunt Ollie foretold) to this place of stunning mystery and beauty on the other side of the earth.

At the time I did not recognize any "religious" element in those feelings but only accounted them as part of the universal unknown that was sometimes tapped into by seers like Aunt Ollie. Now it seems to me remarkable that, in spite of my antireligious sentiment of the time, I went to that land I had heard and read and even sung about as a child in Sunday school and church, the land where Jesus had walked and preached to fishermen and shepherds, and I ended up working myself at those very jobs. I had not consciously gone there for any such purpose, had scorned those religious pilgrims who had come to the Holy Land to pay homage to such faith. Perhaps my experience was simply accidental, or maybe even some sort of subconscious, neurotic "acting out" of a deep-seated childhood fantasy. All I know is that it now seems inevitable, a part of my deepest self, without which I wouldn't be who I am. I carried with me through the trip a historical/journalistic book about modern Israel by Koestler whose title summed up the sense of my own personal journey there as well: *Promise and Fulfillment.*

Then it came literally crashing to an end. I returned from that last trip to the Negev in June to find a letter from my mother announcing that she was divorcing my father after twenty-five years of marriage. I unburdened my feelings in a letter to Sally:

"At Christmas my mother said she might get the divorce and I said if she wanted to she should, and I felt no emotion about it but when I got this letter today I cried, just a little, but I did, and it really hurt—not the fact of the divorce but all those years of unhappiness leading up to it. . . . I am so sorry I couldn't have done anything to help it though I know there was nothing to be done. It was tragic because neither side was wrong, neither was bad, and essentially they destroyed each other not meaning to, only wanting to live, and they could not with any happiness live together. Because of me the kid they stayed all that time and when I left, and rather abruptly, and in some ways unkindly, it all came apart. . . . I brought them some little happiness I think but much more pain I'm afraid, but at least maybe the only happiness there was in it all. . . ."

After crying ("just a little") and pouring my heart out to Sally via aerogram, I thought I would just resume my plans to do a few more articles in Israel and make enough money to move on to Italy, where I would meet one of my New York buddies; we would follow in the European footsteps of our prophet Hemingway. But a few days after the letter came from my mother I hitchhiked to a kibbutz in the north and jumped off the back of a truck that was moving much too fast for such a casual departure. In the painful crash to the road I broke my arm and knocked out most of a front tooth. I was suddenly afraid—perhaps of whatever forces were working within me to cause such a leap to my own self-inflicted injury.

Filled with a deep anxiety that went far beyond my physical injuries, I wired my mother for money to fly back home to New York. A chapter of my life had suddenly closed after six adventurous months, and something lay ahead of me I couldn't discern. I thought of a Spanish phrase that had stuck in my mind. *Tengo miedo.* It means "I am afraid" but the literal translation seemed even more accurate a rendering of my own specific feelings: "I have fear."

6. The Couch

Yes, she said, yes, she would marry me, and yes, she would give me her greatest gift, yes, she said as passionately as Siobhan McKenna reading the Molly Bloom soliloquy on the Spoken Arts record I used to play in anticipation of the long-awaited sexual fulfillment, as well as to gain a deeper intellectual understanding of James Joyce's *Ulysses* (a two-for-one bargain of body and mind). Yes, she was, like Molly, "a flower of the mountain," a virgin ripe and ready at last; yes, she said to marriage and me and love, the whole incredible fantasy and dream come true, yes, just as I had dreamed of it, longed for it, lusted for it, yes, it had finally all come to me, the fulfillment that would save me and shape my life and give it meaning, not only physical pleasure and mental companionship but spiritual union and significance, the highest we humans could know in the era after the death of God, all this was what lay before me in sumptuous splendor that night, yes, oh yes, all that and more, inexpressible, yes, yes, a thousand times yes, oh, essence of yes, but I said no.

No?

No!

That can't be true. Who would say no, and why? Surely not me, a wanting embodiment of hunger—how could I refuse the long-fantasized feast of life and love? Listen again, I know I said yes, I must have said yes. Yes! I can hear it now. Yes! But that was only my mouth, my quaking voice, while at the same time, that crucial time, that essence of time that seemed as intense as what Dylan Thomas described as the "spun bud of the world" (on another of the Spoken Arts records that spoke for my need) my body was mute. I was limp.

I could not make love; I could not live.

One conclusion followed the other like the night the day in my now darkening mind, my blackening empty hole of a soul. She tried to cheer me. But she too was rocked by the unaccountable refusal, the contradiction of verbal yes and physical no, that anguish of irony, awful joke. Impotence. Poor guy couldn't get it up. She had saved herself like all good girls of her time and chosen the man to whom she would give and he wasn't able to take. Had she done something wrong? Did she lack appeal or guile or some secret, essential wile? No, I assured her with heart cracking, nothing, no one could be more desirable than she, no one more desiring than I. Another line of Richard Wilbur (via the Duke d'Orléans) spoke for me: "I die of thirst, here at the fountainside." We tried again, but it didn't work then either, and I sensed her withdrawing, in fear, hurt, frustration, protection. I could hardly blame her when she stopped seeing me. I blamed myself, my debilitating, life-canceling curse, and there was nothing and no one to whom to appeal: *Our nada who art in nada, nada be thy nada.*

What was the reason to live if I couldn't know the essence of life? (I had no idea this failure was not an uncommon experience for novices, but assumed it meant I was doomed, a sexual cripple, unless some unlikely miracle could cure me.) What more exquisite torture was there than to watch other people meet and mate and marry when I was damned from being able to do it myself? One of my buddies was about to be married to a swell girl I'd fixed him up with, and the week before the big day I bourboned myself into near oblivion—the first time I'd done it as a way of not being aware, of blotting out the pain of what I couldn't bear. I locked myself in the bathroom with a vengeance and a purpose.

Our communal apartment of ambitious boys from the boondocks was a kind of postcollegiate dormitory, complete with posters and even impromptu artwork drawn on the walls. In the bathroom someone had painted above the mirror (perhaps to waken our higher consciousness while shaving) the question of the Zen koan that J. D. Salinger had made popular with young people like ourselves all across the country who avidly read his stories of the Glass family as they appeared in *The New Yorker:* "What is the sound of one hand clapping?" In my anguish I painted with slurry strokes another message on the wall beside it, one that confirmed my mood and came from the pen of another of my pantheon of literary gods, F. Scott Fitzgerald: "Life is a cheat, and its conditions essentially are those of despair."

Then I unwrapped a razor blade and stroked it across my wrist, drawing blood. Emboldened, I sliced again, and felt relief as the red badge of rage came, and the flowing tears. I did not dig deep enough to sever anything, but enough to flay the body that betrayed my soul, to protest the refusal of flesh that said no to love and therefore life itself and left me in the deepest and hollowest sense *hopeless.*

Or so it felt. The despair must not have been total, for I hadn't gone so far as to kill myself, nor was that what I really wanted, at least not yet. In fact, in a curious way, I believe the bloodletting eased the pressure of the overwhelming angst, at least temporarily. I learned something I described later in my novel *Going All the Way,* when my unhero Sonny Burns, after just such an experience, ". . . understood that cutting yourself might not have anything to do with suicide or even sympathy, that it was a very private act, a thing of its own; a self-treatment, perhaps, like the lancing of a wound. . . ." Perhaps it served as self-punishment, and so brought a kind of relief. It was not, however, something I wanted to feel compelled to try again. I knew that powerful, destructive forces were at work within me, no matter what they were labeled. What could I do? Where did one turn for salvation in a world without God, a universe the best modern minds had judged meaningless?

Dr. Ernest lit another cigarette, tilted his head back, and blew a stream of smoke toward the ceiling. He said he thought I was among those few people who could benefit from psycho-analysis. I took it as a compliment. He had cited my inquiring mind, my intelligence, my writer's perception, as some of the qualifications that would suit me for this rigorous and demand-ing course of treatment. He was talking about orthodox Freud-ian analysis, a fifty-minute hour five days a week for an unspeci-fied number of years—four or five was about the minimum time for completion of this exhaustive type of therapy, he told me. It was expensive not only in terms of time and commitment but also in cash. The standard charge then was twenty-five dollars an hour, which meant a hundred and twenty-five dollars a week, five hundred a month, six thousand a year. That was a decent annual income in 1956, about double the amount of money I had made and lived on during my first year as a free-lance writer.

It would be difficult to call on my parents for help, since they were going through a divorce. Dr. Ernest suggested I apply for a sort of scholarship that was sometimes given to patients whose background and problems suited the interests of analysts in training at the New York Psychoanalytic Institute. I filled out the forms with difficulty, embarrassed to reveal my shame on paper, couching my sexual impotence in roundabout language and hoping it was exactly the problem some brilliant young analyst was hot to cure (I imagined a kind of latter-day version of Scott Fitzgerald's bright, sympathetic Dr. Dick Diver before he lost his own stability for love of the tragic Nicole in *Tender Is the Night*).

In the meantime I would have to wait and hope, seeing Dr. Ernest for occasional therapy sessions paid for by my mother. Also in the meantime I had to get on with my life, having

discovered that in spite of all the anguish I had just endured I did not want to die. I wanted to try to live, and love, and write, and become whole—healed by the latest, most rigorous modern scientific method of treatment, Freudian psychoanalysis.

The office of the analyst I'll call Dr. Stanley was quietly elegant. Several small, original contemporary paintings hung on the wall (except in museums, I had only seen reproductions) as well as a certificate of membership in the New York Psychoanalytic Society. There was a highly polished tray on the table beside the big leather chair where Dr. Stanley sat, and a monogrammed letter opener. The doctor wore horn-rimmed glasses, a dark, three-piece suit made of some heavy flannel or woolen material, a thin, dark tie with a muted pattern, and a starched white shirt. His dark brown hair was sternly clipped in a crew cut. I could not help wondering if the vest constraining his potbelly contributed to the rather bulging look of his eyes. He reminded me of a bullfrog dressed up as a banker, and his raspy voice contributed to that impression.

"Tell me, Mistuh Wakefield," he asked in his heavy New York accent, "is theah any pah-ticulah paht of a woman's clothing that arouses you sexually?"

He breathed heavily, no doubt from the tightness of his vest. I pondered the question, trying not to panic and give "the wrong answer." But wasn't it the wrong question? Didn't he mean what part of a woman's *body* most aroused me, as in whether I was, in the common male parlance concerning such matters, a "tit man" or an "ass man"? Did his asking about women's clothing mean he was concerned, like my Columbia sex education instructor, about my being inflamed to unhealthy masturbation by the brassiere and hosiery ads in the Sunday New York *Times Magazine?* In fact I was aroused by all women's clothing, as I was by all parts of women's bodies, but I was embarrassed to confess and say "All of it," so I simply said no, deciding that amounted to about the same thing anyway, since it didn't focus on any *particular* item.

That was the only question Dr. Stanley asked me—aside from how the bills would be paid—before beginning a five-day-a-week psychoanalysis with no end in sight, but whose length he estimated, when I pressed the question, to be the minimum of four or five years Dr. Ernest had quoted me. During that time, Dr. Stanley said, until the analysis was completed (which only he as the doctor could determine) I was not to make any major life changes—that is, move to another place, go into another kind of work, or get married. In a sense, I had to agree to put my life "on hold" in regard to such big decisions.

I nodded my assent, though the idea of agreeing not to marry until the end of analysis bothered me—what if I were to meet "the right girl" when I walked out the door, and had to tell her that, even though I loved her and wanted to marry her, we had to postpone the wedding until my treatment was completed?

Entering into this analytic agreement meant a major commitment of my time and energy and my parents' money. I had been turned down for the scholarship I applied for through the New York Psychoanalytic Institute. (Was this good or bad? Did it mean I wasn't screwed up enough to be interesting, or was my case too difficult to be dealt with by someone in training?) My parents—who had decided to get married again to each other—had agreed to pay for this long and expensive treatment, one that would certainly mean a steady drain on their financial resources. I felt guilty about taking their money and vowed I would someday pay it back (which I was thankfully able to do years later), and they no doubt felt guilty about their own responsibility in having a man-child whose problems were such that this elaborate and extensive treatment had been strongly urged by Dr. Ernest, the therapist who had been so highly recommended to them and whose own treatment had seemed helpful to the troubled son.

In fact I had asked Dr. Ernest if he himself could not conduct my analysis. I liked and trusted him and felt I had benefitted from therapy with him. Who better to be my guide on this arduous interior journey? Dr. Ernest thanked me for the confidence I had thus expressed in him but said it would not be the best procedure for him to act as my analyst. He explained that the therapy we had been engaged in was a different type of treatment, and that having established a relationship in that more open, interpersonal kind of communication, it would be difficult to switch to the rigorous, impersonal framework of analysis, in which the patient lies on the couch and the doctor sits behind in a chair out of sight. He did not say further (as I had to learn by reading about the subject) that the rationale for this was that the patient was hopefully to undergo a "transference" of emotions to the anonymous doctor, projecting onto him the feelings toward the parent that were subconsciously blocking his full functioning. In other words, I already knew a little too much about Dr. Ernest as a human being to be able to begin with him as a blank screen on which to make my projections and thus bring about the curative process of transference.

Sadly, I accepted this judgment and then asked Dr. Ernest an uncomfortable key question after my first meeting with the analyst he had recommended, Dr. Stanley.

"Does it matter that I don't like him?"

Dr. Ernest let a smile escape and said, "No, it doesn't matter. In fact, it is something to 'work with' in the analysis."

I protested shyly—feeling like a hick in this sophisticated realm of analytic knowledge—that it didn't make sense to me that I could be helped in such a personal, intimate type of treatment, dealing with the most sensitive private problems, by someone I didn't like. But Dr. Ernest was the doctor, and I accepted his prescription even though I didn't understand it. I also said I didn't understand why the only question Dr. Stanley asked me before embarking on years of the deepest, most personal exploration was what items of women's clothing most aroused me.

Dr. Ernest shrugged, sphinxlike. It was one of those riddles the layman could not understand, and I accepted the mystery—taking it on faith.

I entered psychoanalysis with the high seriousness of purpose and commitment of any acolyte taking his vows to a rigorous religious order. Like many in my generation, I had already made the intellectual substitution of Freud for God. ("Freud" of course meant the world view of the man whose work had made psychiatry and psychoanalysis accepted as a medical science, the ultimate truth of the scientific age which dismissed religion as "illusion," to use Freud's own term.) Now I was acting on my intellectual belief; I was setting out on a search for personal healing through a method that had in my culture replaced religion as the means of achieving salvation. As with many others like me, I had literally replaced religion with psychiatry, for I was seeking the long-lasting, earthly kind of salvation I hadn't gotten from baptism and church and Jesus.

I believed I had started a journey that would guide me to the truth, and I believed that any process involving the pursuit and discovery of the truth was ennobling, if not sacred. I felt ennobled by having the privilege of setting out upon such a path, and I was flattered by Dr. Ernest's evaluation that I was the kind of person well suited to embark on it. I thought it would not only cure my sexual hangups but make me a better writer—in fact, "unblock" whatever was stopping me from writing my novel. It angered me that some people joked about psychiatry and called therapists and analysts "shrinks" when I believed they did the opposite—that, rather than "shrink" the mind of the patient, they enlarged it. I believed in psychoanalysis as a literary as well as a psychological quest, and I took T. S. Eliot's stirring lines as metaphor for my journey:

We shall not cease from exploration
And the end of all our exploring

Will be to arrive where we started
And know the place for the first time.

The answer would be there hidden in childhood, in some
early trauma, perhaps even at birth, and by digging down, by
going through the muck of the years hidden beneath the debris
of the unconscious, with pain but dedication I would finally—
like Galahad reaching the grail—come upon it, recapture it, and
in so doing dispel its power, making myself whole and free as I
intoned the magic name for whatever moment had turned the
screws on my developing psyche. I would shout it from the
rooftops with a happy ring of personal freedom, a name un-
locked from memory that would open the past as dramatically
as it did in recalling the life of "Citizen Kane": *Rosebud!*

I commuted every weekday from the streets of East Harlem,
where I had gone to live while doing research about that neighborhood for my first book *(Island in the City: The World of
Spanish Harlem),* to the couch in the elegant office of the analyst on Park Avenue. The five hundred dollars or so of my
parents' money I paid every month to the analyst for treatment
of my personal neurosis would have fed and clothed the dozen
or so families of the five-story tenement building I lived in. I
tried not to think about that. My psychoanalysis seemed like a
separate compartment of my life, a secret chamber the size of
Dr. Stanley's chic office. I didn't want to talk about "being on
the couch" as it was sometimes called then, since I didn't want
to tell anyone besides close friends about the embarrassing personal problems that led me to it, nor did I want to be like one of
those cliché bejeweled rich ladies or decadent Ivy League
lushes who talked about "my analysis" and "my analyst" to
show how chic they were (come to think of it, I never met any
such characters except in cartoons and bad magazine fiction).
The time on the couch itself, the famous fifty-minute analytic
hour, was not at all what I had imagined. In fact, it was not only

disappointing, it was a crashing bore. How could it be? How could anyone—especially a self-absorbed only child such as myself—fail to be fascinated by talking about himself for almost an hour every day? Well, try it sometime when the person you are talking to is sitting behind you out of sight and almost never says anything other than "Yes, go on." Freudian psychoanalysis is not a conversation.

(Some people use the terms "psychoanalysis" and "analysis" as synonymous with "psychotherapy" and "therapy," and that has led to some confusing discussions and misunderstandings. It's important for me to make clear that the treatment I was in, and my dissatisfactions and later deep disillusionment about it, was distinct from psychotherapy, even as practiced by the Freudian school of psychiatry. Stated basically, psychotherapy may last for a long or short time, with one or more sessions a week or sporadically, with doctor and patient talking to one another face to face, as I had done in therapy with Dr. Ernest; psychoanalysis consists of four or five sessions a week over four or five years or perhaps many more (I once met a man who had been in analysis fifteen years), with the patient lying on a couch and "free-associating" (talking in a stream-of-consciousness manner) with the doctor sitting out of sight behind the patient and rarely making any comment).

I was twenty-five years old when I "went into analysis" in 1957 (my age was another qualification for success of the treatment, I was told by the doctor) and I figured by the time I was thirty I would be a winning combination of F. Scott Fitzgerald (without the hangovers or the angst) and Adlai Stevenson. Little wonder, with this as goal, that I was not only willing but eager to arrange my schedule around the analytic hour. I never told anyone that was where I had to be at a certain hour of day (the appointments were at different times during the week, some in the morning and some in the afternoon) but simply wrote, and did interviews or went to meetings, around those times. Going from East Harlem and later Greenwich Village to the East

Eighties near Park Avenue, I felt like an undercover agent moving between different worlds in a complicated plot to discover dangerous secrets and in so doing to save—not my country but myself.

I eagerly poured out the contents of my mind as I lay on the couch, and of course it came out haphazardly, rambling, repetitious, boring even to me. I was always glad to have had a dream, since that seemed to promise something extra, the hope of some insight that might move this tedious process forward, make something happen. I took in dreams as happily as a dog with a wagging tail takes a stick to its master (but without the resulting pat on the head or words of appreciation—only "Yes, go on"). I even began having what I thought of as "Freudian dreams"— that is, dreams that I thought were the sort of thing one was supposed to have in a good Freudian analysis and so would prove I was a good patient who was making progress. Once I even dreamed I had sex with my mother, and I thought this must be the big breakthrough. In fact, there was little emotion or reality about it, and I felt it was a fake, a dream my unconscious had hoked up just to satisfy what it was supposed to be doing. The doctor said, "Yes, go on."

But less than a year into the analysis came a real breakthrough—the one I had been hoping for, wanting more than anything in life. I made love to a woman. I didn't just do it to prove I could do it, or to pass a test, like losing my virginity in the Upper Broadway hotel room. I did it with a wonderful young woman I loved, at first tenderly and tenuously, on the living-room couch of her apartment one weekend while her roommate was away, not wanting to break the spell by trying to transfer ourselves to the bed in the bedroom, happy to have a full and successful flowering of sexual coupling.

It was the next day in the bathtub, though, that we really lost our fears and found the fun of it, the uninhibited joy of touching flesh, fondling, smiling, splashing, lying in the cool water and linking arms, legs, locking into one another, laughing, lurching out onto the living-room rug dripping wet and feeling free and powerful in our play, our passion, our natural selves, our rightful fulfillment.

"I'm fine," I told the doctor on Monday. "I did it. I can do it." Not just to say I had done it, not just the quick conclusions I had come to with women before like the friend from home with whom I officially lost my virginity, this new experience was one of completion, of knowing command and control of my own body, of being a man, and more than that, hu-man. In the fullness of the feeling I wondered if this meant I was one of those rare analysands who simply completed the course early, a Freudian prodigy, precocious pupil whose free association was so profound, it had freed him early of the very problem that put him into treatment!

The doctor disabused me of such an illusion. He patiently explained that impotence was simply a "symptom." Curing it, I gathered, was not *the* cure but a sort of side effect, a bonus on the way to the real booty, the treasure of knowing and thus being in command of the self. (Such mastery came to my mind as those pictures of ads from the Rosicrucians in the pulp astrology and mental health magazines my mother used to buy at the drugstore in hopes of finding The Answer—mysterious pictures of pyramids, all-seeing eyes, promises of unlocking the secrets of life.) I said I thought maybe this was enough, then realized with the help of the doctor's disapproval that I mustn't settle for less than the full self-knowledge and discovery I had set out to find in the first place, so I settled back on the new tissue, working my back into the hard leather of the couch. "Yes, go on."

I went on to say a few weeks later that I wanted to marry my girl friend, but the doctor reminded me sternly that that was not part of the agreement I had entered into at the start of the analysis. I was not to marry until I had finished the course, and my girl friend should be so informed. She herself was in therapy, had once had what we called then a "nervous breakdown" and been hospitalized for several months. My doctor indicated he did not approve of her as suitable material for marriage and motherhood—the break might occur again (in fact it never did, and she went on to marry, have children, a career, too, and in the most rare and marvelous sense continued to "live happily ever after"). When I told my lovely girl friend I couldn't marry till the unforeseen end of analysis she cried and I did too and then we fought, drifted apart, came together again but never as close, and finally, frayed, fell away from one another for good, as I was afraid to break the analytic pact (or was it only an excuse for getting out of a commitment?).

I settled in then for the long haul, became not only accustomed to but comfortable with the concept of postponing my life. I was morally certified by medical science for not making any commitments; I could meet women, fall for them, get into a relationship, and explain with lofty righteousness that it could go no further, we could not "get serious" in the sense of thinking about marriage, and I was not allowed to make any major life changes until my analysis was over. It gave me a ticket to irresponsibility and made that non-involvement a way of life, a creed of detachment that protected me from the perils of personal involvement, and I think from growth as well. Life was postponed—that included writing the novel as well as getting married, getting into good physical shape, going to Europe—all dreams and plans and responsibilities were put on hold, until the triumphant day when I found my "Rosebud" (the key to the problem, the answer) and was free to move on and live my life. In the meantime, in some deadly way, nothing "counted" or mattered since life really hadn't begun yet.

Looking back at that period, the analysis seems like a black hole that grew larger. The session itself dug a hunk out of every weekday. It took almost an hour to get from the Village to Park Avenue and the Eighties by subway, another hour back, and fifty minutes on the couch, so the greater part of a morning went into this hole. By the second year I started going more often by cab. By the third year I woke with a hangover on more days than not. It became a routine to buy a milkshake at Bigelow's drugstore on Sixth Avenue near Eighth Street, get a New York *Times* and hail a cab to go uptown for the fifty minutes on the couch. The cab fare was often more than I spent on food. I had stopped trying to contribute financially to the analysis as the doctor had said I should when I started (but never asked about later, as long as the checks came in). It was enough of a strain to pay the cab fare.

I had started drinking more, in a regular way, and always when I was out with women. Sometimes the old problem of impotence re-occurred, and drinking became a part of the problem, but I didn't know how to control it. The doctor gave me no advice about it, for that would have meant involvement. He had to remain aloof, detached, the blank screen. I also often drank now when I was alone. Sometimes I had such sick hangovers I couldn't function. In the mornings I gulped down either the chocolate milkshake or, if I was really in a bad way, a combination of orange juice and ginger ale. Sometimes I called friends and asked them to bring those supplies since I didn't think I could even make it to the store. A girl friend had me see her doctor and he said I should drink less. I tried to "cut down," and the effort must have lasted for a month or so. It didn't even occur to me to stop altogether. I postponed doing anything about the drinking because I figured when I hit upon the secret of my childhood I wouldn't need to drink so much, so it would automatically come under control on that magic day of revelation when all my neuroses fell away and my real life began.

But when was it going to happen? Except for my improved sexual performance (which was not to be taken too encouragingly since it was only a "symptom"), things went on pretty much the same. I poured more thoughts and dreams and memories and time and parental money into the black hole, but there was no sign of light, no glimmer of understanding, much less healing revelation. The first dramatic thing that happened in my analysis did not occur until after more than three years, perhaps almost four.

One day when I went in the waiting room a little early for my appointment, I saw that the door to Dr. Stanley's office was slightly open. He had said that whenever the door was open to come ahead into the office, so I pushed the door open and went in. He looked up in surprise from something he was reading and yelled at me. He shouted that I was never under any circumstances to come into his office when the door was closed. I said the door had been open. He said it had only been open a crack, and by mistake, and only when it was fully open was I supposed to come in unless he had come out to the waiting room and told me to enter. He was red in the face and far angrier than seemed appropriate in response to my unintentional breach of etiquette. I knew at that moment that, whatever he might swear about clinical detachment, he simply did not like me, and I knew I did not like him either. I hadn't liked him from the first, and I felt my instincts had been right all along. I yelled back at him. Shaken, and shaking with rage, I rushed out of the office.

I went home and poured myself a drink. I was not only angry, I was afraid. I was entrusting the most private and precious part of my life to someone who didn't like me and whom I neither liked nor trusted. I would never lie down on his couch again. I went back the next day at the proper time for my appointment and I sat on the couch while he sat in his chair and I talked to him, face to face. He apologized for his anger. He said we should go on with "the treatment." I told him I didn't think he liked me and he denied it. I said I did not like him, and never had, and furthermore I didn't trust him. He said all that was something we could "work with."

I refused. For the first time in more than three years of analysis I rebelled. My rebellion was limited—I did not want to give up analysis, not after investing all I had in it for all this time, not when I might be only a year or two away from the fabulous interior recognition that would make me free. So I told Dr.

Stanley I wanted to see another analyst. We discussed this for
three or four sessions, and finally he concluded I would not
reconsider and agreed to find me another doctor.

It occurred to me that, since I didn't trust Dr. Stanley, it
might be wise to find another analyst through the recommenda-
tion of someone I did trust. I went back to see Dr. Ernest, but he
was extremely guarded. It was obvious that he didn't want to
put himself in opposition to Dr. Stanley, and least of all the
Psychoanalytic Institute of which he was a member. He per-
sisted in his original theory that it really didn't matter who the
doctor was as long as he was properly trained in this treatment,
which was insured by his being a member of the New York
Psychoanalytic Institute. I might as well have been going from
one Jesuit to the next. I talked some about my own frustrations
and dilemmas with other aspects of life beside the analysis, and
finally, as I saw that my fifty minutes were up, I asked Dr. Ernest
in a kind of desperation what he thought about my situation. I
think I hoped for some kind of wisdom that I hadn't got from
Dr. Stanley, something to help me continue the journey that
now seemed nearly as hopeless as endless. I remember his exact
words of reply.

"I think that, like all neurotic people, you're in a box."

It wasn't much to go on. I felt a deep sadness when I left, not
only because Dr. Ernest was so obviously not able to help me,
but because it struck me that he had aged quite a bit since I had
seen him last, only three years before. There was a good deal of
gray in his hair now, and there were noticeable circles under his
eyes. There was also a weariness about him, a sense of strain and
fatigue, and I wondered if this had come about because of some
kind of disturbances in his personal life or as the result of his
profession. I wondered if he found himself disappointed with
the effectiveness of the treatment, for I knew he was a good
man and in spite of his professional detachment I believed he
would have felt badly at not being able to help people as he
hoped he could; I wondered if the effort at detachment itself

was a costly and draining process to maintain against natural instincts of sympathy, care, and affection. I don't know. I haven't seen him since, and unless he made a sharp break with his profession, I am sure that if I put those questions to him, even now, he would reply with a slight, enigmatic smile, "What do *you* think?"

I considered trying to find an analyst who was outside of the New York Psychoanalytic Institute, and I spoke to one of my best friends about the possibility, a friend who had himself been in some kind of "analysis" (or so he referred to it) that had involved group therapy and sessions only two or three times a week. Obviously not orthodox. In the end, I did not have the nerve to go outside the sect I had started with. I had the determination to change the priest but not the denomination.

To my rueful amusement, my new analyst was also named "Dr. Stanley." He was also, of course, a member of the New York Psychoanalytic Society, and he also had his office in the same chic neighborhood, the Upper East Side of Manhattan, within a block or so of Park Avenue. Both he and his office, however, at least were done in a different style. The new Dr. Stanley (I thought of him as Stanley II) was not at all chic. His suits were made of some shiny light brown or gray material, and he wore loud ties, with white-on-white shirts. He did not look like a banker so much as perhaps a business agent of a Teamsters Union local in the Bronx. The walls of his office were dull gray, and decorated with framed prints that were a dime a dozen, as well as, of course, the certificate of membership in the New York Psychoanalytic Society in the black wooden frame. On the wall behind his desk was a large print of a boy and his dog by Norman Rockwell. It seemed to me the sort of thing Aunt Minnie would buy at a barn sale.

Stanley II was a sort of shambling, gentle, innocuous-seeming fellow, and my main reaction to him was one of mild pity. I didn't dislike the guy, I simply felt sorry for him. I wondered if he was sent all the castoffs—the difficult patients who got mad at their original analysts and hadn't shown much hope anyway. He looked as if that might be his lot.

The same process resumed on the same kind of black leather couch with the same white thin tissue on the headrest, and I seemed again mired in my own jungle of disconnected dreams, thoughts, desires. In my life off the couch or "real life" the drinking increased and I began to have blackouts.

One night I remember drinking with a girl friend, going back to her apartment, then I remember being on the street by myself, drunk and trying to call Stanley the First to tell him what I really thought of him, to wake him from his complacent sleep and disturb his fat, bullfrog dreams. Of course I got only his answering service. I realized he must be prey to such middle-of-the-night calls from angry or kooky clients and was of course protected from them in advance. I told the operator on his answering service that I had to get through to him, it was an emergency. She said she would have him call me if I gave my name and number. I said I was Dr. Karl Menninger, calling from Topeka, Kansas, and I needed to speak to Dr. Stanley right away. I believed I sounded sober and sincere. I also felt delighted, imagining the bullfrog being awakened with that message. Making that call from an outdoor phone booth on Third Avenue somewhere in the Nineties is the last thing I remember that night.

I woke the next morning and wondered how I'd got to my bed in my apartment on Twelfth Street in the Village. I did not remember getting on a subway or into a cab, I didn't remember talking to anyone or being anywhere else. I remembered being in the phone booth and the next memory was of waking in my bed. In between I didn't know where I'd been or what I'd done. Maybe I could have killed someone. The drunk doesn't have any idea what he said or did during a blackout.

I again tried to "cut down" on my drinking for a while. Everyone I knew drank. I just drank a little more sometimes than others—but everyone drank a little more sometimes, didn't they? Especially if they were writers. It was part of the lore. I was cheered to read a newspaper article about a study of drinking among leading writers that concluded that, of five Americans who had at that time won the Nobel Prize for literature, three were alcoholics, one drank heavily, and the other was Pearl Buck. Drinking, I thought, was simply an occupational hazard of being a writer. It was also a glamorous aspect, as I knew from early Village days drinking at the White Horse Tavern. Veterans there told me with awe how it was in that very back room of the Horse that Dylan Thomas drank his last drink, passed out, and had to be taken down the street to St. Vincent's Hospital, where he died. It was regarded as a noble way to go and we were worshipers in his shrine, honored to follow his example, as we ordered another stein of "arf-n-arf."

One day I woke up with what was now my habitual hangover and realized I had been in analysis for five years. I felt no closer to finding the magic "Rosebud" key to my childhood than I ever had. For the most part, I was able to perform (and sometimes actually enjoy) the sexual act, though trying to get up my nerve and relax at the same time by drinking a lot of liquor sometimes had the effect of getting me so smashed I couldn't function because of the very alcohol I had consumed to help myself function. On two occasions my failure—once with a woman I was absolutely crazy about and had fantasies of marrying—drove me to such despair that I again cut my wrist.

That I had any kind of sexual satisfaction at all I attributed more to the almost saintly patience and kindness of women than I did to Freud or his present-day disciples Stanley I and II. Seriously taking stock of the effects of the analysis aside from sex, I credited one childhood memory about my father with giving me a more sympathetic view of him, though I could not be sure it was not something I would have realized anyway in the course of my life without daily sessions on the couch. Even if that insight and its resulting amelioration of relations with my father were counted as a distinct result of the treatment, it

hardly seemed worth the expense in time, money, and post-
ponement of "real life."

I had stuck to the analysis mostly on faith that it would bring
the salvation I hoped for, and I wondered how much longer I
ought to go on, with such little results to show. Stopping meant
giving up the grand hope it offered, but on the other hand my
life was passing—I had now reached thirty. I had begun to meet
people at parties or through friends who had been in analysis for
ten, twelve, even fifteen years, still with no end in sight.

At the end of my fifth year I told Stanley II (just as if I, instead
of he, were in charge of my fate) that I did not intend to continue with analysis indefinitely. I had decided to give it one
more year and then terminate the treatment, regardless of
where I was in it or whether or not I had achieved the progress I
or he had hoped for. I explained my reasoning about this in
detail, saying I felt that a total of six years was quite enough time
to devote to any such effort, and that I would not invest any
more time or money in it. He did not express either his approval
or disapproval. He said, in the same flat monotone as always,
"Yes, go on."

One morning when I woke with an especially painful hangover, intensified by the warlike growl of the garbage trucks
outside my window, and my whole life suddenly seemed like a
losing battle, I thought for the first time that maybe I ought to
get out of New York. The city I had so loved, that I thought I
would never leave, had become fogged over in the growing
blur of bourbon and the endless repetitious cycle of the daily
visits to the couch. As the black hole of analysis grew larger it
finally came to engulf even New York City. I also, on some level,
knew I was physically sick, and a change of scene sounded
beneficial.

I had lunch with Harold Hayes, the editor I worked with at
Esquire whom I'd come to regard as a friend, and asked him
how I could get out of New York. I was making a living as a free-
lance writer of magazine articles at the time, mainly profiles of

famous men for *Esquire* (I had just done Bobby Kennedy as Attorney General, after Adam Clayton Powell, Jr., and William F. Buckley, Jr., and later that year John Dos Passos, one of the last living literary heroes of the twenties) and I didn't even have an idea where I could go and continue to make a living. Harold said I ought to take a break and apply for a Nieman Fellowship in journalism, which gave you an all-expense-paid year at Harvard. I had heard of the Nieman Fellowships but thought they were only given to daily newspaper journalists. Harold said the foundation was broadening its concept; he had got a Nieman as a magazine editor and would nominate me for one as a magazine journalist. I applied that autumn of 1962 and hoped for the best. If I got the fellowship it would take me up to Cambridge a month after I had ended (if not "finished") my analysis, which was just the kind of new beginning I was hoping for.

I was giving a party at my apartment on East Twelfth Street in the spring of 1963, for what I don't know; for the excuse all such occasions provided, I suppose, for men and women to gather together and flirt, dance, talk, drink. Drink up! Drinks are on the house. If the booze runs out, just run down the street and buy a few more bottles. Drink till you lose your blues, or at least your inhibitions. I did. So did others. I kissed a new woman I met that night, and the woman I was dating disappeared with one of my friends and I found them necking in the bathroom. I raged. I broke a wine bottle and threatened to beat people up. My party was over. The guests fled. I drank more, and so did my girl friend, and then in despair I got out the razor, as of old, and cut my wrist again. The next morning I woke with a throbbing head and a wrist with a red slash. That afternoon was my interview with the Nieman Fellowship Selection Committee at the Harvard Club.

I called my old friend Jane, who always helped. I told her I had ruined everything. How could I go before the Nieman Committee and smile and talk about journalism, in my condition? Would they give a fellowship to a guy who had just got drunk and cut his wrist? Was this the fruit of nearly six years of analysis? It was all over. There was no hope. But Jane said not to worry. She made me the magic elixir of ginger ale and orange juice, put me into a shower, bandaged my wrist, got me into a suit, secured the sleeve at the cuff with a safety pin so it wouldn't slip down and reveal the wound. Then she took me to the Palm Court of the Plaza, ordered us frozen daiquiris, told me I looked terrific and would definitely do a great job of beguiling the committee. I guess I did, because a month later I got a letter in the mail saying I had won a fellowship—I would go to Harvard that fall. The doctor said, "Yes, go on."

I did. Boredom seemed the only enemy between me and the finish line I had marked off for the analysis. I droned on as always, with little insight or interest. Then it came. The nightmare. One day toward the end of April, with only three months left in the black hole of analysis, I told Stanley II about an especially disturbing dream. In the dream the face of one of my best friends was disfigured, blighted leperlike, in an even more disgusting mask than I had worn with the worst of the acne. When I told the doctor the dream it became more real. It was sickening. I walked out of his office with it still erupting in my mind. I tried to shake it, but it only came back multiplied in greater distortion. Suddenly my whole waking consciousness was overwhelmed by it. I was nauseous and terrified. That night I got drunk. When I woke, the hallucinations were worse. I couldn't get them out of my mind. They were there if I closed my eyes or opened them. They were there like a living hell everywhere I turned, everywhere I looked. I couldn't stand it. It was like an incarnation of ugliness, the quintessence of my worst nightmare, and it was with me constantly, waking or sleeping.

The only thing I had ever heard of that resembled what I was going through was the account of a horrific mescaline experience by the French writer Henri Michaux. At that time mescaline and LSD were not yet widely known (as they soon would be in the drug culture about to explode in the mid- and late sixties) but I had read about this ungodly nightmare experience of Michaux in some little magazine, and it had the crazy, overpowering quality of what I was going through. But I had not taken mescaline or LSD or any other drug, except alcohol, and I had never heard of any alcoholic hallucinations as severe, sustained, and unrelenting as this. (Obviously the alcohol wasn't helping matters, though the doctor never suggested I stop drinking, even during this hallucinatory nightmare.)

I tried to put other pictures in my head, pictures of beautiful things, like flowers, but as soon as I did the flowers became distorted themselves; in my sick mind's eye the lovely leaves became eaten away and blackened with disease. The only relieving image that came to my mind was a human skull without any skin, and I told someone about it, sobbing, explaining that it was the only thing I wanted to picture because it was "clean." I was terrified, for I knew it was death, and I knew death was luring me.

I told the doctor I needed help. I thought I was going crazy— if I didn't stop seeing these things I would surely go crazy. He prescribed some tranquilizers. I slid off the couch in agony and onto the floor of his office. He remained immobile in his chair. I crawled to the chair next to it and began picking up one leg of it and hitting the bottom of the leg against my face. I couldn't get off the floor. He told me the hour would soon be up and asked if I had a friend he could call to come and get me.

Friends kept me alive. They took me home from the doctor's office when I couldn't get off his floor, they sat up all night with me and held me in their arms. Alice kept the longest vigils, trying to soothe me when I could stand it no longer and screamed in panic and sobbed and pummeled my head with my fists. Once in her apartment I was so unhinged, so desperate in my desire to "disappear," to hide myself from the onslaught of unbearable visions, that I actually tried to crawl into her fireplace. When Alice went to work I went to see Ivan or Robert or Jane. I went from one friend to another. I couldn't be alone. I wanted to be in a hospital. I asked the doctor if he couldn't put me in a hospital and give me some kind of sedative so I could at least get some rest and nourishment. I was exhausted, and the sight of food sickened me. Maybe I could be fed by a needle or a tube. Anything. Please, couldn't he get me into a hospital?

He told me in his analytic monotone that this raised a difficult dilemma. He said that, if he put me in the kind of hospital he would approve of my being in, he would no longer be the principal physician in charge of my case. On the other hand, the kind of hospital he could put me in and remain in charge of my case, was not the kind of hospital whose care he approved of. It was a Catch-22—either I could go to a hospital where he would be in charge of me, but whose care he did not approve of (he did not say why he did not approve of the care in such hospitals), or I could go to a hospital whose care he approved of but where someone else—a stranger, a doctor I had never met before— would be in charge of my fate, which meant such a doctor would have the power to declare me insane or in need of incarceration in a mental hospital or perhaps of electric or insulin shock treatment (I had seen those life-wrenching convulsions administered to patients at the Brooklyn Mental Hospital while I was a student in a psychology class at Columbia) or any other treatment this hypothetical doctor deemed fitting. Fearing I might end up in a loony bin for the rest of my life, I did not take that alternative, nor did it seem reasonable to go to a hospital the doctor who had been treating me all this time did not approve of, in which case if things went badly I would have only myself to blame. The doctor, in other words, gave me no alternative, nor any other kind of guidance, nor any kind of help.

I cursed the doctor and accused him of irresponsibility and deception, of unethical and immoral behavior. I told him he had got me into a life-threatening situation which he did not himself understand and obviously did not know how to deal with. I told

him he had unleashed something through the analytic process
of free association that he had no right to do since he did not
now know how to help me through it or handle it. I said that
both he and the first Stanley had deceived me in saying this was
a "scientific" medical treatment I was undergoing. He insisted
it was exactly that. I said, "Do you mean to tell me that what we
are doing here, the process that has led me to this unbearable
madness, is as scientific as diagnosing and setting a broken leg?"
He looked me in the eye and said that was exactly the case. I
asked him then to tell me what was happening to me. He said
we had entered "the heartland" of the analytic experience. I
asked him whether, if I could survive this ghastly torture, I
would be "better" and if undergoing this hell would somehow
bring me greater understanding that would make me a health-
ier human being. He assured me that was the case, that all this
was a medically scientific treatment with proven results, just as
certain as setting a broken leg.

I called him a liar. I have not had reason in all the years since
to change that opinion.

The living hell of the ever changing hallucinations lasted for
nearly six weeks. Then it began to ease, and though the hallucinations came back for a while in full force—off and on while I
was walking down the street or simply reading a book, just as
the mescaline nightmares returned to Michaux long after the
"trip" (and very occasionally in brief flashes years later, as was
my experience as well), by the summer I was able to sleep and
eat and live again more or less as I had before. During the
season in hell the only thing that brought relief was drinking
cold, clean water out of a metal cup I found in a friend's kitchen,
and the memory of a fragment of the Twenty-third Psalm,
which I began to pray as continually as I could, as incantation
against the hell raging within me:

". . . though I walk through the valley of the shadow of
death, I will fear no evil, for thou art with me."

By the end of that summer I was living in a small house in New Hampshire by a pond, and another part of the psalm came to mind, bringing with it a deep and thankful sense of peace, like the calm that comes after surviving a terrible storm and at last lying down on the shore:

> "He leadeth me beside the still waters; he restoreth my soul."

I am neither qualified nor interested to make a psychological evaluation of my experience in analysis. From a spiritual point of view, I know it was my own dark night of the soul, in the deepest sense of that concept. My literary-journalistic "guide" to our times, Arthur Koestler, described his own 1930s generation's disillusionment with Communism in *The God That Failed*. The same title could apply to the effort of those like myself in my 1950s generation who tried to to find through Freudian psychoanalysis a substitute for God, a "scientific" formula for self-gratification, for "having my own way." As happened so often with his work and thought, that wasn't what Freud intended at all. I later found help, as I had before with Dr. Ernest, using psychotherapy as an aid to understand and cope with the pains of life, rather than provide a meaning for it. I am sure there are people who are able to use psychoanalysis that way also, but I was not one of them.

I consider myself blessed. Even in my darkest night of the soul I did not perish. I read years later in Psalm 139 the real metaphor for my analytic journey:

> "Whither shall I go from thy spirit? Or whither shall I flee from thy presence?
> "If I ascend up into heaven, thou art there: if I make my bed in hell, behold, thou art there.
> "If I take the wings of the morning, and dwell in the uttermost parts of the sea;

"Even there shall thy hand lead me, and thy right hand shall hold me.

"If I say, Surely the darkness shall cover me; even the night shall be light about me.

"Yea, the darkness hideth not from thee; but the night shineth as the day: the darkness and the light are both alike to thee. . . ."

7. Guides

I had gone into psychoanalysis to save myself, and at about the same time I went to East Harlem in the hope of helping others. Looking back from the vantage point of thirty years, it seems quite clear in a literal way that what I did to save myself nearly killed me (I have never been so close to annihilation as I was in that extended waking nightmare at the end of the analysis) and what I did in the hope of helping others nourished and sustained me and maybe even saved my life.

Since whatever gift I had for writing was not yet ready for the task of fiction when I came back from Israel, I thought I might as well use it in the service of something worth while (and at the same time gain the experience and validation of writing a book —my motives were certainly not devoid of self-interest). By describing the slums of Spanish Harlem in my first book, *Island in the City*, I hoped I might not only expose injustices that plagued the people who lived there but also make known their humanity to the outside world in a personal rather than abstract way. My wish was expressed in a kind of charge to the reader in the introduction to the book: ". . . may you become involved in this life. May its faces haunt you and its dialogues disturb you. May its tragedies sicken you and its love make you glad, and may you, if only in your mind, if only for a moment, become a part of Spanish Harlem."

I was only a part of that neighborhood for a moment in time

myself—I lived in East Harlem six months while doing research
for the book—yet I kept being drawn back there. I returned not
only during my years in New York but even much later, in a
time and from a place that I could never have foreseen. I can
now discern that I really arrived at that place thanks in part to
my experience in Spanish Harlem, through the deep way in
which I was moved and influenced by the people I got to know
in that neighborhood. But how did a boy from Indiana ever get
to Manhattan's East 100th Street, which then was described by
the New York *Times* as "the worst block" in the city?

Following the spiritual thread of one's life sometimes seems
like the plot of a science-fiction novel, one of those good ones
like Isaac Asimov's "Foundation" series, in which forces are at
work moving people here and there in ways they don't themselves see and for purposes they don't yet even know about. (It
is also common in the Old Testament, as when Joseph forgives
his brothers and tells them, ". . . it was not you that sent me
hither, but God.") That seems the kind of plot by which one
could understand how the angry atheist I was at the time was
drawn to a place that was probably the most powerful focus of
genuine spirituality in New York City: the Catholic Worker
"hospitality house" in the Bowery.

I was introduced to the Catholic Worker by a Jewish classmate and writer friend from Columbia who shared my own
image of the writer as a seeker, a person on a quest to learn
about humanity from all the varied experience and people one
could encounter. Sam Astrachan had won the respect and admiration of students and faculty alike by writing a first novel that
was accepted for publication by the distinguished firm of Far-
rar, Straus while he still was a senior in college. His accomplishment gave him the status of mentor as well as friend of mine,
even though he was a year younger than I, and when the summer after we graduated he suggested I go with him to the
Bowery to meet the author of a book with the unlikely title of

The Autobiography of a Catholic Anarchist I was eager to join him.

I don't remember how Sam got to know Ammon Hennacy, who was then a sixty-three-year-old antiwar radical with bushy gray hair and a single tooth in his mouth, but I took it as part of Sam's wisdom as a novelist (didn't you have to know everything to write a novel?) as well as a native New Yorker. Sam was fascinated by Ammon as a "character" and respected him as one of those rare people who lived his convictions. Hennacy had served time in the Atlanta Penitentiary for refusing to register for the draft in World War I, and in the 1950s he was going around New York with picket signs protesting the draft, the atom bomb, and the civil defense laws that gave a dangerous illusion of protection against nuclear attack. Sam also appreciated Ammon's dry wit, and laughed that day he introduced me when he told Ammon with a flourish of literary pride that the title of his forthcoming novel was *An End to Dying.* Ammon scratched his chin in thought and said, "Well, that might be all right."

Sam as a Jew and I as an atheistic lapsed Christian were both rigorous in our intellectual idealism, and it was the integrity we saw in the people at the Catholic Worker that drew us to them in spite of their being openly and unashamedly religious. These were not your country club Christians who were thinking positively for greater success in business, they were living their beliefs by befriending and sheltering and feeding the poor, and their soup line was known as the only one in the Bowery that didn't require confessions of faith or promises of conversion; you only had to be hungry in order to be fed. The people at the Worker (as the movement, its mission house, and its monthly newspaper all were familiarly known) might be crackpots, but by any God you chose to swear by, they were not phonies.

Later that fall, when Ammon and some of the others were arrested for protesting civil defense air raid drills, I returned and wrote an article about them called "Miracle in the Bowery" in which I explained that the people at the Catholic Worker were "not all Catholics and not all workers. A few, like the aims of the movement, are pacifists and anarchists. Some are former monks. Some are former soldiers. Some are alcoholics. Some are just hungry." None of them, needless to say, would have been welcome at a Northwestern University fraternity rush, and I felt a kinship as well as an admiration for them, especially the young intellectuals like Michael Harrington who had come from St. Louis to live and work in the Bowery at the Catholic Worker Hospitality House (that more gracious name than the more common "mission" indicated their attitude that the people they served were not heathens or castoffs but "guests"). It was there that Harrington began to see and understand with compassion the congenital poverty built into our affluent society that he would later bring to national attention in his book *The Other America.* I immediately liked Mike and felt he was the kind of guy John Reed would have wanted to hang around with, and so did I.

When I came back from Israel I gravitated back to the Worker, wanting a kind of sustenance people found there that was less tangible but just as nourishing as bread and soup. I would never have gone to a church at that time, but I could justify going to the Catholic Worker as a writer and intellectual. I was deeply saddened to learn that Dorothy Day, the cofounder and guiding spirit of the Worker, had been offended by something in the article I wrote. I had mentioned Malcolm Cowley's reference to her in his book *Exile's Return* as a writer in the twenties who was admired by the gamblers at a certain Greenwich Village bar because she could drink any one of them under the table. I had taken this part of her bohemian past to be an endorsement of Dorothy as a "real person," more interesting and credible than if she had been a lifelong saint, but she evidently didn't want to be reminded of it. Though this great lady was cool to me from then on, others at the Worker assured me "that's just how Dorothy is" and made me welcome anyway.

To me, it was Dorothy Day's past as a hard-drinking Village writer that gave her credentials I could admire, and enabled me to read her more recent work, with its deeply and frankly religious frame of reference. She wrote in the introduction to Hennacy's autobiography, "If it is necessary to repeat, he repeats, and perhaps when he has repeated his fast in penance for Hiroshima, repeated his picketing, repeated his statement forty times, forty days—he will have put on Christ to such an extent that people will see more clearly Christ in him, and follow more in his steps. That is our job here, to put on Christ, and to put off the old man, so I am not talking of an excessively religious person, an un-balanced person when I talk of Ammon so living year by year he 'puts on Christ.'"

Dorothy Day, as you can see, did not beat around the bush. *"That is our job here, to put on Christ."*

What in the world kind of talk was that for an avowed young atheist to be listening to, and why after my article about the Catholic Worker was published did I keep going back and hanging around a place where people said it was their job to "put on Christ"? I would have defended myself then from any suspicion of spiritual motivation by saying I went purely for intellectual stimulation to their Friday night meetings where guest speakers talked about socialism or James Joyce or the threat of nuclear war to an audience composed partly of homeless people the world called "Bowery bums" and the Worker thought of as "guests," and partly of idealistic young intellectuals from the hinterlands like Mike Harrington.

I might have even said I went there to meet girls, though I would have had much better odds by spending that time at Julius', Louie's, the White Horse, or any of the other Village bars I frequented. But I did meet three bright, attractive young women at the Worker. Helen Russell had left a convent in California—she had read a copy of the *Catholic Worker* penny newspaper, gotten on a bus to New York and gone straight to live and work at the Hospitality House in the Bowery. There she met two like-minded young women from New York, Mary Ann McCoy and Eileen Fantino. The three of them joined together to open a day-care center for the children of 100th Street in East Harlem and moved to the neighborhood in order to gain the trust of the people who lived there.

This was not the sort of thing any of the other bright, young, attractive girls I knew were doing in those days, and I was fascinated by their dedication, their own clear and delighted sense of mission. I also had a crush on the Irish blond Mary Ann McCoy (it never became a romance, but a treasured and permanent friendship). An invitation to dinner at the girls' apartment took me to East 100th Street, and as soon as I saw it—a colorful, chaotic, culture-clashing world of its own—I wanted to write about it. First I thought of an article, but after going back several times to the neighborhood and beginning to take in the rich complexity of it, I knew it should be a book.

There was a hitch—of course there would be many obstacles in such an undertaking, but this was a particularly annoying one for me. It turned out that the three Catholic Worker girls were not the only "missionaries" from the outside (white) world who lived in the neighborhood. Mary Ann explained there were ministers and their wives and families from a group called the East Harlem Protestant Parish who lived and worked in these streets, and that I should get to know them if I wanted to learn more about what went on here.

Well, radical Catholics were one thing, but white Protestant do-gooders sounded too much like the emissaries of the God of my teenage years who had caused all my problems, the God of Indianapolis morals and manners I had turned against and denied. I went with a sense of cynicism to meet the Reverend Norman Eddy, the Protestant Parish minister who lived on 100th Street, but he was not what I expected. Instead of a long-faced puritan, I encountered a bright, vital man who went about his work with a genuine sense of joy. I described him in the book as "a tall, vigorous, articulate man in his late thirties, easily spotted walking down 100th Street by the thick crop of hair that—even before he moved to this neighborhood—had turned prematurely, totally white. Norm explained to me once that one of the reasons he was so vitally interested in working with narcotics addicts was that the people who were trapped by addiction were forced to come—mentally and physically—face to face with the deepest questions of existence. 'Those are the questions I am most interested in,' Norm said."

I had found a Protestant minister whose goals were quite far from the easy path to success in business made popular by Norman Vincent Peale, and closer to the difficult, demanding way of love and sacrifice preached by Jesus of Nazareth. When I asked in my book the rhetorical question about whom Norman Eddy could talk to within the Marble Collegiate Church, I was at the same time saying I had finally found a minister *I* could talk to, even about the religion I had declared myself an enemy of. Norm listened to my anger and fear, taking it all with respect and good humor, and I have continued talking to him through what is now thirty years of friendship.

Like Norm, I too was "most interested in" those "deepest questions of existence" that narcotics addicts were forced to face, and I too was drawn to the addicts themselves and the committee that Norm had founded to help them, the first such local effort of its kind. Even after I finished my book, I returned to the neighborhood to go to Narcotics Committee meetings, helping with publicity and press releases for some of the group's social action efforts, like the picketing of Metropolitan Hospital that opened up the first beds for treatment of narcotics addicts anywhere in the country outside of prison facilities.

I was not just trying to assuage my social conscience and white guilt by returning to East Harlem to be involved with drug addicts. I felt a kinship with them, a rapport on some deep level of identification, an empathy (not just sympathy) with their plight, for I understood how a person—*me,* for instance—could easily become addicted to a potion that numbed the pain, blotted out the daily angst that any sensitive human is subject to and that is so much more intensified by the poverty and despair, the no-exit hopelessness of life in the slums. Who in such circumstances wouldn't at some extreme moment want a "fix," a temporary relief from problems and pain, no matter what the cost or danger or even risk of death?

I was getting my own fixes with booze and daily analytic sessions, both of which had the nature of addiction, and I'm sure I had, along with these junkies hooked on the illegal substance of heroin, a basic "addictive personality." In fact I found the addicts as a whole more interesting and creative, more attuned to humor as well as pain, than most people I met up with in the straight walks of life. I found it easier to talk with them about painful or embarrassing problems, for they knew depths beyond any I had reached, and their experience stripped them of any need or tolerance for sham and hypocrisy.

I felt a brotherhood with the addicts, and in the small way of going to those meetings and doing off-and-on publicity work for the committee, of hanging around and drinking beer with those guys, or inviting them to drink with me in the Village, I perhaps was affirming not only that sense of brotherhood but also my own humanity. As something like humanity seemed to be draining out of me day by day on the analyst's couch, in the unceasing self-absorbed process of consciousness-letting, I believe it was in some vital measure replenished by my connection to East Harlem, the addicts, and Norm Eddy, all of whom kept me in touch with a reality beyond my own psychic navel. Perhaps the significance of that whole experience is spoken of in another way in one of the key messages of Jesus, repeated in each of the gospels, and stated in Luke as: "For whosoever will save his life shall lose it: but whosoever will lose his life for my sake, the same shall save it." From the rest of Jesus' teaching it is clear that "for my sake" also means for other people: "As ye do it unto the least of these, ye do it unto me."

Somewhere between the world of Spanish Harlem and the analyst's couch was my daily life or "real" world of work and play and love (or the usually frantic efforts to find love, and then, when found, to turn and run from it) and mentors and friends. I have always been blessed with good friends, so richly that I've sometimes thought that perhaps to make up for my lack of brothers and sisters I was given an extra portion of friends. There were in those days in New York (and thankfully still are in my life) Ted "The Horse" whom I've known since high school, Mike "The Governor" from Columbia days, "Nurse Jane" who got me to the Nieman interview in one piece and always knew how to put me together when I'd yet again come apart, and a host of others to whom I sometimes could also reciprocate care, and the healing of kindness, and share the happy hysteria of rolling-on-the-floor laughter as well as the gut-wrenching twists of defeat and disappointment and four-o'clock-in-the-morning dark fear.

There were friends who were also mentors, like Murray Kempton (who saved the introduction to my Spanish Harlem book from overblown generalizing by advising me to "take out of it anything that didn't happen while you were living there") and C. Wright Mills, who encouraged me to bake my own bread as well as to "think big" in my work. There was a blessed host of other, older, accomplished writers who gave me the kind of boost that they had once been given when starting out, in a spirit of traditional generosity that is often left unmentioned in references to the literary life that emphasize the dog-eat-dog, backbiting aspect, the self-centered shadow side of the dream.

James Baldwin gave me bourbon and inspiration on Horatio Street, bestowing confidence through those giant eyes that penetrated a whole social order and seemed to look even deeper into the soul, holding court in the small, almost bare apartment with the Billie Holiday records playing from a phonograph on the floor and the friends and hangers-on drifting in until it got so crowded and late he would lead everyone across the street to El

Faro for Spanish food and sign a personal check for the bill.
There was the time he wrote an eloquent letter defending me
in response to a bad review I got on my journalistic book about
the civil rights movement *(Revolt in the South),* and when I
thanked him he said, "No, baby, I'm doing it for *myself.*" Once
in the depths of the analysis I went to sit beside him at a
drunken Village party and simply cried without explaining anything and knew that no words were necessary.

The critic and novelist Robert Phelps, adopted as "Uncle
Bobby," was a life-saving spirit advising and cajoling and in-
structing, introducing me not only to the works of James Agee
(Robert edited the posthumous novel *A Death in the Family*
and had the idea of putting the poetic "Knoxville, Summer"
piece at the start) but also to Agee's still living mentor, Father
James Flye, who spun stories for us of his own beloved protégé
"Jim." The ebullient all-round writer (novelist, journalist, critic)
Harvey Swados kidded me out of it whenever he caught pomposity cropping up in my prose, and invited me to his home
with that radiant family for dinner and overnight stays up the
Hudson in Valley Cottage when he knew I needed physical as
well as literary sustenance.

May Swenson, whose poems I memorized because of their
quiet power and because they spoke most eloquently my own
thoughts and feelings ("The Key to Everything," "Mortal
Surge"), gifted me with the gentle and firm attention and support due an innocently dewy-eyed younger brother (a friend of
hers told me I reminded May of her little brother). Like Baldwin, she has a way of looking at you with a steady intensity of
gaze that pierces all protective sham, and she is the only person
I have ever known who, while engaging in the most meaningful
and revelatory conversation, is able to chew gum with total
dignity. When no one else believed in my efforts to break from
journalism into fiction she inscribed a book of poems to me with
a "prediction that he will be known as a great novelist before
the century is over" (thank God she took the long view) and

signed "May Swenson hath spoken, March 23, 1963." The book
was *To Mix with Time,* and now, with gratitude, I do, invoking
generous friends and mentors whose faces, words, and voices
from a quarter century ago in New York materialize in this
room where I sit now in Boston.

There are in all our lives important mentors or "messengers"
(that particular definition of "angels" applies here) whom we
never meet in person but whose thoughts and ideas reach us in
stories, books, essays, and poems. The process I am thinking of is
best described by a teacher in J. D. Salinger's *The Catcher in the
Rye,* when he assures Holden Caulfield:

"Many, many men have been just as troubled morally and
spiritually as you are right now. Happily, some of them kept
records of their troubles. You'll learn from them—if you want
to. Just as some day, if you have something to offer, someone will
learn something from you. It's a beautiful reciprocal arrangement. And it isn't education. It's history. It's poetry."

It is "the history of human trouble and the poetry of love," I
wrote in my own appreciation of Salinger in an essay in *New
World Writing* in 1958 entitled "Salinger and the Search for
Love." On rereading now I think I might have more accurately
called it "Salinger and the Search for God." I pointed out that
Salinger at the time was the only new American writer to
emerge since World War II who was dealing with "the grandest
theme of literature: the relationship of man to God, or the lack
of God." I cited Marcel Arland, a French writer who believed
that (as I summarized his message) "all problems boil down to
the single problem of God." I discovered that back in 1924,
when "all the sad young men" like Scott Fitzgerald were ro-
mantically lamenting that all wars were fought, all gods were
dead, Arland wrote an essay calling for a "moral literature" in
the *Nouvelle Revue française* that proclaimed:

"God, the eternal scourge of men, whether they are intent
upon creating Him or destroying Him! Virgil's work is ex-

plained by His permanent presence; Rousseau's by the search for Him; Stendhal's by the attempts of passion to cover up His absence."

I identified with those men Arland described as "no longer feeling within themselves the idol but still feeling the altar"; not believing in God but feeling a need to fill the emptiness left by His absence, for which at that time I sincerely believed psychoanalysis would be the answer ("Substitution: Freud for God"). And yet, and yet . . . even then, when I was in the first hopeful flush of excitement and promise of analysis, I wrote this essay that clearly showed a need for something higher than my own consciousness, deeper even than the powerful *un*conscious I was trying to bring to the surface every day on the couch. I would never have dreamed at that time of going to church or reading the Bible (which my letters from Israel complained I found wanting even as literature) or the work of any ministers or monks, from Norman Vincent Peale (except to study for scorning) to Thomas Merton, yet I eagerly read with fascination and respect Salinger's writing, not only about God but, even more remarkably, Jesus Christ.

After *The Catcher in the Rye* became a best-seller and a byword, a kind of Bible for youth in the 1950s, the word spread like wildfire when a new Salinger story came out, and I remember literally running to the newsstand to buy *The New Yorker* for the latest installment in the saga of his fictional Glass family. For several months after the short story "Franny" appeared, it seemed that at every party I went to where other young college graduates gathered there were heated discussions about whether Franny in fact was pregnant, or having a nervous breakdown, or a religious conversion, or any (or all) of the above, when at the end of a depressing Ivy League football weekend she finally could only repeat to herself the "Jesus Prayer" that she read in a book by an anonymous Russian holy man called *Way of a Pilgrim:* "Jesus Christ, have mercy on me, a sinner."

At this time neither I nor most of my friends used the name "Jesus Christ" except as a curse or exclamation or in satirical drunken renderings of country-western songs from childhood camp days such as "I don't care if it rains or freezes, I am safe in the arms of Jesus. . . ." In other words, Jesus was a joke (provoking nervous laughter) to us sophisticated young intellectuals, a symbol of the old hometowns and their corny values we had left in rebellion; yet Salinger somehow managed to make him a subject of serious, eloquent, personal significance in the lives of characters of our own time whom we admired, identified with, cared about, and talked about as if they were real people.

I followed with eager absorption—along with several hundred thousand other readers—as Franny's crisis was continued in another story Salinger published in *The New Yorker* called "Zooey" (one of Franny's brothers). The saga reached its emotional climax with Zooey in a long phone conversation as he tried to talk Franny out of her depression and her wish to withdraw from the world by telling her how their beloved older brother Seymour used to urge him to shine his shoes before going on a radio program, even though he didn't see the point; Seymour said to shine them for "the Fat Lady." Zooey tells Franny in the final emotional climax of the story:

"But I'll tell you a terrible secret—Are you listening to me? *There isn't anyone out there who isn't Seymour's Fat Lady.* . . . Don't you know that. Don't you know that goddam secret yet? And don't you know—*don't you know what that Fat Lady really is?* . . . Ah, buddy. Ah, buddy. It's Christ Himself. Christ Himself, buddy."

So there in the pages of our most sophisticated magazine, between the ads for diamonds and furs and fancy restaurants, in a story about a troubled Ivy League college girl by one of the most beloved American writers of his generation, was the message of the New Testament: not only that all men are brothers and should treat each other as such ("Do unto others as you would have others do unto you") but that, as Paul wrote to the Romans, "So we, being many, are one body in Christ; and every one members of one another"; and as he elaborated the idea further in his first letter to the Corinthians: "And whether one member suffer, all the members suffer with it; or one member be honored, all the members rejoice with it."

The "Fat Lady" as Christ became part of our idiom, and Salinger's daring fictional revelation inspired and stirred a spiritual sense in young people hungry for such sustenance not only in this country but abroad. The London drama critic Kenneth Tynan expressed it when he asked in the *Declaration* of the "angry young men" of his English generation:

"Do I speak for you when I ask for a society where people care more for what you have learned than for where you have learned it; where people who think and people who work can share the common idiom; where art connects itself instead of separating people; where people feel, as in the new Salinger story, that every fat woman on earth is Jesus Christ . . . ?"

In a time when most of our writers began their work from the premise of the death of God, when Christianity seemed to have been co-opted and tamed by professional positive thinkers and the New Testament was shilled as a handbook for "how to succeed in business," Salinger created fiction in which Jesus Christ became a living factor and a force for change—for personal salvation—in the daily experience of educated, sophisticated, heretofore stylishly cynical readers. Though I have never met Salinger, any more than I have met many of the other writers, both living and dead, whose gifts have nurtured me in spirit as well as in intellect (from Dostoevsky and Henry James to Carson McCullers and Chaim Potok) he served through his work as a guide for me as he did for so many others during a spiritually arid period of our culture, and in my own life during the progressively dark interior journey of psychoanalysis.

In the latter days of my analysis I was stirred and heartened by an article in the *Atlantic* that expressed some of my own misgivings and questions, fears and anger about psychiatry. It was called "A Young Psychiatrist Looks at His Profession," and the author was identified as "Robert Coles, M.D." Speaking critically of his own profession, this Dr. Coles wrote:

"Though we talk a great deal about our scientific interests, man's thoughts and feelings cannot be as easily understood or manipulated as atoms. . . . Our work is the human condition, and we might do well to talk with Reinhold Niebuhr about the 'nature and destiny of man,' or with J. D. Salinger about our Holden Caulfields. Perhaps we are too frightened and too insecure to recognize our very brothers. This is a symptom of the estranged."

What astounding and refreshing thoughts from a psychiatrist! Dr. Coles's essay articulated some of my feelings that I had doubted as perhaps only manifestations of hostility and aggression, the neurotic "symptoms" of a patient who had not yet "worked through" his problems. The fact that a certified psychiatrist had written and published such thoughts made me feel less isolated, less "crazy" in my misgivings about the process I was involved in.

When I went up to Harvard on the Nieman Fellowship I met Dr. Coles at a dinner party in Cambridge and we immediately began a conversation that continued through the year. We shared a passion for the work of James Agee, and we talked about literature, journalism, politics, education, sex, society, religion, and of course psychiatry. Coles was probably the one person in the world I would have felt free to talk to about my near catastrophic experience in psychoanalysis, for I knew from his article that he had his own questions and doubts about psychiatry, and that he was a person of deep compassion as well as understanding.

My anger about psychiatry was such that I would not have dreamed of "seeing" a psychiatrist in any kind of further treatment then (to heal me of the wounds received in the *last* treatment) but I poured out my feelings to Coles. I did this not as a patient in his office at the Harvard Health Services, but as a friend and fellow writer, drinking Jack Daniels and something called Heaven Hill bourbon in my dorm room at Dunster House or at his house in Concord after satisfying dinners of shepherd's pie (so good they made me wonder if this was not Anglo-Saxon soul food) made by his lovely wife Jane, and walking through Harvard Yard consuming ice cream cones from Brigham's (he liked them with lots of the chocolate shavings called "jimmies" on top). I got rid of much of the pain and hurt and leaden dead weight of the years on the couch as Coles lamented along with me, helping me do it as he shook his head and rubbed his hand through his black hair with the passionate intensity he put into all he said and did, an intensity of concentrated intelligence and emotion so powerful as to seem almost uncontainable. I felt sometimes he would burst from it, from the fury and love that have since created the significant and humanizing body of work contained in his books about our culture and especially the people in it, from children to blacks, whose voices we have tried to shut out. For our own health as well as theirs, Dr. Coles has made us listen.

Coles recommended a book by another psychiatrist named Allen Wheelis called *The Quest for Identity,* and reading that was also part of my healing. Dr. Wheelis wrote as a psychoanalyst who questioned some of the basic tenets of his own professional technique, and summed up one of my own conclusions about the process when he said:

"By proclaiming itself clothed in the raiments of science, psychoanalysis becomes acceptable to the sophisticated who search for magic. It seems to promise the transformation of self, to be the hidden door to all the lost certainties."

That was the door I had opened to find instead the contents of my own Pandora's box of hallucinatory fright-mask images. Those visions snapped back at me sometimes during the Nieman year, while I was simply walking down the street or listening to a lecture or sitting in a restaurant, though with less frequency and intensity. When they did come, I had found a new weapon with which to ward them off, something from a book I first heard about from Salinger's Franny Glass called *The Way of a Pilgrim*. I had not known there was really such a book when I read the story in *The New Yorker* but thought it might have been part of the fiction; I was thrilled to see it one day in the window of the Thomas More bookstore in Harvard Square. I used the "Jesus Prayer" as my own weapon of defense against the horror show that sometimes still flashed into my mind: "Jesus Christ, have mercy on me." I did not add "a sinner" because I didn't feel like one, but I did want to say the name of Jesus and ask his mercy, though I still wasn't sure I believed. It was at least an incantation, an appeal to some force or power higher than the unconscious, and it gave me a kind of solace and a point to focus on away from the mental demons. It helped.

Once in the following year I went to a Sunday church service but felt uncomfortable and out of place and didn't try it again. As my nightmares faded I stopped praying, pretty much forgot about Jesus and the "Jesus Prayer" and the Twenty-third Psalm and God, and resumed my search for personal pleasure and fulfillment, hoping to "have my own way" and not be bothered by some divine "potter" trying to shape the clay of my life and experience into anything I didn't want or enjoy or that wouldn't bring me the fullest satisfaction.

I did find many satisfactions in the years following the analysis. The Nieman year provided a much-needed time of respite after the exhaustion of my last frenetic days in New York during the ghoulish finale of the psychoanalysis. I found that everyone used the Nieman opportunity to his own best advantage—some by going to classes every day and staying up late at night cramming every last bit of knowledge it was possible to wrench from Harvard, like Morton Mintz, the dedicated investigative reporter of the Washington *Post;* some by savoring the works of classic American authors missed in earlier years, and exploring the literary and historic New England heritage that lay all around us, like Roy E. Reed, the wry observer from the Arkansas *Gazette*. He went on to write of the South for the New York *Times* and then settle into teaching at the University of Arkansas, imparting his singular vision in a series of essays and articles collected in *The View from Hogeye*. I used the Nieman myself to recoup, read, listen to Crane Brinton lecture on the French Revolution, and with my new friend Wayne Kelley drink at the old Cronin's in Cambridge, and look for a good time—or, as Roy Reed more colorfully put it, "try to find some banjo music." Restored and refreshed, in the year that followed the Nieman I had the most productive year of writing I'd enjoyed, and sold my first fiction.

I was married at the end of the Nieman year to a lovely woman I'd gone out with off and on for several years in New York. We moved to a small town in New Hampshire, hoping to find peace and serenity in bucolic surroundings, but the same problems and conflicts we had in the city emerged in the country, and I panicked and fled from both the marriage and the sounds of silence and crickets. She went West, and I went back down to Cambridge, a compromise between the clamor of New York and the different but equally threatening stillness of rural New England.

Though I never quite felt comfortable in Cambridge, I was drawn instinctively to Boston and knew when I first saw Beacon Hill the special solace of *place* Henry James described when he returned again after twenty years in Europe: "Oh, the wide benignity of brick, the goodly, friendly, ruddy fronts, the solid *seat* of everything . . ." When I moved there in the sixties the Hill was rather like a happily down-at-the-heels dowager, with a nice mix of Brahmin and hippie-bohemian flavors, a funky back side of rooming houses and students mixed in with stately manses and staid matrons. When I bought a town house on Revere Street in 1972 I joined the Beacon Hill Civic Association and really felt rooted for the first time since leaving Indianapolis. Greenwich Village had seemed not so much like home as *exile* from home, but Boston and the Hill became the real thing for me.

A few blocks away and around the corner through the Boston Public Garden I found a professional home at the *Atlantic Monthly,* where Robert Manning had become editor about the time I was settling into Boston. He liked a piece I wrote for them, called me in, and began an editorial relationship that lasted throughout his sixteen-year stewardship of the magazine and a friendship that endures to this day. He commissioned me to travel through the country in 1967 to write about the effect of Vietnam on the United States, and the assignment turned into an entire issue of the magazine, called "Supernation at Peace and War." After it was published I was named a contributing editor of the *Atlantic* and given a desk and office space that made me feel like a citizen of the real world with my own corner of it. Although no salary came with the position it gave me a kind of security that was welcome and significant, a rooted sense that is sorely missed by the free-lance writer, who seems to be in a sort of continuous free-fall condition.

Along with this journalistic work I still nurtured the dream of writing a novel, and for a long time my most tangible hope of someday doing it was, literally, a dream. After I wrote my Spanish Harlem book I hunkered down in earnest and managed to grind out fifty pages of a coming-of-age novel at nights while I wrote and researched my *Nation* pieces (and went to analysis) during the days, only to have it rejected by my publisher with the advice that I should stick to journalism. I was devastated, and depressed about it for months, until one night I had a dream in the form of a novel; that is, the dream began with a "title page," proceeded with a story (in which I played a part, under a different name and identity), with a beginning, middle, and end, and when it was over, a final "page" of a book said "The End." I woke up elated, knowing I could someday write a novel; it was as if the dream was telling me that the capacity to do it was within me.

I got another, more tangible "message" of encouragement about writing fiction the year following the Nieman, when I sat down one beautiful autumn afternoon in New Hampshire feeling a joy and fullness and wanting to write, yet having no idea of what I would write about. I simply started writing down what came to my mind and I kept writing steadily for three hours or so and when I finished I had a short story, called "Autumn Full of Apples," that my agent sold to *Redbook,* and which was then published in *The Best American Short Stories of 1966.* I almost felt as if I had simply transcribed the story rather than consciously written it, that I was serving as a "channel" for the story's transmission. (I don't mean in the current use of the term "channeling" as being the conductor of a voice of some other persona of the past, but as a conduit of spirit flowing through me and transmitting my own experience into form or "song.") It was an exhilarating and somewhat frightening feeling, and I automatically said a prayer of thanks.

I finally wrote the first novel in 1968 and 1969, hurling myself at it and into it with all the force I could summon, feeling at first discouraged and then frustrated, and finally desperate. I wrecked a relationship with a woman as well as an automobile in the course of it and, with the finish not even in sight, somehow ended up in the basement "family room" of my dear friend Wayne Kelley whom I'd met as a fellow Nieman and introduced to Margaret, who became his wife. When I went to hide out with the Kelleys in Alexandria, Virginia, I knew I had come to a real crossroads and that if I didn't somehow finish the novel then I never would.

That Sunday morning Kelley, who'd become the publisher of the *Congressional Quarterly,* brought in the "Book World" section of the Washington *Post* that I read as I tried to sober up with coffee and orange juice. It had a review of the latest volume of Leon Edel's biography of Henry James, who had always seemed to me a sort of "guide" in a spiritual (or, as I would have said then, "personal") as well as a literary way, someone whose integrity and purpose shone through his work and inspired the highest aspirations. There was a quote in the review from James's journal entry after the play on which he had counted so much had failed in London and he was prescribing his own cure for the devastation he felt. Through the painful haze of my hangover, the words seemed to light up and give me purpose and hope:

"Produce; produce again; produce again better than ever, and all will be well."

I knew I was going to do just that. I was going to finish the novel.

My coming-of-age first novel, set in Indianapolis, *Going All the Way* (in which, as in the dream, I played a part under a different name and identity), was published by Seymour Lawrence/Delacorte in 1970. It was blessed with a wonderful endorsement by my fellow Shortridge High School alumnus Kurt Vonnegut (though not received well by many alumni who remained in Indianapolis); it was chosen as a Dual Main Selection of the Literary Guild; it hit the *Time* magazine best-seller list for three weeks (leaping from number 10 to 9 and back again), sold more than 800,000 copies in paperback (it actually totaled more than a million copies in the United States counting the book club edition), and foreign rights were sold in England, Italy, Sweden, and Japan. It was widely and, for the most part, respectfully and well reviewed, and movie rights were optioned. I had finally written my novel and it was not only published but successful.

The dream of a lifetime had been realized, and I was delighted. I was also nervous and anxious. When the book made the *Time* magazine best-seller list I immediately fretted that it hadn't hit the New York *Times* list; when foreign rights were sold to Italy I brooded over why it wasn't taken in France! I learned what people have testified since the beginning of time, but that no one really believes until he has the experience—success and achievement and rewards are all fine, but they do not transform you, do not bring about a state of built-in contentment or inner peace or security, much less salvation (and in fact sometimes increase anxiety, raising the stakes, as in my worry about the other best-seller lists and the other foreign rights). I was still the same person. The novel was not The Answer to all of life's problems. I had another drink.

I was drinking to numb myself, to blank out the psychic or existential pain or whatever is the name we give to a feeling of emptiness of soul and the resulting anxiety and lurking terror of it. I added drugs to the booze when I suddenly took off for Los Angeles one day on a whim of boredom, impulse, and anxiety, imagining that the motion of travel and change of scenery and weather would also help block out the void. I lived for nearly a year at the Chateau Marmont, doodling with a movie script, hanging out with people on the fringe of the music business, adding cocaine to my daily diet of booze, and experimenting with LSD three times (I was wary of this because of the fear of unleashing the hallucinatory nightmares, and knew I was lucky when I stopped after three trips on the brink of a black hole, teetering there until I came out from under the influence). The only reason I didn't smoke marijuana is that I had never been able to inhale so I didn't get high from it. I had once sniffed heroin and found it by far the best and most complete painkiller. It was only my memory of the addicts I knew in East Harlem that kept me from doing more, since I knew first hand from those people that junk was a one-way street to destruction and not just another fun way to get high.

I used drugs the way I think most people really do, not primarily and habitually for "kicks" or glamor but for blotting out pain, the pain of that interior or psychic void that I think is the absence of spiritual substance, the hole that is left by the lack of any power higher than the human, or what some people call God. The irony is that the very substances—the drugs or alcohol

—that one uses to numb the pain in this chemical, artificial way have the real effect of enlarging the very void they are seeking to fill, so that more and more booze and drugs are always needed in the never ending quest to stuff the hole that is inevitably made larger by the increasing efforts to eliminate it.

As I stepped up my own intake of alcohol and drugs during those years I of course blotted out the spiritual perceptions and impulses that were actually the very qualities and forces that might have begun to fill the emptiness and heal the pain. The very idea of church seemed an anachronism, and I stopped praying, even those old reflexive prayers that used to come to mind in times of stress or panic. How deeply and effectively I had squelched such impulses can be measured by the fact that sometime in the early 1970s, while on a plane forced to circle a fogged-in airport, I proudly refused to revert to prayer but recalled the words of some William Butler Yeats poems I had learned in Lionel Trilling's class at Columbia. When the plane finally landed I was proud of myself. I had not "given in" to any divine superstition, but even in the face of death had proved my mettle as a pure atheistic intellectual.

What seems miraculous in retrospect is that any sort of spiritual sensations at all pierced through the heavy armor of my atheism and the fog of my alcoholic/narcotic consumption during that era. And yet they did, as I think they most often do for us, through the guardian-angel "messengers" or "guides" whom we meet in the flesh or through their thoughts expressed in writing (and, for some people, in painting and music as well). Those hands or words reach out to us and somehow, sometimes, touch us, even through the intellectual and chemical defenses we have thrown up around ourselves.

Something of that kind happened to me in the midst of the year I was so hard at play in Los Angeles after the novel's publication. At a time when I had just begun practicing the twin habits of brandy and cocaine consumption I got a letter asking me to teach the following spring at the Iowa Writers Workshop, and in my jangled state my visit to the University of Iowa was confused and bedeviled with on-the-spot controversy. I went to try to sort it out (not an easy process when your system is as besotted as mine was at that time) on a visit to my staunch friends the Kelleys in Alexandria, Virginia, where I'd stopped off during the novel crisis.

I sat up most of the night drinking bourbon with Wayne and listening to Don McLean's "American Pie" (trying to glean some message from its marvelously mixed-up pop imagery so suited to my scrambled brain at the time), debating whether to go teach at Iowa the following spring semester of 1972, or to stay on in Los Angeles partying it up with my music business pals or to go to London and try to write my next novel in a literary-charged landscape where I didn't know a soul. My bad time on the Iowa visit was surely an "omen" not to go there, I decided, and I was tiring of the Los Angeles toyland despite its many numbing attractions, so I figured the best plan was to "escape" to London where I could begin a new life with the advantage of having no one there who knew about my old one. That was my decision when I staggered to bed.

I woke the next morning with a hangover and paced around the house swilling orange orange juice and looking at some interesting new posters Margaret Kelley had hung hung—quotations from great men written on colorful backgrounds by an artist named Patricia Ellen Ricci. There was something profound about literature by James Joyce, and other erudite insights by artists, but the one that seemed to leap out at me was by Albert Schweitzer, whom I considered a boring German Jesus-freak. The message was not at all in keeping with my current thinking, yet it "spoke to me" in a very clear way, as if I were reading my own instructions in a game that gave me "clues" to my next direction. It said: *"I don't know what your destiny will be but one thing I know, the only ones among you who will be really happy are those who have sought and found how to serve."*

It was then absolutely clear to me that I was going to Iowa. I had taught before at the University of Massachusetts at Boston and felt I had contributed something to some of the students, conveyed some angle of insight or provided a measure of personal support or belief, and I thought I might be able to do that again. When Kelley got up he was amazed that I had decided to go to Iowa; Margaret was even more surprised when she offered me one of the posters I had admired the night before and I chose not the one with the James Joyce quote she had expected me to choose but the Schweitzer, which hangs on the wall of my study today.

Iowa was a happy interlude, and I was able to help one of my students I thought showed particular talent by introducing him to Bob Manning, who gave him an assignment for the *Atlantic*. A few years later another *Atlantic* editor, Richard Todd, gave this budding journalist an assignment to write about computers so that lay people could understand them, and this work grew into a book called *The Soul of a New Machine* that brought its young author, Tracy Kidder, a Pulitzer Prize.

Another student I got to know and like at Iowa was a young black man from my own hometown named Ron Clark. I recommended him for a teaching job at the University of Rhode Island, and it turned out to be lucky for *me* that he was close to Boston. After I had ended a promotion tour for my second novel, *Starting Over,* with an alcoholic binge that left me sick and frightened, I called Ron and simply, in a shaking voice, said, "Help." He and his wife and their small daughter Justina came up and stayed with me for a week in my new town house on Beacon Hill (not even my own house had proved to be The Answer!), feeding me sweet rolls and sugary desserts to take the place of the booze, cooking and talking and nursing me back to sobriety in the first dry-out period of my life.

I especially had an incentive for shaping up and trying to pull myself together because I had just met a woman I knew I wanted to live with for the rest of my life. Eve had been married and divorced, as I had also by then, and neither one of us wanted marriage, but we made a commitment to live together that we meant just as deeply as anything said in a church with vows or endorsed by papers of the state. The fact of our not wanting the official bond of marriage seemed to deepen the personal bond between us, the specialness of our relationship.

Eve came up from New York to share my house and my life and I tried to be worthy of her and of the opportunity. I even made a decision to give up hard liquor for good and to limit myself to wine and beer, which at the time seemed like an enormous and nearly miraculous change. It occurred while I was sitting in a barber chair getting my hair cut by a woman "stylist." I had the shakes with one of my familiar severe hangovers, and when she went to trim my sideburns with the electric razor I had such a bad spasm of trembling that it was difficult for her to trim the line evenly. I was so embarrassed by my "fit" of uncontrolled head shaking, which I knew was due to the booze, that the thought and the decision came to me at the same time that I would not humiliate myself (or Eve!) by being so out of control, and that I would at least moderate my alcohol intake by swearing off the hard stuff and sticking to wine and beer.

It was one of those decisions in which I could almost feel a kind of inner shift, and I knew I would never go back on it. At the same time, in a much more remote region of my mind, I had an additional thought, as tiny as the point of a pin, that someday I would give up drinking alcohol of any kind—but the very notion of that was so wildly out of the range of my conception then (and the idea of living in such a way so terrifying) that I immediately dismissed it.

This new life with a woman I loved brought many blessings, and even though I didn't turn to God or church there was a spiritual influence, another "guide," who appeared at this time and who I felt was a kind of "adopted" guardian angel for both me and Eve. This woman I met when I went to write about her popular soap opera "All My Children" was Agnes Nixon, who became a friend for life. She was the only person in my life then who was "religious," that is, who openly believed in God and made religion a part of her life.

In the book *(All Her Children)* I wrote about Agnes and her show, I described a visit she took me on to St. David's Episcopal Church in Radnor, Pennsylvania, near her home in Bryn Mawr. This was my first time inside a church in many years. Even though no service was being held I felt deeply moved by the experience, which seemed a stark contrast to the rest of my life. When Agnes took me inside the empty church I became aware of my own breathing. I described the experience in the book:

"It is both a surprise and a comfort, hearing that breathing that is the only sound in the midst of the otherwise unusual stillness. It reminds me I am alive. Most often that seemingly simple perception is drowned out in the chaos of our clangorous existence. We are alive here. We can hear it.

"We pause a moment, agnostic and Catholic, man and woman of very different styles of life, not looking at one another, but sharing the almost silence. I think, though there are no words, or perhaps because of their absence, this moment can appropriately be called a kind of prayer."

Perhaps because I didn't want Agnes to think badly of me, I described myself as an agnostic rather than the harsher designation of atheist (or maybe things had been going so well in my life since the advent of Eve that I didn't want to deny completely the possibility of God, but at least to leave room for the possibility). Obviously the idea of prayer seemed very strange to me then, and I evidently couldn't come right out and write about it without hedging it around with "a kind of" and the "I think" (meaning "I don't really know"). I was glad to have Agnes as a friend, and I felt the spiritual nature of her own life as a benign influence, but I didn't think I needed any more than that secondhand spirituality.

I believed I was self-sufficient now—with a little help from a woman psychiatrist I had met socially, liked and respected, and saw in a sort of informal therapy off and on before and during my time with Eve in Boston. Several earlier postanalysis attempts at therapy had quickly ended with my anger at the therapist (who I'm sure got the spillover of my anger at Stanleys I and II) but the counseling of this woman doctor seemed a kind of practical and levelheaded support, and I felt it was helpful and steadying.

I thought that in joining my life with Eve's I had beat the game. I had found the answer John Reed promised about the love of a woman in his essay "Almost Thirty." When I was almost forty-three I felt so self-satisfied that I reviewed with a kind of wry condescension a book about the male mid-life crisis for the New York *Times*. From the comfort and security of my town house on Beacon Hill, with the woman I felt was my mate for life in residence with me, I wondered what all the fuss was about this alleged "male menopause." Compared to my adolescence, I reflected, mid-life was "like a calm day on Walden Pond." I thought little about God or His absence. Who needed Him? I had Eve, the house, and a three-book contract.

There was even more to come in this period of largesse—an offer from out of the blue to write a television script about a teenage boy, and NBC liked it so much they commissioned a series. Our move to Hollywood seemed to promise more of all the good things of life: money, love, success; plus warmer winters and a wider variety of California wines.

I had become a connoisseur.

A decade later I had become a connoisseur of the works of Ralph Waldo Emerson. I was reminded of that era I have just described when I read this passage from his essay on "Self-Reliance":

"A political victory, a rise of rents, the recovery of your sick, or the return of your absent friend, or some other favorable event, raises your spirits, and you think good days are preparing for you. Do not believe it. Nothing can bring you peace but yourself."

In Emerson, had I read him back then, I could even have found a passage from "Compensation" to offer solace for the loss of those things whose promise I found at the time so enriching: "The changes which break up at short intervals the prosperity of men are advertisements of a nature whose law is growth."

III
RETURNING

8. The Blood Tie

I realized the journey that brought me home to Boston from Hollywood had skipped a crucial part—perhaps the hardest part of all. Five years after I'd settled back into my old neighborhood on Beacon Hill and returned to my religious roots when I joined King's Chapel, I still had not made peace with the home I was born and grew up in. I'd avoided Indianapolis for many years, only going back when circumstances forced me, even then returning in the style of a thief in the night, not telling anyone except the few people I had to see. In the fall of 1985 I looked uneasily at a headline announcing a talk I was scheduled to give at the Indianapolis-Marion County Public Library; "Dan Wakefield—A Prodigal Son Returns." I was going to try again.

When my flight out of Boston was delayed I began to get nervous. The last time I'd boarded a plane to make a public appearance in Indianapolis I never got there. That was fifteen years before, when my leaving-home first novel was published in 1970. It was called *Going All the Way* and a lot of people in Indianapolis who read it thought I had gone too far. Phone calls and letters and secondhand rumors (as well as painfully censorious silence from old friends) had made it clear there was a lot of hostility toward me and my book back home in Indiana. Some people (mostly ones I barely knew) firmly believed I had exposed their most intimate secrets or those of their wives or daughters, and threatened to wreak vengeance. Others felt I had cast aspersions on their community and its values, the place of my own birth and upbringing. All this made me wish I had followed an early anticipation of such misunderstanding and set the damn book in Cleveland.

There was also disapproval in some quarters from people unaccustomed or unsympathetic to the manners of current fiction, who felt that my frank use of "language" describing sexual experiences and fantasies was shocking and immoral. At the twenty-fifth reunion of my high school class, which I was too chicken to attend, my old classmate Dick Lugar, then mayor of Indianapolis, got a big laugh when he said he had read my novel, after receiving it through the mail "in a plain brown wrapper."

My publisher's publicity director had assured me I was being oversensitive when I didn't want to go back home for book promotion, especially after an Indianapolis television station offered to pay all expenses for me to come and be interviewed on their talk show. I grudgingly agreed to do it, even though discomforting omens warned me otherwise. That morning of departure was foggy, with rain, and someone in the office of my publisher had clipped out a picture for me from the New York *Daily News* that showed a woman accused of murdering her boyfriend being led out of a brownstone by armed police. I asked what the story had to do with me and was told to look closer at the picture. The accused murderess was shielding her face from the cameras with a book—it was a copy of *Going All the Way*. Did my novel promote mayhem in people? I laughed nervously, downed a morning drink, and went to the airport.

The flight was scheduled to go to Indianapolis, Kansas City, and San Francisco, but we made an emergency landing in Pittsburgh because of a bomb threat to TWA from a caller who said, *"That plane will never get to Indianapolis."* Quivering in the concrete blockhouse where passengers huddled while the aircraft was searched for bombs, I told my story to an FBI man who said he didn't believe the threat was linked to anything like a novel or its author—they thought it had to do with a stewardess and a broken date—but when I confided my fears to a woman passenger who taught high school in Bloomington, Indiana, she said, "I've heard people talk about your book, and if I were you I wouldn't go back either." The wail of police sirens rang in my mind from the end of a popular song of the season called "Indiana Wants Me." How many signs and portents did I need? I joined those who took the airline's offer to return to New York instead of continuing the interrupted flight, and told the publicity director over a stiff brandy that Thomas Wolfe was right: "You can't go home again."

In the decade that followed I practiced Wolfe's preachment. I only went back once to Indianapolis on a quick trip to see my parents (pledging them not to tell anyone of my arrival), preferring to send them tickets every year to visit me wherever I was at the time. I justified that arrangement because it seemed to be less emotion-charged for all concerned. I lost track of dear friends from high school I'd kept in touch with over the years (the ones who stayed home, not my fellow migrants like Hickman in Tampa or Ted "The Horse" in New York, with whom I not only shared the experience of Indiana but also of leaving it), fearing they felt I'd betrayed them. The book was seen by some as the final cap to my earlier transgressions of going East and becoming an alleged pinko, bohemian, beatnik, hippie (to match the changing times and styles), a middle-aged divorced man without children, a turncoat against the values and beliefs I'd been nurtured on while growing up, making me seem a sort of Indiana Benedict Arnold, betrayer of my own roots. (As if this image weren't bad enough, I'd heard rumors out of Indianapolis over the years alleging me to be at different times a drug addict and a homosexual, which added to my other alleged sins might make me the first Hoosier-gay-pinko-junkie-pornographer.)

When I went home in 1980 for the funerals of my father and mother I was surprised and relieved and unutterably grateful to see old high school friends I hadn't talked with in more than a decade—some I had not even seen since high school graduation thirty years before. When I flew in for my father's funeral, having just broken up with Eve and feeling more alone than I ever remembered, I put on my best suit and smile and stationed myself at the front of the antiseptic room with my father lying in a coffin behind me and wondered how the hell I was going to get through it.

A handsome man with distinguished white hair came toward me and I dutifully stuck out my hand and said, "Hello, I'm Dan Wakefield." The man smiled and said in a voice and accent I knew and loved, "It's Harpie." My best friend from high school. I remembered once doing a story for *Esquire* on Happy Chandler when he came out of retirement to run again for governor of Kentucky. He had gone to a funeral at which the father of the family, an old friend and ally, came up and threw his arms around the candidate and said, "Good God, Governor, there's no one on earth I'd rather see." That's how I felt when I recognized Harpie, though in Indiana we men don't embrace and express emotion the way they do unashamedly to our South, so I simply shook hands with my old friend and said, "Thanks."

At those times of death the support of friends from home was the most saving grace I was given. No matter what some may have disapproved of about my life or what rumors they had heard of it, those friends were there in that experience of grief because I had shared with them that precious era that Jerry Burton, my friend since kindergarten, described in a letter as "those wonderful heartbreaking days when we lived so much of our lives, in such a few short years." Even had I been the first Hoosier gay-pinko-junkie-pornographer, I also was, more importantly, one of *them*, and they were there to stand by me. There is a loyalty of place as deep as blood, something in and of the flat, true heart of the Midwest, a slowly grown sentiment born of the very plainness of the land, something solid that takes root and holds, and that sticks forever. I saw that in the old friends from home who came at those difficult times, so many years later, and I loved them for it.

Something held me back, though, from returning to re-establish those old friendships after my parents had died. It seemed as though there still was some kind of invisible barrier between me and Indianapolis that I couldn't manage to cross. I didn't go back again until four years after my mother's and father's funerals, but even then I still didn't tell my old friends I was coming. In my old thief-in-the-night manner, I kept my trip a secret from almost everyone I knew in Indianapolis except my Cousin Paula, who I knew I could trust not to let anyone know I was coming.

Maybe my reluctance was simply due to a revival of old guilt, for I was going back to show my writer-producer friend Don Devlin around the city to scout locations for a movie version he wanted to make of *Going All the Way*. Even though the film he hoped to produce was an "update" of the story from the 1950s to the 1980s and bore little resemblance to the original, I still feared the project might upset people again, reopening old wounds. On the other hand, I'd rationalized that Don's movie was not really a film of the novel. Like the movie version of my novel *Starting Over,* it would only use the book as what the writer of that script described as a "launching pad" for the movie. Nevertheless, I didn't want to open the whole can of worms by bringing up the subject to old friends in Indianapolis. I told myself to stop worrying and just enjoy the trip.

One of the worst blizzards in recent Indiana history covered the city the week I was scheduled to meet my writer-producer friend in Indianapolis that February of 1984. Don called me in Boston from Hollywood and asked if we ought to postpone the trip, but I wanted to do it and get it over with. He and I shivered and slid around a frozen Indianapolis for several days, enjoying good conversation about potential locations if he got the project

into production and decided to do the shooting there, which he
realized wasn't essential to the new version of the story.

The Sunday morning before going back to Boston, I decided
to visit my parents' graves. I wanted some kind of reconciliation
with them, and even though I had prayed for it, I wanted to do
something else, specific and tangible, to try to bring it about. I
knew that the bones of my mother and father were in the
ground, and I had no illusion their incarnated bodies were floating around somewhere in the atmosphere, yet I'd sensed ema-
nations of their essence, or whatever unknown, unnamable
quality it was Aunt Ollie had sensed and sometimes communicated with in her own rapport with the "spirits" of those who
had left this earthly life. Once in the year after my mother's
death, when I had just made a decision that troubled me and in
fact turned out very badly, I clearly heard my mother crying, as
close and "real" as if she were in the same room.

I had never visited anyone's grave before, and never been
able to understand what seemed the barbaric practice of standing over a plot of ground that covered the bones of the dead.
Now it seemed at least a symbolic spot for paying respects to
whatever manifestation of the deceased still remained in this
realm of the living, even if it only remained in the heart or soul
of the mourner. Whatever the case may have been, I was nervous. Cousin Paula had drawn me a map showing my parents'
plots in Crown Hill Cemetery, but I got lost in that immense,
eerie landscape, made more stark and somber by the covering
of ice and snow. No other visitors had come to pay respects on
such a bone-chilling morning, nor were any officials or atten-
dants in sight. I was not made more comfortable by the observation that I seemed to be the only living soul in the huge, other-
worldly kingdom of the cemetery. I was alone with my parents
and the rest of the dead.

I knelt in the snow beside my parents' graves, feeling cold
and discomforted. I said the Twenty-third Psalm, going through
it pretty briskly, muttered a request for forgiveness for not

more freely expressing my love to them in their lifetime, then shifted on my knees. The layer of snow crunched beneath me. I wondered if the earth might open and swallow me, sucking me into a grave beside my parents. That had been a painful point of contention with us. On a trip to New York in the mid-seventies my mother blithely told me the "good news" that she and my father had just purchased their cemetery plots at Crown Hill, and that there happened to be bargain sale, "three for the price of two," on grave sites, so they had got one for me right beside them.

"No!" I shouted. "No way!" We were having lunch in the main restaurant of the New York Hilton, where I had put them up on that visit, and other tourists at nearby tables turned and stared at my unseemly outburst. I felt an awful panic, a fear that my parents had found a way to trap me at last, to keep me "home" with them through eternity, thus negating my noble escape and establishment of independence! My mother answered my spontaneous rejection of their generous offer by pointing out, "You have to be buried *some*place!" I denied this, explaining I wanted to be cremated, but my mother, whose hearing difficulty always became more acute with information she didn't like, cupped a hand to her ear and asked what I'd said. With heart pounding, I threw down my napkin, stood up, and shouted:

"I want to be cremated and have my ashes scattered on Beacon Hill!"

The entire population of the large dining room turned toward me as my father heaved one of his heartrending sighs and I sank back down in my chair, trembling. When I got back to Boston I went to my lawyer and made up the first "last will and testament" of my life, spelling out my wishes for interment in no uncertain terms.

All that came rushing back to me as I knelt on the cracking ice beside my parents' graves, perhaps on the very plot they had purchased for me. I bade them a hasty farewell and clambered up from the frozen ground, slipping and sliding to the car. I jumped in and slammed the door, jammed the key in the ignition, and prepared to turn the key to escape to my airline flight, whose time of departure was drawing close. The key wouldn't turn. It wouldn't budge. Not at all. I frantically searched my pockets for other keys, but this was it. I took it out and stuck it in again, with no better results. I flung open the door and scrambled out of the car, calling for help. There of course was no one. On that freezing Sunday morning the place was quite literally dead. I felt as if some kind of force field had formed around me, a trap that had sprung from my parents' graves to hold me there with them. I could feel the anger and power of my mother and father, their sense of disappointment in what they interpreted as rejection by their only son. I could feel their presence. I started to run.

I ran as fast as I could up the winding paths of the cemetery toward a large mausoleum that seemed to be the focal point of the whole place. Part of my mind saw myself from an aerial view, a lone man running through a deserted, snow-covered cemetery, past the whitened statues, the memorial crosses and blocks of marble—a figure in a frieze from an outtake of a Bergman film. The rest of my consciousness was filled with pure, unreasoning panic.

There was a guard on duty in an office in the mausoleum, and he came out and tried to get my borrowed engine started but had no better luck than I did. The key simply wouldn't budge. Back at the mausoleum office I called Cousin Paula, who came with a neighbor and was not able to turn the key to start the car herself, though she said she couldn't understand it, they had had that car for years and nothing like this ever happened before. The neighbor took me to the airport and I just made the plane to Boston. When I got home safe I called Cousin Paula to learn that her husband had gone back with her to the car that afternoon and the key worked perfectly, no problem at all, and

Jim couldn't believe that neither I, nor the cemetery guard, nor Paula, nor her neighbor had been able to get it to turn.

The memory of those previous "prodigal son" efforts I had made didn't give me lots of confidence for the new attempt when I went back for the library talk in the autumn of 1985. When my flight out of Boston was delayed I got even more nervous. I tried to reassure myself by thinking about the church retreat on "Reconciliation" I'd gone on the previous weekend, where we'd studied the story of the prodigal son. Surely that gave me the best kind of preparation and blessing for this latest try. As I waited for my flight to take off, I knew I was ready to renew old ties with the high school friends I hoped to see, but I wished now I didn't have to do it as part of a public appearance. I'd agreed to speak at the library as part of their series of Conversations with Indiana Authors, and to help promote the event with interviews on local television and in the press.

What if some of those irate fathers or husbands who were angered when *Going All the Way* was published came to my talk to avenge what they imagined were personal slurs on their loved ones; or those who felt my novel had insulted their entire *community* and way of life? What if they hurled tomatoes or eggs, or at least hostile, heckling questions?

"I see myself on this return like the aging warrior, wrinkled and weathered, with feathers turned to gray, raising a hand in blessing and saying, 'I come in peace.' "

That's what I said in an interview about my upcoming lecture for the Indianapolis Public Library newsletter, but that didn't guarantee how other people would see me. *Dear God, may I really find reconciliation.* I twisted in my seat as the plane began to taxi down the runway for takeoff, lifting into thick, gray skies and hurtling west toward the heartland.

The next day I was shooting baskets with Harpie in his back-yard. The smack and echo of the basketball on the grassy ground, the feel of its grainy skin on my fingers, thud of the banked shot against the wooden backboard, then a run for the rebound, breath coming clean and sharp in the chest—all of this was deeply reassuring and made me feel this trip back home was not only safe but *right*. Harpie and I were playing ball in the falling sun and shadow of a late October afternoon, with the dizzying fresh perfume of new-mown hay coming over the long flat fields, the whole of it creating a full harmony of home, a blood- and bone-deep rhythm of casual order, a ritual I relaxed into like a warm bath or a deep bed of the most complete imaginable comfort, the comfort of deepest inner self, of soul.

I was home, as I had been, and would be—now, then, again, it was all one. Time seemed fluid rather than fixed, not linear but spiraling, mysterious and luminous beyond our grasp. Playing basketball in Harpie's backyard, I was (am) a child, boy, gray-haired man, old coot I've yet to become.

The sunset that evening was one of the most spectacular displays of intense essences of colors—fiery, molten golds and reds—I can ever remember seeing, more brilliant even than the ones I had witnessed in the clear air of the Caribbean. Harpie said the sunsets were often like that this time of year in the farm country north of town because of a kind of dust that gets into the air from the harvesting of the corn. It acts as a filter that intensifies the light. It made me think of the word "glory" as in "The glory of the Lord shone round about them." (I realized it did more often than we think, but we're too preoccupied to notice.)

Our high school is unabashedly called "glorious Shortridge" in its anthem and we sang it that night at the tops of our lungs at the party at Harpie's, several dozen men and women who more than three decades before had befriended one another in a bond that seemed as strong and real in our early fifties as it had been in our teens. After I accepted the invitation to speak at the library I had called Harpie, whom I hadn't seen since my mother's funeral, nor sat down for a real talk with in more than twenty years, and asked if he'd mind getting some of the old gang together the night before my public performance. Realizing what a presumptuous request this was made me feel nervous, but as soon as Harpie started talking about it, going over names of people we'd like to see, the whole thing seemed as natural now as it had when we planned such parties back then, in high school.

Everyone looked so much the same except for whitening hair that I had the eerie feeling we had all gone back *from* the future to our high school selves for a party that required everyone to wear a gray wig. The talk was much the same—we spoke of favorite teachers like Dorothy and Abie and joked about "Krazy Kate," who enacted history by sticking her foot in the wastebasket and shouting, "I claim this land for Spain!" Bugsy spontaneously gave an account of the game with Withrow of Cincinnati we went into undefeated; he was playing quarterback and thought he heard the referee's whistle while he had the ball so he set it down on the grass and an enemy player jumped on it and the ref said, "First down, Withrow," and they went in and scored and beat us by a touchdown. "I know I heard that whistle," he said. I knew it too; and I couldn't believe the game he described was played any longer ago than the past weekend.

Like most of us there, I was drinking no more than Diet Coke and I know the warmth and trust we felt was not just a boozy illusion. Linda said her own kids never understood what the big deal was about her high school. Everyone agreed their own children had not enjoyed the special sort of bond we shared that still drew us together with a sense of loyalty and love no less than it had been three decades and more before. As I talked to Linda, Jerry, Janet, Ferdie, Pat, and the others I had such a sense of relief and trust that I got the deep feeling that these people, their faces and voices and love, this place we were born and grew up in—this was "real," and the rest of my life, the part since I left home to go to college and stay on living in the East, all that was "the dream." I used to think it was just the other way around. I remembered Eugene O'Neill's concept of youth

and middle age being the "strange interlude" between childhood and old age, and wondered if that was part of this sudden
sensation I had at the party with the old gang.

The next night at the library I announced that I wanted to
dedicate the evening to the memory of my mother and father. I
felt it was not just a gesture of piety but a true declaration of my
love that would somehow be communicated. I was addressing
my parents as well as the audience when I explained some of
the deep feelings I had about this place and its people, feelings
most brilliantly articulated by Eudora Welty in her essay "Place
in Fiction":

"There may come to be new places in our lives that are
second spiritual homes—closer to us in some ways, perhaps,
than our original homes. But the home tie is the blood tie. And
had it meant nothing to us, any other place thereafter would
have meant less, and we would carry no compass inside ourselves to find home, ever, anywhere at all. We would not even
guess what we had missed."

No hecklers were in the audience, only friends and readers
and old neighbors from back before high school. I did not quote
anything from *Going All the Way* but closed my talk by reading
the nostalgic short story "Autumn Full of Apples" that had
poured from me like a love song to home twenty years before
on a bright fall day in New England: "We cheered because we
thought we had outrun everything—the day and the season and
the year and all years—and we would never be caught by them,
never pulled anywhere beyond this sixteenth sweet-and-sour
apple autumn, cursing and kissing as if we had invented them
both." And there we were in the library, "caught" and pulled
ahead by time, but circling back in it, too, feeling those sixteen-
year-old selves alive and vivid in memory real as flesh.

I now saw a new dimension to the great key line that expresses the moment the prodigal son decides to go home: "he
came to himself." It meant on this trip of my own return a
coming to terms not only of acceptance of a true inner self but

also of the place in which that self was born, took root, was nourished, and grew.

I did not have the nerve to go back to visit my parents' graves on that trip, not wanting to risk any conflicting feeling to spoil the tremendous spirit of reconciliation with home, as well as—I hoped and prayed—with my mother and father. I went back to visit their graves on a trip to Indianapolis the following spring. On a day of soft sunlight and gusty, clean breezes I knelt again beside them. The weather inside me had changed, too, in part because I felt a real reconciliation had taken place when I honored my parents in public and also accepted in some deeper way the love for them I had buried so long in angry denial. There was an aura of calm around their graves now, and I felt my parents' presence again, but this time with peace, like a blessing. I took it with me and prayed to leave them mine, with love.

I felt I had two homes now, that I no longer need deny Indianapolis or relegate it to some compartment called "the past." I was able to enjoy and appreciate it as part of the very love of home that informed my feelings for Beacon Hill, feelings I had expressed not only in journalistic accounts of my adopted city but also as the healing setting of a new life for the divorced man in my novel *Starting Over.* I recognized the dynamics of the two homes in my life and work in another insight offered by Eudora Welty in her discourse on "Place in Fiction":

"It is noticeable that those writers who for their own good reasons push out against their backgrounds nearly always passionately adopt the new one in their work. Revolt itself is a reference and tribute to the potency of what is left behind."

What draws us to one place and not another, what force or magnetism pulls us back and forth across continents and oceans to settings that for seemingly unexplained or unexplainable reasons speak to our inner selves, our need? When I met Christopher Isherwood at a dinner in Hollywood in 1978 I told him I had just been to a part of the California desert he described in his novel *Down There on a Visit,* and he brightened at once and became animated with enthusiasm as he spoke of that landscape. He said when he first saw the desert in Southern California he felt an immediate sense of "being home," which made no sense at all to someone who grew up in England; yet the colors, the air, the whole look and feel of the place seemed to strike some deep chord in him, and it was that response more than work in the movies or the climate or any other factor that made him want to stay on and live in Los Angeles, as he did from the time he first saw it in the 1940s to his death in 1986.

When I first saw Beacon Hill I had that feeling of "home" but I didn't know why. After all, I grew up in pancake-flat Indianapolis in the landlocked heart of the country, in a neighborhood of small white frame houses and porches with swings, little front yards with grass and maple trees, backyards big enough for clotheslines and victory gardens and basketball rims. There was nothing from scenes of my childhood that hinted of any connection to the brick sidewalks and iron street lamps of Beacon Hill (they looked to me like a drawing of Dickens' London), yet I felt an immediate connection to the place, a haunting sense of ease and familiarity, like the *déjà vu* from a dream.

When I went up from New York City to Cambridge on the Nieman Fellowship and my parents came out to visit, they reminded me that Cousin Katherine Wakefield of Kentucky had told us we had an ancestor in the historic Granary Burial Ground in Boston, and we went to pay a visit to his grave. I think we wanted to make sure he was really there. Cousin Katherine was (like her father, my Uncle Jim) a gifted and colorful storyteller whose exciting tales of recent family history (including her own romantic sagas) sometimes seemed so melodramatic that we wondered whether the accounts of early family history she so assiduously traced as a devoted Daughter of the American Revolution were altogether dependable. When we found the simple slate marker, not far from Ben Franklin's parents' tomb, marking the grave of John Wakefield, a ship-wright of Boston who died in 1667 at age fifty-two, we were impressed, and also a little embarrassed at doubting Cousin Katherine. My mother took snapshots of me and my father standing at the grave of our forebear.

After I returned to Boston from Hollywood I walked past the Granary Burial Ground and remembered my ancestor. I turned in and stood for a moment by John Wakefield's grave, paying respects and offering thanks, as if somehow his presence had helped me get back. When I started going to King's Chapel I walked by the Granary every Sunday, and whether or not I went in to stand for a moment of silent prayer by his grave I always thought of my ancestor as I passed.

Once when I was walking up Tremont Street to attend a midweek service, lost in thoughts of work and problems, I came just parallel to the Granary and I suddenly stopped or was stopped by what felt like a gentle but firm blow to my midsection. I gasped, both from surprise and a sharp need for air. There was no one in front of me or anyone even paying attention to me in the crowds of preoccupied pedestrians hurrying past. I turned instinctively and looked across the street. I was standing almost precisely opposite the site of my ancestor's grave. I felt a sense of him, as if he were sending a signal or simply a greeting, across the street and the centuries. Like the feeling of the "blow" itself, it was gentle, yet firm enough to get my attention. A warmth rose up in me and tears came to my eyes. I leaned against a building for a moment, said a silent prayer, then slowly walked on, feeling blessed.

I mentioned my ancestor's grave in a magazine piece about Boston several years ago, and got a letter from a man whose middle name is Wakefield saying that he, too, was related to our namesake in the Granary Burial Ground. He asked if I also knew that the John Wakefield in the Granary had two children in the King's Chapel Burial Ground, next to the church. No, I had not known until I read that letter. By then I had been a member of King's Chapel for several years, and the church had become not only a spiritual home but a family. Knowing that the ancestors of my genealogical family were in the very ground of the place to which I had been so naturally drawn seemed part of the whole intricate pattern of my journey and return.

After my original family was taken from me, I had no idea that another one was already waiting.

9. Family

I saw myself at the end of a barren tree limb, hanging on. The picture came to my mind the winter of the year my parents died, when I realized the closest family I had left was a cousin in Indianapolis and another in Atlanta. I was a divorced man with no children, living alone again at age forty-eight. I had good friends, surrogate families like the Kelleys and O'Connells, and later Joanne Spitz and her brood. (I am godfather of her and Richard Geller's three kids, one of whom was given the middle name "Wakefield.") But I had no "official" family of my own, no people with whom I was bound whether we liked it or not, by some force beyond our own personalities and good will, and suddenly that seemed like a real void.

Given the way I had lived my life, the situation was hardly surprising. What surprised me was that a few years later I looked around and saw people I related to as aunts and uncles, sisters and brothers, children and parents and grandparents, even though I didn't yet know all their names. When I joined King's Chapel I felt I'd become a member of a family as well as a church. If multiplying fishes and loaves to feed a crowd was regarded as miraculous, having a ready-made family spring up around me after my own was gone seemed no less impressive.

I knew it was a family and not just a pretty illusion because its members called on me for help and support, which not only made me feel valued and included but also assured me I was free to call on them, too. It was nothing grand or flowery that gave me the feeling of family, but the everyday details, the commonplace stuff. Elizabeth Thomson, a neighbor from my pre-church days who chaired the Hospitality Committee, asked me to cook the chili I used to serve at parties on Revere Street for a Sunday church lunch at the King's Chapel parish house. I nervously explained I'd never cooked for more than ten people at a time and I didn't know how to make enough for forty, but Elizabeth patiently pointed out that if I made four times the recipe it would probably do the trick. Lo and behold, I multiplied my old chili recipe and fed the multitude of forty—miraculous.

The most filling part for me wasn't the meal but cooking in the kitchen of the parish house, which more than the beautiful, historic sanctuary on Tremont Street where Sunday services are held came to seem like the real home of the church. Shedding onion tears and chopping tomatoes in the kitchen incorporated the feeling of family into my flesh and bones as well as my heart and mind.

I was asked to write a skit for the Sunday school to perform at the postholiday Candlemas celebration, and took time I didn't think I had from working on a novel to knock out a silly, soap opera version of *A Christmas Carol*. Another miracle—the kids liked it, and people laughed at the right times.

I was flattered when Johanna Chapin, one of the congregation's bright teenagers, interviewed me for a term paper on daytime television because she found out I had written a book about the making of a soap opera *(All Her Children)*. Harriet Parker, a Boston lady of great wit and charm who served as a naval recruiting officer in World War II and became the first female to hold the position of junior warden of the church, invited me to serve on a committee to suggest revisions of the midweek service for the new prayer book. Informally and officially, by young and older members of the church family, I was given the most important gift of all, the chance to *serve*.

I responded not from "selflessness" but a sort of "enlightened selfishness"; not because it made me holy but because it made me happy. I found in the bottom of an old trunk the poster with the Albert Schweitzer quote I had taken from the Kelleys' house without knowing quite why, a decade before:

"I don't know what your destiny will be but one thing I know, the only ones among you who will be really happy are those who have sought and found a way to serve."

Our magnetic former assistant minister, the Reverend Yvonne Schaudt, asked me to serve on a committee to plan a retreat on living alone (I was becoming an expert on starting over). I had never been on a church retreat and I feared brown rice and a bed of nails, but found instead fried chicken and a room with a view of a lake in a big stone house built to look like a French château in nearby Andover.

I took part in discussions of subjects I had hashed over hundreds of times before but never with the sense of extra dimension that comes from a group who share a common belief in something beyond themselves and concern for more than their society's newest crises; or rather, how those issues related to beliefs that went deeper than headlines, deeper even than politics. We raised questions but did not feel compelled to agree on answers.

I joined in singing on Saturday night when Ciael Hills—a teacher and copy editor with a quick smile who came to seem like a favorite sister—got out her guitar and led us in songs I hadn't sung since Scout camp and college and early days in Greenwich Village. I closed my eyes and moved back and forth through my life as I sang. "I am climbing Jacob's ladder . . . I sailed on the sloop *John B.* . . . How many roads must a man travel down? . . . Michael, row the boat ashore. . . ." Hallelujah. I was home.

Retreats in spring and fall, on the Cape and in New Hampshire, at the Unitarians' Senexet House in Connecticut and the

Benedictine monastery Glastonbury Abbey only forty-five minutes from Boston, became a part of the order of my life, refreshing time-outs from routine and pressure to reflect with prayerful discussion and meditation on matters like healing,
reconciliation, and "discernment," or, in the words of one of our
retreat titles: "How do we know when it's God?" At Glastonbury I found a special depth of prayer provided by the hospitality of the monks, who allowed us to join in their daily services
from morning prayer at 6 A.M. to compline at seven-thirty in
the evening, chanting the clean notes of psalms in plainsong, an
inner as well as an aural experience of harmony and clarity.

We went on retreat not simply to find uplift but to examine
and share the downsides of the journey, to confront the dark as
well as enjoy the light, as one retreatant did when he wrote:
"Darkness is terrible. I celebrate the darkness in which I
grope." He wondered if perhaps it is only in the darkness that
"we discover our true selves because we are too distracted in
the light." As I wrote in my own response to the subject of God's
darkness on that retreat: "One thing certain—it is better to be
in this soul darkness with others, who are also seeking the light,
than to be lost in it alone."

The age-old human questions that we wrestled with were not
just spiritual or intellectual abstractions but became sometimes
starkly immediate matters of how to deal with life and death in
the family. At the minister's course in religious autobiography I
paired up with a woman in one of the exercises when we were
asked to explain to one another the "road map" of our lives. We
had drawn these with crayons on a big sheet of paper, illustrat-
ing with pictures and symbols the curving paths and broken
bridges of our journeys. I knew nothing of my partner except
that she was a beautiful, vibrant woman in her early forties, a
wife and mother of teenage twin daughters. As we questioned
one another about our "life maps" I asked her what the cluster
of colors meant in the middle of her "road"—was it some kind of

flowers? No, she said, those represented the blood cells that indicated the leukemia she learned she had the year before.

The disease was in remission and there was no way to imagine Lola Minifie was not the healthiest member of the church family. She had responded to her own troubles by forming a group called Lifeboat for others who knew they had fatal illnesses, and they met together to share their feelings and provide mutual support. Lola came from her job in the Radcliffe admissions office to have lunch with me and a few other members of our Adult Religious Education Committee to help plan a series on healing for our program. We were sitting in an outdoor café in Cambridge on a bright, warm September afternoon, sipping iced tea and finishing salads. It was simply not possible to imagine that Lola, the youngest and most vital person at the table, was doomed to be taken from the life she so brightened in the middle of the journey.

She went back to the hospital that winter and did not recover. Her memorial service filled the church with the largest crowd I had ever seen at King's Chapel. There were friends from all different areas of a life that served diverse groups of people with the most complete kind of giving of self. Her death made no sense. Her death raised doubts, anger, fear, and resentment in me, and others who knew her more closely; we wondered what this meant about God except to show us again His darkness, and our inability to comprehend His mystery.

Our minister said that in one of his talks with Lola he had told her that what she was going through sounded like a crucifixion, and she had said yes, she realized then that our religion gave us "a language to describe what happens to us." At the wake at her home I stood in the midst of relatives from all her families pressed close in reassuring flesh and realized this was something else our religion described—that we were part of a "body" larger and more meaningful than our own bag of bones, not just isolated flecks of dust lost in the universe. Through faith it was possible to see ourselves as pieces of a jigsaw puzzle that made no sense when spilled haphazardly on the floor but formed a meaningful picture when fitted together.

I realized we kept searching for the meaning at the same time we knew it could never be fully grasped, and I was awed by the dedication of the members of my church family when I saw how some conducted their quest with the unspoken, underlying understanding that everything was at stake. Some of us who had found a special power in Bible study met to discuss continuation of the program at the apartment of Judy Dimmett, and when it was explained that owing to a variety of logistics and circumstances the church would not be able to offer it again in the coming year, our hostess said politely that if in fact there was no way our church could offer Bible study, she would find a church that did. Lo and behold, a way was found for our Bible study to continue.

Judy became a sister and ally as we joined in a mutual exploration of the method of Bible study our minister taught us based on Walter Wink's *Transforming Bible Study,* which we used as a kind of handbook. It came out of Wink's attempt "to heal the split between the academic study of the Scriptures and the issues of life," and used Socratic questioning of the self as well as the text. It was the kind of approach described by Father Diarmuid McGann in *The Journeying Self,* which saw the Scriptures "not only as a story of Jesus, but as a story of me, of who I am and who I am becoming."

In the five years that followed Judy's declaration of her commitment to Bible study—a turning point and opening not only for her but also for a number of us in the church—I saw her become not only a key leader in King's Chapel, I saw her move up and out from her job as a legal secretary to become director of the Bethany Union women's residence in Boston's Back Bay. With her commitment as example and inspiration, I became cochair with Judy of the Adult Religious Education Committee for four years of very "active service."

I learned the church was really family because we worked

hard and close enough with one another to get mad and argue as well as sing hymns together. I found myself one evening, after an inspiring session of a class called "Introduction to the New Testament," standing in the downstairs hall of the parish house shouting at Judy in an argument over the course of the *religious education* program while our family members walked past us. I knew we were family because we went to our minister as the mediating father, and we got our mutual frustration out. We realized what had brought us together in the first place in the work we had done, and we got past our differences. I knew we were family because I heard gossip about all this and other human conflicts of other family members, and we kept returning to ties that went deeper even than our own egos, and I knew that only happened in families that shared some vision beyond their individual beings.

After our blowup, Judy and I, suffering from burnout which comes from work in church as well as career, took a break from our committee duties, handing them over to a fresh "relative" with new and exciting ideas. Judy and I then joined forces in taking the Bible study that meant so much to both of us into other churches, as well as to a place in the community where it was wanted and needed.

I knew we were a family because we often behaved toward our minister as if he were the father of all 395 of us, as well as (through his office) the local representative of God, "our Father who art in heaven." The Reverend Carl Scovel makes no claim to power or glory and yet we see him walk up into that high pulpit every Sunday morning, and that is a lot closer to Whoever is up there above than we are. Sometimes we seemed to me like those early Israelites, a small band of people looking for security and freedom, with Carl as our Moses on Tremont Street, going up to get the Word and bringing it back down to us as we grumbled and strayed and returned.

I saw that the minister served as a kind of lightning rod for us, and by the very nature of his position he drew the emotional charge of our deepest hopes and fears. Talk about "transference"! I sometimes "projected" onto the minister angers and suppositions that I later realized had nothing to do with the man Carl Scovel because when I examined the matter he had said or done nothing whatsoever to provoke such a response. I noticed that he rarely ever gave advice but, like a good therapist, listened well and asked questions, and out of that I created my own amazing interior dramas, and usually came away from any private conference with him feeling much better.

I wondered how Carl the man withstood the pressure of being the Reverend Scovel. At first I wondered how he did it simply on the level of overwork, as I had to revise my naive prechurch assumption that a ministerial career was a soft life whose principal duty was a Sunday sermon and some casual weekday visits to the ill and elderly. I soon found out the job was a fulltime, high-pressure, professional hot seat, demanding that one person fill the roles of psychiatrist, orator, fund raiser, teacher, dishwasher, marriage and career counselor, singer, social director, mediator, cook, writer, scholar, and politician. The hardest part was that, unlike any of those other jobs, the minister was expected to be on call at any time of the night or day.

As I began to appreciate the pressures the minister was under I tried to restrain myself from bothering him at home and yet there *were* those few times when it seemed to me absolutely essential to phone him around ten o'clock in the evening and I did. Sometimes I worried that my own ripely aging immaturity made me unique in my need for the minister's attention, and then one day I saw one of our most distinguished parishioners, a man of great savoir faire and accomplishment in what I still sometimes regarded as the "real world" of business, waiting for Carl to get through with a meeting to talk to him privately. As this man, with a smile of almost childlike relief, saw Carl come out of another meeting and turn to him, I realized to my own astonishment: *My God, he needs him too!*

I knew that Carl kept in good shape by running on weekday

mornings—I sometimes saw him charging past me through traffic on Charles Street as I sleepily schlepped myself to breakfast coffee and scones at Romano's Bakery—and by working out on a portable rowing machine. Hiking in the White Mountains not only gave him good exercise but provided his one sure chance of really getting away from us all. Few have the stamina to pursue him up Mount Washington, though I wouldn't be surprised if some hardy and desperate parishioner tried to entrap him right on the trail to ask some burning question about God, sex, salvation, or all the above.

Granted that he kept in good physical condition, I still wondered how Carl withstood the psychic pressures of the job. After more than seven years of watching him work I began to realize that our minister taught us in two principal ways. One was by his sermons, which I admired as a writer because they were crafted like model stories with a beginning, middle, and end, with language deceptively simple because it was straightforward and struck at the heart as well as the mind. His sermons fulfilled Emerson's dictum in his eloquent address to the senior class of the Harvard Divinity School in 1838: "The true preacher can be known by this, that he deals out to the people his life—life passed through the fire of thought." In other words, Carl didn't give us abstractions but specifics, the true key to any good storytelling.

I also saw that he taught us by his actions as well as his words. By my own observation I concluded he was able to perform the enormous amount of pressurized work he did by "emptying"; that he nourished himself by constantly giving himself, and the giving out was what renewed him.

I saw it once specifically in a very simple incident on a retreat. A man had come on the retreat who wasn't a member of the church, and most of us didn't know him very well. He was in the grip of painful personal problems growing out of a divorce and other kinds of loss. He was a walking embodiment of grief. Most of us avoided him. I did myself, almost unconsciously, like a reflex. He was in that condition I knew because I had been there myself, that wounded state when you give off an air of defeat that frightens people because they know they have it in themselves and they are terrified of it.

As the man stood off by himself toward the end of the retreat, Carl went up to him smiling and said how great it had been to have him with us. *(Are you kidding?* I thought. *He was a real downer!)* Then Carl asked him if he might get together with him for lunch someday back in the city; if the man had time, Carl said, he'd really enjoy that. (I thought, *You liar, Carl! No one wants to have lunch with that guy—he's a loser!)* Then I saw the man's face. I saw the shock when he was asked, then the realization he was wanted, he was all right, another person desired his company if *he* had the time. I saw his face transformed by relief, and gratitude, at this simple act of kindness and interest. His expression came alive. I saw Carl smile with genuine pleasure and I thought: *that's how he does it.* I saw that Carl kept renewing himself by giving himself out, that he was preaching the Gospel—love thy neighbor as thyself—by doing it.

The goal of loving one's neighbors did not just apply to each other, the neighbors of our own church "family," but meant our brothers and sisters in the human family throughout the world. Though I'd kept my head in the sand politically for many years, the church made me look up and see the anguish of Central America when we co-sponsored (with Harvard Divinity School) the Reverend Medardo Gómez of El Salvador on a visit to this country. He brought us from our own pulpit the personal message of his people's struggle to preserve their lives and dignity and religious beliefs in the face of the government death squads.

Medardo and his struggle were incorporated into the life of our church when crosses handmade by people of his parish were given to the members of a confirmation class of our own teenagers, who included Johanna Chapin and the late Lola Min-

ifie's twin daughters Sarah and Polly. In action as well as sym-
bolism, the church responded to Medardo's visit when my
friend Ciael Hills—the guitar player of our retreats—formed a
committee for Central American Refugee Assistance (CARA)
that found a number of ways to serve these new neighbors in
our own city. Through CARA I assisted at services for men
whose fate hung in the balance while they were interned at the
Immigration Detention Center in Boston.

The church turned me outward to a personal awareness of
the poor I had avoided since I stopped writing about Spanish
Harlem and the civil rights movement, when I went to assist at
the refugee services, and to help serve dinner to the homeless at
the Pine Street Inn. I saw in my own experience of church that
Jean-Pierre de Caussade's Christian concept of "Abandonment
to Divine Providence" did not mean giving up responsibility for
oneself or one's fellow humans, but rather that prayer and faith
directed attention toward such responsibility. In Caussade's
own words, "It is a waste of time to try to picture any kind of
self-abandonment which excludes all personal activity and
seeks only quiescence, for if God wishes us to act for ourselves,
then action makes us holy." In terms of waiting on God to act in
the world, I believed St. Theresa's view when she asked:
"Whose hands are God's hands but our hands?"

After seven years I saw that the gospels were enacted in
many aspects of the life of the church, that the words and
lessons had power because they had flesh and substance. There
were family members taken from us not just by death but by
absence when some circumstance required them to move to
another part of the country, and each time that happened,
especially with someone from the staff, it was a loss that seemed
at the time irreparable and I knew things would never be so
good again. That's how I felt when Donna DiSciullo left.

I got to know Donna because I went to church by mistake on
the one morning of the year devoted to the Sunday school, and I
thought, *Oh, Lord, I am going to have to sit through some*

Christian version of "Mister Rogers' Neighborhood," delivered by this woman who barely seemed tall enough to look over the pulpit. The moment Donna began to preach, I was transfixed by a powerful, intense voice telling us how the children had chosen from all the possible projects they might undertake for the year to raise money and work for the cause of nuclear disarmament. The message was radical and disturbing and inspiring. I learned that Donna had worked as a volunteer at the Catholic Worker Hospitality House in the Bowery with Dorothy Day, which had been the beginning place of my first book. The Worker gave us a bond, and I went to Donna with some of my early questions about spirituality and found her clear and tough-minded in a way that was always helpful. When her minister husband was called to a church in Seattle and Donna became a minister out there too, I feared King's Chapel would never be the same.

I felt the same sense of loss, like a hole in the body, when Sue Spenser, who had been our seminarian from the time I started going to King's Chapel, left after her own ordination to take a ministerial position in Vancouver. What was going on? Was God grabbing all the good people from Boston and putting them out in the Pacific Northwest? A strong and thoughtful woman who had given up a career as a lawyer to go into the ministry, Sue had made me comfortable at that first Bible study in the parish house, and led the unforgettable retreat on "Zen and the Art of Bread Baking." When Sue left I was convinced, once again, King's Chapel would never be the same.

At first I didn't even notice Pamela Barz. She was terribly quiet and unobtrusive, and I guessed she was shy, perhaps because she had gone fresh from college to divinity school and was the youngest of the seminarians to work at King's Chapel since I'd been going to church there. She started coming to the Bible study sessions and other activities of the Religious Education Committee and didn't really say much except to always ask politely how she could help. Without my really being aware of it, she did begin to help, in all the little ways, from doing dishes (following Carl's ministerial example) and setting out Bibles for classes, to being on hand to open up the parish house and greet people coming to events. I got to know her better when Carl gave a new religious autobiography class and asked me to be his assistant since I'd taken it before. Pam took the course too, and her own religious autobiography had what I thought was the best first line of any in the class: "My mother and father talked about God on their first date."

Pam had a wry wit and sharp intelligence behind her quiet demeanor, and she began to use them in her homilies at the midweek services, and in a talk she volunteered to give in our committee's series on "Religion and Life" in which we asked parishioners to tell how their work and their spiritual lives connected. Pam told us how her own questions about God had led her to major in mathematics at Wellesley in hope of finding the answers to the great questions of life through logic, and when that was obviously not going to work, she turned to religion itself, and church and theology. Finally the search she began with mathematics led her to Harvard Divinity School and a career in the ministry.

We watched Pam grow and mature in confidence and poise and compassion, with the pride of any family in a favorite daughter. There was a solidity about her, a standing fast to her goals and beliefs. Her ordination to the ministry was one of the great events of the year, with more than two hundred members in attendance at the rite whose high point was a laying on of hands by members of the church to pass on the power of the love of those she would serve. I had my greatest honor as a member of King's Chapel in presenting her with one of the tokens of ministry—the cup of communion.

I knew Pam would soon be leaving to take on her own first ministry of a church, and of course King's Chapel would "never be the same." I finally realized it was never the same because it was not supposed to be the same, it was supposed to be always changing, renewing itself, like all the rest of life. If it stopped changing it would wither and die. That did not mean the church was not strongly tied to its past, its distinguished history, for that was part of the particular power and resonance of King's Chapel.

When I interviewed Carl at the time of the tercentenary about the significance of the church's history for its members, he told me, "I think our parishioners are people who like to feel they are part of a 'flow,' of a stream of events. We have a very strong sense of history, and I think that's important for people who do not feel 'isolated in time'—who do not feel this year is totally different from all other years, but want to know they are part of what's *happened* and will be part of what *happens.*"

I realized that being influenced by history did not mean being stuck in the past, but rather being aware of the connections of past, present, and future, of what Carl called "the flow" of events. I saw that change was not only part of the history of King's Chapel but part of its theology as well. I had written in my journal about six months after Pam had come to us, when I first became aware of her own unique style and growing power, that in spite of my sense of loss at the passing of Donna and Sue to other ministries, "The church gets what the church needs." What finally dawned on me as I recognized the gift we got in Pam was that the church enacts its own resurrection.

Pam gave a sermon on Henry Whitney Bellows, the nineteenth-century Unitarian leader who did so much to organize the denomination because "He believed that individual religion was not enough, that only in community could human beings fully worship and know God." Pam concluded her sermon with an explanation that told me more than any other I had heard why I belonged to a church, why I wanted to be part of the church "family"—not just because I had lost my own family, but because the church and its congregation provided an essential part of my own spiritual life and quest.

"Bellows knew what the individualists had forgotten, or never realized," Pam explained. "Yes, as separate women and men we are making our own journey and God speaks in our souls to each of us. If we ignore this voice we are lost. But we are also lost if we forget that we are parts of the whole, that together we form the body of Christ. For it is by coming together for worship and work that we see God—in and between and among each other."

Yesterday I went to a midweek service at which the Reverend Pamela Barz administered the sacraments of communion. She gave me the cup to drink from that I had given her in behalf of the church. There was a sense of life flowing back and forth, as the sacrament itself renewed the risen Christ, the ongoing resurrection in which we partake. At the end of the service Reverend Barz raised her arms and said the blessing: "Go in peace to love and serve the Lord." I walked out onto Tremont Street, into the crowds, not alone.

Epilogue: On the Way

"Faith is elliptical," our minister told us.

Of all the things the Reverend Carl Scovel said in the seven years I'd been going to church, that was perhaps the most important. It was not the most inspiring or dazzling or uplifting bit of wisdom he imparted in sermons and classes and personal counseling, but it was the most practical and useful admonition. It was foot-soldier knowledge for the spiritual journey, hardtack and C-ration nourishment for the long haul.

By "elliptical" he meant that the spiritual path was not a straight line, that at times we moved away from the God we searched for as surely as we moved back again toward Him, and the periods of feeling remote and out of touch were not aberrations or indications that our faith was not "real" but rather were a natural part of the journey. No matter how intently we set upon the path, there were bound to be detours and dry places, stretches of darkness we feared we might never emerge from, and such doubts and distractions were not unusual, in fact were built into the very process of spiritual growth. It was deeply reassuring to learn from the minister himself—our contact man with God—that I was not the only one who strayed, who stumbled and fell, forgot all the lessons of faith, and sometimes felt abandoned *even though I tried so hard!* (Where was my merit badge from God, the Divine Scoutmaster?)

My stumblings and gropings always resulted in my wanting to learn how to better find my way again. I wanted to know more about prayer and meditation and how to relate them to the rest of my life. When I learned that a growing number of lay people went to clerical advisers for "spiritual direction" I sought out a person trained in that discipline and asked for instruction and guidance. I was delighted to see a nun for such direction, for I hoped she might give me some clandestine Roman Catholic formula, an arcane style of prayer that provided a special link to God. I was determined to follow whatever set of complex instructions the Sister suggested, even if they involved such popish artifacts as beads and incense.

She told me to go look at a tree.

"Look at a tree," she said, "and think about what God had in mind when He created it, what we can learn about God from meditating on it." I thought that must be the kind of instruction a person of advanced spiritual enlightenment would give to a child, or a Protestant (especially a Unitarian). Sheepishly, feeling like a kid sent out on an embarrassingly simple assignment, I went to the Boston Public Garden and sat down in front of the biggest tree I could find. I looked up at it with Sister's instructions in mind and felt completely overwhelmed. The tree was too big and complicated and intricate to begin to comprehend. Instead, I picked out something to look at that seemed more suited to my own powers of understanding: a blade of grass.

I meditated while looking at a blade of grass for twenty minutes every day for two weeks and was amazed that I kept seeing something new all the time—different facets of color and texture, the way it moved in the wind, its relation to the grass around it, the *aliveness* of it. I wrote in my notebook, as Sister instructed, the words that seemed to describe the qualities of God as He manifested Himself in the grass He created: "tenacious," "resilient," "alive," "communicating," "dancing," "dependent," "surprising," "reaching," "responding."

I saw that each blade was a separate, living entity, just as I was, and also a part of a whole amazingly rich and interrelated landscape—just as I was. One day as I sat staring at the grass I became aware of its connection to the rest of the Garden and to the world. I saw the grass, and myself, in relation to the pigeons, squirrels, bugs, pond flies, and people moving all around me. I had a brief sense of them all being part of the same thing I was, all of us being manifestations of the same source of aliveness. I felt it in my deepest self, like hearing a perfect chord in a symphony, and then it faded away. I kept it as an idea, a memory, though I couldn't recapture the actual experience of it.

I continued to meditate twenty minutes every day, switching after a while from grass blades to trees to passages of Scripture and psalms, and sometimes pieces of music I loved. Sometimes I just kept silent and tried to do the kind of "listening" described by Jean-Pierre de Caussade in *Abandonment to Divine Providence*, trying to achieve a state "rather like one who believing himself on the point of hearing music makes himself alert and attentive. . . ." The twenty-minute prayerful meditation became a part of my daily routine, like the Exercycle, and I knew after several years that this practice created a kind of interior calm that was cumulative and strengthening for the soul, just as exercise was for the body.

There were times I was shaken out of the calm and it took all the discipline I could muster to hold myself in the meditation for twenty minutes when I wanted to jump up and go out for coffee or make a phone call or turn on TV to anything that moved (whatever could serve as a substitute for getting stoned, which was no longer part of my arsenal of self-distraction and destruction). It was only after three years of the daily meditation that I found I could do it even in times of extreme anxiety, that I could sometimes at least "pray through" the rending sense of all-consuming, immediate crisis, and reach some still point in myself.

There were times when prayer itself brought up uncomfortable, distressing thoughts and feelings, emotions that shook me up inside, and I remembered our minister telling us once of a Yiddish proverb that said "God is an earthquake, not an uncle." There were times when I made myself pray even though it seemed I was only doing it out of habit, for the idea of God sometimes seemed more remote than the planet Mars.

The feeling of faith, of seeing and believing my life and the world as a part of the whole unknowable immensity of God, came and went like the working of a highly sensitive camera lens that sometimes brought everything into brilliant focus and then slipped away into fuzziness. The moments of focus sometimes came in church, when I was hearing a sermon or singing a hymn or reciting a psalm with the congregation, like the time I said aloud the line from Psalm 118 that painted one of my favorite images of spiritual ease and freedom: "I called upon the Lord in distress: the Lord answered me, and set me in a large place."

Once the sense of focus came while I was sitting in the dentist's chair and looking up at Cindy, the hygienist I knew felt genuine gratification in her work of caring for patients in the most immaculate possible way. I saw for a split second, in the aliveness and absorption of her eyes as she bent above me, a connectedness to other people and the source of being and life she was serving, the source some people call nature ("the force that through the green fuse drives the flower" in Dylan Thomas' phrase) and others call God.

For most of my life I kept a journal to record thoughts, impressions, conversations, scenes, and events, and after I started going to church I got another notebook to keep as a kind of "spiritual journal" for all that was happening to me in the new and growing awareness of that realm. I kept those segregated journals for several years—the orange loose-leaf notebook for my secular or "everyday" life, and the newer green one for my church or "spiritual" life—until one day I started to write something down and hesitated because I didn't know whether I ought to put it in the orange notebook or the green one. In the moment of hesitation I started laughing at the naiveté of my notion that it was possible to compartmentalize the spiritual or religious side of one's experience like a separate subject or course in school, and I combined the pages of the two notebooks into one.

My eagerness to find God sometimes led me astray. It led me to an island called Iona off the coast of Scotland that was supposed to be a holy place, charged with spirituality, because a saint named Columba had gone there in the sixth century to use it as a base for missionary work among the Celts. A friend of mine was in charge of a guest house there and on an impulse— at a time when a trip enabled me to avoid facing difficult questions at home—I went over in hopes of getting a special zap from God, a "quick fix" of holy experience.

The island was the most barren, bleak spot of land I had ever seen *(Godforsaken,* I thought of it), with cold rains falling and sickly-looking sheep, stained with red streaks of dye for marking that looked like blood, roaming the rocky hills. Only later did I learn Columba had gone to Iona not for inspiration but for penance. On my second night there I woke in the eerie white light of that northern climate at three in the morning and saw in my mind's eye a gray wall and black letters splattered onto it that said, "There is no God." I left a day later on the quickest transportation I could get, and back in Boston, in my prayer group that met in the parish house, and at my bench by the pond in the Public Garden, I felt again in touch with the God I had gone halfway around the world to find and instead got a nightmare jolt. It was a lesson I should have known before starting. I took comfort in what was becoming one of my favorite and most reassuring statements in the New Testament: Paul's declaration, "I'm a fool."

After I told the others in my prayer group about my depressing experience on Iona, one of the women brought me a quote from St. Augustine she thought might be helpful: "Do not plan long journeys because whatever you believe in you have already seen. When a thing is everywhere, the way to find it is not to travel but to love."

My church and my Christian faith were at the heart of my continuing search but did not confine it. I found new insights from others outside, who brought different visions that enriched and illuminated my own way. At a time when I felt stuck in a sort of spiritual bog, my writer-teacher friend Marcie Hershman urged me to try again to read Martin Buber's *I and Thou*, a book I had found too formidable when I first tried it a few years before, but on this new attempt it seemed to open to me. I felt renewed by the profound spiritual vision of the great scholar of Judaism; the sometimes painful changes I experienced through the passages of my own journey were illuminated in Buber's eloquent words: "Creation happens to us, burns itself into us, recasts us in burning—we tremble and are faint, we submit. We take part in creation, meet the creator, reach out to him, helpers and companions."

I did not want my own companions in this greatest of all journeys to be limited to members of my own church or faith, even though others had different rituals and rules for serving and finding God. I did not want to feel cut off from my Jewish friends whose quest was described by Paul Cowan in his book *An Orphan in History* in terms that seemed so familiar to the emotions of my own experience:

"I was on a lifelong journey to find faith . . . Now as I sat in our synagogue, I realized I was no longer an orphan in time, but a wandering Jew who had come home."

I felt we were all wanderers looking for home, and we all had insights and experience to share. I joined in a Bible study group of Christians and Jews who gathered last spring in different people's homes to explore the books of Genesis and Exodus, which are part of our common heritage, and I found more depth in my own faith as I gained some understanding of the Jews'. I learned that the laws God issued after the Ten Commandments—the many laws that as Christians we sometimes skipped over and skimmed as "trivial"—were held especially sacred by the Jews because, as one of them in our study group put it, "Those provide the context in which one is able to follow the Ten Commandments. Those laws with their intricate details make holy the actions of everyday life."

I was reminded not only of Father Jean-Pierre de Caussade's phrase "the sacrament of the moment," but also of Thoreau finding not in church but in nature the "newer testament" he called "the Gospel of the moment." In Peter Matthiessen's Zen journals, *Nine-Headed Dragon River,* as well as in the search of Paul Cowan as a Jewish *Orphan in History* or Annie Dillard as a Christian *Pilgrim at Tinker Creek*—or Thoreau marching to a different drummer—I found nourishment and guidance for my own journey that enriched my personal faith as a Christian. No matter what the religious form, there was a path toward a greater power, a more lasting home than we had known and yet yearned for. There were people of all colors and creeds who had in common the search—those people who in the phrase of the Navajos were "on the gleaming way."

Being on "the way" for me came to mean seeing the connection of body with mind and spirit for the first time in my life. The health program I had embarked on out of desperation when I came back to Boston in 1980 led to a kind of physical version of the spiritual "turning" I'd experienced—like blending my two notebooks together. I wasn't "born again" as a muscle-builder who bench-pressed weights in the gym—in fact I even found the popular Nautilus workouts too much of a strain —but simply enjoyed getting in touch with my body through exercise instead of numbing it with drugs and alcohol.

When I took a yoga class for exercise at the Boston Center for Adult Education, the teacher began each session by having us say the Sanskrit word *Namaste,* which means "I honor the light within you." I liked that acknowledgment, and I didn't feel the light was limited to any one faith or sect or set of experiences. I honor those who find the light regardless of where they find it.

Though we hear in the media far more about the flashy and controversial signs of our society's turn toward spiritual concerns, there are growing indications of a quiet and personal search for religious roots and values. While scandals of TV evangelists and political crusades by the Moral Majority make news, there is a quiet majority of people who simply go to the church of their choice, like my friends at King's Chapel, for whom Sunday services and activities in their congregation are a natural and essential part of their daily lives. So little is this remarked on that I was surprised to learn from the latest research of The National Council of Churches—statistics published in *The Yearbook of American and Canadian Churches 1987*—that church membership in the United States is "growing gradually," that there is in fact a literal majority of sixty percent of Americans who are members of churches and synagogues, and seventy percent of Americans polled say they are "involved with a church, or synagogue," even if not formally affiliated.

"God Comes Home" was the title of a recent article in *Boston* magazine reporting on the increasing number of small groups of all faiths gathering in churches, synagogues, and homes for the purpose of prayer ("They call it Bible study, prayer group, fellowship, *havurah* or minyan.") I imagine such assemblages are not unlike my own prayer group that meets on Monday nights in the parish house of King's Chapel, made up not of zealots or "flakes," but esteemed good citizens whose professions include banker, librarian, consultant, technical writer for a computer company, teacher, housewife/graduate student. I doubt we are all that different in temperament or education from the professional people described in an article on "The New Orthodox" in a recent issue of *New York* magazine describing a "Jewish revival on the Upper West Side" of Manhattan.

I'm sure we share the sentiment of one who said in explanation of his religious return: "Once you've played all the tennis you can play, what then? There had to be more." I was fascinated to learn that many of these new synagogue members grew up with little religious training, and were called in Hebrew *"baalei teshuva,"* which means "those who have returned."

There is a return if not necessarily to a personal faith then at least to an interest in the subject within the intellectual community that I have become increasingly aware of in the past few years. In an article called "The Third Parent," adapted from a speech delivered by George W. S. Trow at the Whitney Museum in New York, the author said "I believe that humans are unable to live without some contact with what I call the third parent; God, or some culture growing up around a tradition of thinking about God or gods." God is "alive" again as a subject of intellectual inquiry. The point was brought eloquently to the newsstands with the December 1986 issue of the *Atlantic,* featuring a picture of Jesus on the cover and a lead article ("Who Do Men Say That I am?") by the magazine's managing editor, Cullen Murphy, brilliantly surveying the recent rise of historical and theological scholarship on the subject growing out of findings from archaeological discoveries like the Dead Sea Scrolls and new types of historical and literary criticism. The article quoted Catholic priest David Tracy of the University of Chicago faculty, who said "More has been written about Jesus in the last twenty years than in the previous two thousand."

A course on Jesus taught by the noted theologian Harvey Cox at Harvard has become one of the most popular offerings at the college in recent years, and last spring burst the bounds of the biggest classroom when more than nine hundred students signed up and the lectures had to be moved to Sanders Theatre. Professor Cox, whose books include the bestseller *The Secular City,* told me, "When I came to Harvard twenty years ago I wouldn't have dreamed of offering a course on Jesus—I wouldn't have thought enough students would come." The change he attributes to the fading of the sixties popularity of the Eastern religions among the young—"people have finally found out Zen Buddhism is difficult"—and a resulting student interest in examining their own religious traditions. That is another kind of "returning," of intellect if not necessarily of belief.

For any of us who return to faith, whatever that faith might be, the process is not a static one, not a single act in which by joining a church or synagogue we have completed our search, but rather, such an action means we're beginning it again. "Returning" to me does not just mean "going back" to something, but rather, re-turning as in "turning again," for the process is continuous and lifelong, a constant renewal and discovery. It is not a comfortable excuse for hiding out in old certitudes, but rather a constant pushing forward to test one's belief and use it, a challenge to respond to an interior pull as instinctive as tropism toward whatever source for each individual is the light.

For me the light is Christ, and it is not just a light as in "sweetness and light" but an illumination of pain as well, and a force for understanding and bearing it. When I went to our minister once at a time of particular anguish I asked him suddenly, with a challenge, "Where is Christ in all this?" and he answered without hesitation "He is in the pain." I learned that resurrection is not just the "happy ending" that follows crucifixion but, as our minister put it, those events are "two aspects of the same experience, even as Easter and Good Friday are the same reality."

It came as a relief to me to understand that my religion was as real in times of anguish as it was in the fullness of joy—the kind of welling up of life described in the line of the Twenty-third Psalm, "my cup runneth over," and in Jesus' words in Luke: "Give, and it shall be given unto you; good measure, pressed down, and shaken together, and running over . . ." The presence of Christ in pain as in joy reminded me again of the words of Psalm 139, "the darkness and the light are both alike to thee."

Light flooded in through the big windows of the chapel at Glastonbury Abbey, the Benedictine monastery near Boston where I sometimes go on retreat, as Father Nicholas shared in the homily his own sense of confusion that morning. He said he had read and reread the Old Testament lesson and the New Testament lesson in the lectionary that day, and the different view of God they presented was difficult to reconcile. He said he had before been confused by the sometimes conflicting images of God he found in the Bible, and that he had come to believe that "we must take God as he comes to each of us." With thanks, I added my own "Amen."

ABOUT THE AUTHOR

DAN WAKEFIELD was born in Indianapolis in 1932, graduated from Shortridge High School there in 1950, and from Columbia College in New York City in 1955. His nonfiction books include *Island in the City: The World of Spanish Harlem,* and *Supernation at Peace and War,* which first appeared as the entire issue of the March 1968 *The Atlantic.* Four of his five novels have been Literary Guild selections, including *Going All the Way* and *Starting Over,* the latter becoming a movie starring Burt Reynolds. Mr. Wakefield created the NBC-TV series "James at 15," and has written television movies for CBS and the Public Broadcasting System. He was awarded a Neiman Fellowship in Journalism at Harvard, a Rockefeller Grant in Creative Writing, and has been a Visiting Lecturer at universities and writers' conferences, including the Iowa Writers' Workshop and Bread Loaf. He served as a staff writer for *The Nation* magazine from 1956 to 1960, and as a contributing editor of *The Atlantic* from 1968 to 1980. His articles, essays, and reviews have also appeared in the New York *Times Magazine, Esquire, Harper's, Redbook, Rolling Stone, Commentary, Gentlemen's Quarterly, TV Guide,* and other magazines.